INTERNATIONAL POLITICAL ECONOMY SERIES

General Editor: Timothy M. Shaw, Professor of Political Science and International Development Studies, and Director of the Centre for Foreign Policy Studies, Dalhousie University, Nova Scotia, Canada

Recent titles include:

Manuel R. Agosin and Diana Tussie (*editors*)
TRADE AND GROWTH: NEW DILEMMAS IN TRADE POLICY

Mahvash Alerassool
FREEZING ASSETS: THE USA AND THE MOST EFFECTIVE
ECONOMIC SANCTION

Robert Boardman
PESTICIDES IN WORLD AGRICULTURE
POST-SOCIALIST WORLD ORDERS

Inga Brandell (*editor*)
WORKERS IN THIRD-WORLD INDUSTRIALIZATION

Richard P. C. Brown
PUBLIC DEBT AND PRIVATE WEALTH

Bonnie K. Campbell (*editor*)
POLITICAL DIMENSIONS OF THE INTERNATIONAL DEBT CRISIS

Bonnie K. Campbell and John Loxley (*editors*)
STRUCTURAL ADJUSTMENT IN AFRICA

Jerker Carlsson, Gunnar Köhlin and Anders Ekbom
THE POLITICAL ECONOMY OF EVALUATION

Jerker Carlsson and Timothy M. Shaw (*editors*)
NEWLY INDUSTRIALIZING COUNTRIES AND THE POLITICAL
ECONOMY OF SOUTH–SOUTH RELATIONS

Steen Folke, Niels Fold and Thyge Enevoldsen
SOUTH–SOUTH TRADE AND DEVELOPMENT

David Glover and Ken Kusterer
SMALL FARMERS, BIG BUSINESS

William D. Graf (*editor*)
THE INTERNATIONALIZATION OF THE GERMAN POLITICAL
ECONOMY

Betty J. Harris
THE POLITICAL ECONOMY OF THE SOUTHERN AFRICAN PERIPHERY

Jacques Hersh
THE USA AND THE RISE OF EAST ASIA SINCE 1945

Bahgat Korany, Paul Noble and Rex Brynen (*editors*)
THE MANY FACES OF NATIONAL SECURITY IN THE ARAB WORLD

Howard P. Lehman
INDEBTED DEVELOPMENT

Matthew Martin
THE CRUMBLING FAÇADE OF AFRICAN DEBT NEGOTIATIONS

James H. Mittelman
OUT FROM UNDERDEVELOPMENT

Paul Mosley (*editor*)
DEVELOPMENT FINANCE AND POLICY REFORM

Dennis C. Pirages and Christine Sylvester (*editors*)
TRANSFORMATIONS IN THE GLOBAL POLITICAL ECONOMY

Tony Porter
STATES, MARKETS AND REGIMES IN GLOBAL FINANCE

Stephen P. Riley (*editor*)
THE POLITICS OF GLOBAL DEBT

Alfredo C. Robles, Jr
FRENCH THEORIES OF REGULATION AND CONCEPTIONS OF
THE INTERNATIONAL DIVISION OF LABOUR

Frederick Stapenhurst
POLITICAL RISK ANALYSIS AROUND THE NORTH ATLANTIC

Arno Tausch (with Fred Prager)
TOWARDS A SOCIO-LIBERAL THEORY OF WORLD DEVELOPMENT

Nancy Thede and Pierre Beaudet (*editors*)
A POST-APARTHEID SOUTHERN AFRICA?

Peter Utting
ECONOMIC REFORM AND THIRD-WORLD SOCIALISM

Trade and Growth

New Dilemmas in Trade Policy

Edited by

Manuel R. Agosin
Professor of Economics
Universidad de Chile
and UNCTAD, Geneva

and

Diana Tussie
Senior Research Fellow
Latin American School of Social Sciences (FLACSO)
and National Council for Scientific and Technological
Research (CONICET)
Argentina

St. Martin's Press

Selection and editorial matter © Manuel R. Agosin and Diana Tussie 1993
Chapters 1–10 © The Macmillan Press Ltd 1993

First published in Great Britain 1993 by
THE MACMILLAN PRESS LTD
Houndmills, Basingstoke, Hampshire RG21 2XS
and London
Companies and representatives
throughout the world

A catalogue record for this book is available
from the British Library.

ISBN 0–333–59917–9 hardcover
ISBN 0–333–59918–7 paperback

Printed in Great Britain by
Mackays of Chatham PLC
Chatham, Kent

First published in the United States of America 1993 by
Scholarly and Reference Division,
ST. MARTIN'S PRESS, INC.,
175 Fifth Avenue,
New York, N.Y. 10010

ISBN 0–312–09987–8

Library of Congress Cataloging-in-Publication Data
Trade and growth : new dilemmas in trade policy / edited by Manuel R.
Agosin and Diana Tussie.
p.   cm. — (International political economy series)
Includes index.
ISBN 0–312–09987–8
1. Developing countries—Commercial policy.   I. Agosin, Manuel.
II. Tussie, Diana.   III. Series.
HF1413.T688   1993
382'.3'091724—dc20
93–1303
CIP

This book is dedicated to the memory of
Sidney Dell

Contents

List of Tables and Figures

Tables

ix

Figure

Notes on the Contributors

Manuel R. Agosin is Professor of Economics at the University of Chile in Santiago. He has held several positions with the United Nations as a research economist and as director of research and technical assistance programmes. He has also been adviser on international trade negotiations to Chile's Ministry of Foreign Affairs. He has published in several international journals. He holds a PhD from Columbia University.

Yilmaz Akyüz is Senior Economist with UNCTAD in charge of macroeconomic analysis. He has taught at universities in Turkey, the United Kingdom, Norway and Switzerland and has published widely in Turkish and international journals on topics related to development economics, macroeconomics and international finance. He holds a PhD from the University of East Anglia.

Alice H. Amsden is a well-known specialist on development policy and management issues in development, and teaches at the New School for Social Research in New York City. She has also taught at MIT. She has written *Asia's Next Giant: South Korea and Late Industrialization* (1989).

Mario Damill is Senior Research Fellow at the Centro de Estudios de Economia y Sociedad (CEDES) in Buenos Aires. He also teaches at the University of Buenos Aires. He has published numerous articles on macroeconomic issues in Argentina.

Ricardo Ffrench-Davis is Senior Adviser with the UN's Economic Commission for Latin America and the Caribbean in Santiago. In his long and distinguished career, he has held numerous academic and government positions in several economic fields. His most recent position was Director of Research at the Central Bank of Chile. He holds a PhD from the University of Chicago.

Saúl Keifman is an Argentinian economist with the Facultad Latinoamericana de Ciencias Sociales (FLACSO) in Buenos Aires. He has taught at several universities in Argentina and has published several articles on Argentina's trade and structural adjustment policies.

Robert Z. Lawrence is Albert L. Williams Professor of International Trade at the John F. Kennedy School of Government, Harvard University. He has been Senior Fellow at the Brookings Institution and has been consultant to a large number of international organizations in the United States. He has published widely in the field of international trade policy issues. He holds a PhD from Yale University.

Patricio Leiva is Chilean Ambassador to the European Communities in Brussels. He has been Chilean representative to the Uruguay Round of trade negotiations. He has held numerous government and international posts and has been consultant to several international organizations. He was formerly Professor of Economics, University of Chile, and Director of the Centro Latinoamericano de Economía y Política Internacional (CLEPI), Santiago.

Roberto Madrid is Associate Director at CLEPI, and has authored several studies on international trade issues of relevance to Chile.

José Antonio Ocampo is Colombian Minister of Agriculture. He has been Director and Senior Research Fellow at Fundación para la Educatión Superior y el Desarrollo (FEDESARROLLO) in Bogotá, Columbia. He has been high-level adviser to the Colombian Government on issues related to trade policy. He has taught at universities in Colombia and abroad. He has published widely in international and Colombian academic and policy journals on issues related to macroeconomics, international trade and economic history. He holds a PhD from Yale University.

Adriaan Ten Kate is a Dutch economist with a broad experience in the problems of developing countries. He has taught at universities in the Netherlands, Mexico and Costa Rica. He has been adviser to the Mexican Government on international trade policy issues, including the negotiation of the North American Free Trade Agreement. He holds a PhD in economics from Erasmus University in Rotterdam.

Diana Tussie is Senior Fellow at Facultad Latinoamericana de Ciencias Sociales (FLACSO) in Buenos Aires, where she has coordinated the Masters' Programme in International Relations. She is the author of *The Less Developed Countries and the World Trading System* and of numerous articles. She has recently edited *Developing Countries in World Trade: Policies and Bargaining Strategies*. She has been

Notes on the Contributors

consultant to several international organizations and adviser to
Argentina's Foreign Affairs and Economics Ministries. She holds a
PhD from the London School of Economics.

Ercan Uygur is Professor of Economics at Ankara University and
adviser to the Central Bank of Turkey. He has been a consultant for
several international organizations and has published widely in Turkey
and abroad. He holds a PhD from the University of East Anglia.

Preface

The role of trade policy in development strategies and the kinds of trade policies that are most conducive to development have been constant areas of enquiry in development economics. They have acquired new urgency in recent years with the growing perception that a greater and qualitatively improved integration into the international economy is now necessary in order to accelerate economic growth. Export expansion and diversification are seen as particularly important for sustained growth: production for exports does not come up against the limitations in market size (at least not for small producers) that constrain growth under an import substitution strategy; in sectors where economies of scale are important, these are more readily reaped exporting; and, perhaps most importantly, export growth yields the foreign exchange needed to import capital goods embodying ever more rapid technological advances and the intermediate goods that small developing economies cannot produce efficiently by themselves.

Therefore, there is a growing consensus that export-oriented development strategies are more conducive to long-term growth than strategies that put the accent only on import substitution. There is considerably less consensus on how to achieve the objective of export-oriented growth. The conventional approach emphasizes the need to achieve neutrality in the incentive structure and to align domestic to international prices. According to this approach, all import barriers should be dismantled as quickly as possible, and tariffs ought to be brought down to a low and uniform level. Once imports have been liberalized and the structure of incentives no longer favours import substitution, the market alone will reallocate resources towards sectors in which the country has comparative advantages.

Others argue that markets work slowly and imperfectly and that a more activist approach is required. It is argued that trade liberalization is a purely negative impulse and that it is likely to lead to output and capacity losses and to a very slow reallocation of resources towards more efficient activities. Therefore, this line of argument goes, trade liberalization programmes need to be designed and implemented carefully and, in addition, they need to be complemented with positive impulses that encourage the creation of capacity in sectors with actual or potential comparative advantage. This requires *selectivity* in trade policy and strong guidance through the exchange rate. Most of the chapters in this volume adhere to this view of the world.

This book also incorporates the *international* dimension, so often left out of *national* policy debates. Developing countries, particularly the more industrialized among them, have been under increasing pressure to cede an important degree of autonomy over their trade and industrialization policies and to conform to international disciplines that sometimes not even developed countries abide by. This book also explores this issue and places the current debates surrounding trade policy in the context of the international policy environment that is emerging in an increasingly globalized world economy.

The chapters contained in this volume were prepared for an UNCTAD project of research and technical co-operation directed by Manuel Agosin and entitled 'Trade Policies for Developing Countries in the 1990s'. This project was made possible through the generous financial assistance of the governments of Germany, Italy, Norway and Sweden. Versions of these chapters were presented at two international conferences. The first one was co-sponsored by the Central Bank of Turkey and UNCTAD and was held at Antalya, Turkey, during the period 25–29 April 1992. We are very grateful to the staff of the Central Bank of Turkey, and particularly to Dr Rüstü Saraçoglu, Governor, and Hassan Ersel, Vice-Governor, for the financial and intellectual support that made this conference possible.

Some of the chapters that the reader will find in this volume were also presented at an international conference entitled 'La Dinámica de los Mercados Internacionales y las Políticas Comerciales para el Desarrollo', held at El Escorial during the period 8–12 July 1992 and co-sponsored by UNCTAD, Universidad Complutense de Madrid and the Instituto de Cooperación Iberoamericana (ICI). We wish to express our recognition to these institutions for their financial support. Our very special thanks go to Osvaldo Sunkel and Carlos Abad Balboa (Editor and Managing Editor, respectively, of *Pensamiento Iberoamericano*, the journal published jointly by ICI and the UN's Economic Commission for Latin America and the Caribbean, where preliminary versions of some of these studies were published in Spanish) for their belief in this project and their work towards making the conference a great success.

The project itself was a collaborative venture of a number of people in UNCTAD who patiently and efficiently worked to bring it to fruition. Although their names do not appear in these pages, their contributions deserve special recognition. In particular, our heartfelt thanks go to Ian Kinniburgh, Gunilla Ryd and Christine Wyatt for their important substantive contributions to the entire project. Susana Navarro and Sylvia Robin provided indispensable administrative and secretarial support. A special word of thanks must go to John Burley, who supported this project from its beginning – when it was no more than a glimmer in the project director's eye – through to its final shape as this book. We are also indebted to Melania Bravo, of the University of Chile in Santiago, for efficient and cheerful secretarial assistance.

Both the project and this book would not have been possible without the support of Enrique Ganuza (then Chief Economist with the Swedish International Development Agency) and Magnus Blomström, Professor of Economics, Stockholm School of Economics. We wish to express our deep appreciation to them.

Santiago and Buenos Aires   MANUEL R. AGOSIN
                                               DIANA TUSSIE

List of Abbreviations

ACP	African, Caribbean and Pacific Countries
ATKE	American-trained Korean economists
BIS	Bank for International Settlements
EC	European Community
ECLAC	Economic Commission for Latin America and the Caribbean
EERM	effective exchange rate for imports
EERX	effective exchange rate for exports
EFTA	European Free Trade Area
ERP	effective rate of protection
ESP	Economic Solidarity Pact (in Mexico)
FDI	foreign direct investment
FTA	free trade area
GATT	General Agreement on Tariffs and Trade
GDP	Gross domestic product
GSP	Generalized System of Preferences
IMF	International Monetary Fund
KIET	Korean Institute for Economics and Technology
MFA	Multifibre Arrangement
MFN	most favoured nation
MOSS	market opening sector specific
NAFTA	North American Free Trade Area
NTB	non-tariff barrier
OECD	Organization for Economic Cooperation and Development
POSCO	Pohang Iron and Steel Company
QR	quantitative restriction
R&D	research and development
REER	real effective exchange rate
SD	special and differential (treatment)
SII	Structural Impediments Initiative
TFPG	total factor productivity growth
TRIP	trade-related intellectual property (rights)
UNCTAD	United Nations Conference on Trade and Development
VER	voluntary export restraint
VRA	voluntary restraint agreement

1 Trade and Growth: New Dilemmas in Trade Policy – An Overview

Manuel R. Agosin and Diana Tussie[1]

INTRODUCTION $F13$ 019

Trade policy in developing countries is the central focus of this work. It has been inspired by the need to assess the adequacy of the recent experiences with trade policy reform in the developing world in the light of current trends in the world economy and the new policy dilemmas that developing countries must confront.

During the 1980s there was a sea-change in the attitudes towards trade policy in both developing and developed countries which represented a reversal of previously held positions. Developing countries stepped to the vanguard of trade liberalization as a growing number of countries undertook a fundamental change of direction towards a greater degree of openness. On the other hand, while they continued officially to espouse a free-trade doctrine, in practice the governments of developed countries increasingly embraced selectivity and continued to make use of non-tariff barriers to manage imports from developing countries.

The causes for the conversion to trade liberalization in developing countries are manifold. Some are related to the growing interpenetration of markets, an unfolding process summed up in the concept of globalization. The main traits of the process of globalization are a more rapid growth of international economic variables than national ones and a step-up in the rate of technological change, which, for developing countries, is embodied mainly in imports of capital goods and foreign investment. Globalization has raised the perceived advantages of closer integration into the international economy. Thus a growing number of developing countries are seeking to establish conditions for faster growth of both exports and imports and for larger inflows of foreign direct investment. In many countries, these objectives have led to trade liberalization, which has been pursued with varying degrees of intensity in different countries.

But globalization has also brought along increasing pressures on these countries that may make outward-oriented growth harder to achieve (or to sustain). Developing countries (and particularly the most industrially advanced among them) are being pressed to abandon the use of discretionary trade and industrial policy tools and to accept new disciplines in areas previously out of bounds of international scrutiny. This trend is reflected in the use that developed countries are making of trade negotiations. Increasingly, trade negotiations are becoming a vehicle used by the most powerful trading countries to dictate the terms of a single worldwide model of economic policy-making. The trade door is being used to go to the heart of a range of laws, institutions and other governmental practices sometimes labelled as 'structural impediments to market access' or 'distortions to trade'.

There is also a complex array of domestic and international factors that have operated to induce more open trade regimes in the developing world. The dynamic performance of the export-oriented South and East Asian countries has had a demonstration effect on other countries and has influenced prevailing economic philosophies. In some instances, governments came to realize that import substitution had been taken too far and sustained for too long. In addition, important segments of public opinion showed signs of 'protection fatigue'; there was growing criticism of the costs incurred by such policies, as firms lived off the rents provided by protection and failed to reach adequate standards of international competitiveness. The need to promote exports in order to ease foreign exchange stringencies was another contributing factor. Several countries also came under pressure from international financial institutions to implement structural adjustment programmes. The change of direction has been most marked in Latin America, but it is a widespread trend in most of the developing world.

In short, perceptions have shifted away from the traditional support for import substitution towards greater reliance on the growth of exports and the opening to trade. The general stakes of developing countries in the evolution of the trading system are thus higher. Yet this shift occurs at a time when the game is harder and harder to play, with increasing pressures on them to surrender policy autonomy in a widening range of fields.

Stimulated by these waves of change, discussions over trade policy have regained centre-stage. The subject has recently been rekindled, on the one hand, by the process of globalization and, on the other, by new contributions to the theory of international trade and its applicability to developing countries. The centre of the controversy is whether sustained outward-oriented growth is best achieved through trade liberalization and incentive neutrality or whether it requires selective trade policies and activist pro-industrialization government stances, the right to which is being increasingly challenged in international negotiations.

The chapters in this volume seek to pull together the strands of these different dimensions and show how they interact. Part I deals with the emerging conditions in the world trading system which serve as the parameters within which trade policy must operate. Part II addresses new conceptualizations in respect of trade policy issues. Part III assesses the trajectories and performances of selected Latin American and Asian countries that have undertaken different varieties of trade policy reform.

The basic message of the chapters on the international context in which trade policy reform is taking place is that developing countries are under increasing pressure to tie their hands with respect to traditional tools of trade policy and to accept new disciplines in an ever-widening number of areas. At the same time, developed countries have shown themselves loth to grant developing countries the significantly enhanced market access on which successful outward-oriented growth depends. On the other hand, the essays on the implications of the new trade theories for policy in developing countries and those on the experiences of individual countries with trade policy reform suggest that strong government guidance of the economy and the retention of incentive selectivity are more likely to induce outward-oriented growth than passive government policies. Section IV of this chapter examines how the conflict between the trends in the international policy arena and the policy needs of developing countries can be reconciled.

The selection of countries as case studies was motivated by an interest in shedding light on the most recent trade policy reforms in the developing world. Three countries where trade liberalization has been particularly thorough are Chile, Mexico and Argentina. We have sought to contrast these reforms with the trade policy experience of two countries, South Korea and Turkey, both of which have had a successful track record with export-oriented growth. No attempt was made to address the policy problems of very poor and commodity-dependent countries, such as those of Africa; a set of issues that requires a book to itself and on which there is little knowledge – and even less agreement.

I   THE INTERNATIONAL CONTEXT

Unilateral or Negotiated Liberalization?

An external environment that is conducive to outward-oriented growth surely entails the incorporation of developing countries as full partners into the international trading system. This is in itself a significant challenge, given that perhaps one of the most contentious international trade issues has historically been the relationship between developed and developing countries. While tariffs in developed countries have been brought down on average to very low levels, non-tariff restrictions remain on a variety of products and in a number of sectors. These discriminate against the manufactured exports of developing countries, which are concentrated in sunset (mainly labour-intensive) industries in which developed countries have ceased to be competitive. The unwillingness of developed countries to adjust to these shifts in competitiveness has led to the configuration of a lopsided system whereby large segments of international trade have been partially excluded from the process of liberalization. The periodic rounds of tariff negotiations in GATT have focused on sectors that have been at the core of the trade concerns of developed countries. These sectors are characterized by intra-industrial specialization, economies of scale, product differentiation, imperfect competition, and a significant amount of intra-firm trade (Tussie, 1989, chapter 3).

Where factor endowments and inter-industrial characteristics are dominant in trade flows, tariffs remain relatively high and, moreover, ingenious non-tariff restrictions have mushroomed, rendering insignificant whatever tariff liberalization may have been achieved. Such 'sensitive', mainly labour-intensive, sectors are riddled with a multitude of quotas, voluntary export restraints (VERs), price undertakings and the protectionist use of antidumping and countervailing duties. A significant proportion of the manufactured exports of developing countries (not to mention their agricultural exports) to their main developed trading partners are affected by measures of this nature.

Therefore, trade liberalization in sectors of export interest to developing countries is the core of the issues that are normally included under the heading of 'GATT's backlog'. Crucial in this backlog of issues is the non-applicability of GATT disciplines to temporary safeguard action. Safeguards have been GATT's 'black hole'. They are supposed to be applied as a means of temporary protection to allow industries threatened by a sudden surge in imports to adjust. Yet, once in place, safeguards acquire a life of their own and are rarely withdrawn; in fact, many have remained in place for decades. More seriously, they take the form of quantitative restrictions (QRs) or so-called 'grey-area' measures (e.g. VERs or orderly marketing agreements) and they are seldom applied on a most favoured nation (MFN) basis, discriminating disproportionately against developing countries, thus contravening both the letter and spirit of GATT. In such circumstances, all trade becomes subject to permanent negotiation.[2]

Whole industries in which developing countries are competitive have been excluded from the liberalization exercises of GATT negotiating rounds and even effectively removed from GATT governance. From 1961 a system of discriminatory restraints against exports of textiles and clothing from developing countries has been in force; and as more and more countries built supply capabilities in this sector, restraints have become increasingly tighter with each renewal of the Multifibre Arrangement (MFA). Since 1977 there has been a progressive movement towards a similar system of restrictions on steel. VERs and the abuse of antidumping and countervailing duties also hit developing countries particularly badly in a host of industries, from cut flowers to consumer electronics.

While the great majority of developing countries had restrictive import regimes and relied heavily on government intervention in trade, it could be argued that systemic bias against them was a result of their own self-exclusion. Developing countries were caught in the awkward position of demanding market access coupled with a reluctance to endorse a freer trade regime at home. The conventional argument on their inability to obtain significant market access opportunities could hold that: 'An inherent limitation on the bargaining strength of developing countries in the past rounds of trade negotiations has been the lack of liberalization offers of their own to serve as bargaining chips' (Bergsten and Cline, 1982, p.29).

The mushrooming in the number of developing countries seeking a more dynamic integration into world markets has produced a mirror image of that situation. As developing countries have shifted to more orthodox trade practices, they have been increasingly prone to reduce and even abandon their formerly defensive style, centred on obtaining derogations from GATT principles to allow them a free hand to pursue inward-looking trade policies. The gist of that stance aimed at preserving special and differential treatment (S&D) in trade negotiations and the right not to grant reciprocity for tariff reductions in their favour, which resulted in their retention of high unbound tariffs. In addition, they expected lax treatment in the resort to Article XVIIIb, which allows the application of QRs to tackle balance of payments problems.

That defensive stance is rapidly disappearing. Now that they are showing widespread willingness to accept fuller GATT disciplines unilaterally, a growing number of developing countries have turned into faithful upholders of genuinely free-trade principles. Today the largest stumbling block to their full integration into the system rests on their very inadequate market access in the sectors in which they enjoy or are developing comparative advantage. Moreover, there has been relentless pressure on a number of developing countries to give up S&D permanently, to make further concessions and to bind all commitments. These demands are summed up in the concept of 'graduation'.

It is not difficult to understand why developing countries have been willing to liberalize unilaterally without negotiating concessions from their developed country partners (or from other developing countries, for that matter). It has partly been a result of the perception that, as small markets, each individual country could extract limited *quid pro quos* and that, in any event, trade liberalization was a good thing in itself, regardless of what trading partners did. Moreover, the lack of agreement with regard to development strategies among developing countries themselves precluded negotiating a joint liberalization. As the number of countries adopting more liberal trade policies rises rapidly,[3] this situation is changing, and there is now considerably more consensus among developing countries about the desirability of opening their economies.

Thus, in broad terms, a growing number of developing countries seem to be upholding an enfeebled system which has yet to address their needs in a balanced fashion. In the absence of significant improvements in market access for the products of concern to developing countries, the question can be rightly raised as regards the suitability of a continued uncritical acceptance of more stringent disciplines on their trade and industrialization policies.

Whether the kinds of trade liberalization that are taking place at present in the developing world will produce rapid export growth is a subject that is taken up in the next two sections. Suffice it to say here that the promise of a new engine of growth has certainly been the chief incentive for the widespread changes in trade strategies. Therefore, a legitimate question that needs to be raised is whether, under the conditions that are likely to prevail towards the end of the 1990s, it will be possible for a large number of countries to sustain *simultaneously* an export-oriented growth path. Most individual developing countries are insignificant suppliers in international markets and can effectively be considered to be price takers. Therefore, for a country viewed in isolation, export-oriented growth would appear to be desirable regardless of conditions of market access. Yet, in the aggregate, the simultaneous emulation of these policies by a large number of countries is likely to lead to an escalation of protectionism which would render the *ex-ante* expansion of manufactured exports infeasible at unchanged export prices and exporting countries' exchange rates. This point was forcefully made a decade ago by Cline (1982), who argued that the experience of export-led growth of the South-east Asian countries could not be replicated by a significant number of developing countries.

This fallacy-of-composition problem gains more relevance when analysing the sectoral breakdown of international trade flows. De Castro (1989) conducted an econometric study which showed that pressures for protection in developed countries are greatest in sectors where the levels of import penetration (i.e. the share of imports in consumption) are already high, where output is growing slowly, and where intra-industry trade flows are not significant.[4] Thus the sectors where a protectionist response is most likely are precisely those that loom large in the exports of developing countries. Under current political realities, a large increase in exports of manufactures from developing to developed countries would surely encounter serious resistance. This would result in deteriorating terms of trade for the manufactures exported by developing countries, it would call for steeper devaluations than might otherwise be the case in order to hit any given export target, or both. In sum, increasing export orientation in a significant group of developing countries *at the same time*, unaccompanied by reciprocal liberalizations in developed countries, can result in immiserizing growth for the former group of countries. At the same time, the persistence of protectionism in the sectors where developing countries are most likely to enter international markets will certainly endanger the sustainability and political viability of the trade liberalizations that are taking place in the developing world.

The Driving Forces behind Globalization

A process of rapid internationalization of the world economy has been
gathering momentum in the past couple of decades, as foreign direct
investment (FDI) has been more dynamic than aggregate domestic
capital formation, and the growth of international financial flows has
far outstripped that of national financial variables. Table 1.1 docu-
ments the growth of outward and inward FDI stocks relative to GDPs,
both in developed and developing countries (see also Julius, 1990).[5] As
a proportion of the GDPs of originating and recipient regions, the
stocks of FDI have grown remarkably since the late 1970s. It should be
noted that the recipient (and even more so the originating) countries
continue to be mainly those of the OECD. Among developing
countries, in recent years the fastest increases in FDI stocks have
been recorded by the Asian exporters of manufactures, which have
come to replace the Latin American countries as the favoured location
for foreign investment in the developing world (UNCTC, 1991; and

Table 1.1   World FDI stocks, by region, 1960–89

	Outward stocks	Inward stocks		
	Developed countries	Developed countries	Developing countries	World[a]
In millions of current US				
1960	67.0	n.a.	n.a.	n.a.
1975	275.4	185.3	61.5	246.8
1980[b]	535.7	401.0	134.9	539.4
1985	693.3	478.2	159.0	637.2
1989	1,276.3	944.2	258.0	1,202.2
As % of GDP in originating and recipient regions				
1960	6.7	n.a.	n.a.	n.a.
1975	6.7	4.5	6.4	4.9
1980[b]	6.7	5.1	7.4	5.5
1985	8.0	5.5	8.5	6.1
1989	8.7	6.4	9.7	6.9

Notes: [a]Excluding Eastern European countries.
          [b]1983 for inward stocks.
Source: Based on data of UNCTC, the United Nations Statistical Office and
          the World Bank.

UNCTC, 1992). In Latin America, the fall in FDI during the 1980s was highly correlated with the debt crisis; in recent years, there have been signs of revival in the interest of foreign investors in the region. Trade in manufactures has been for several decades one of the most dynamic segments of world economic activity. In recent years, that trade has become increasingly inter-linked with investment, and this may have accelerated the rate of growth of FDI and increased its importance relative to domestic economic magnitudes. While one of the principal objectives of FDI in the 1960s and 1970s was production for the domestic markets of host countries, more recently FDI has been increasingly undertaken by companies with a global outlook and has gradually shifted towards projects oriented to regional and global markets.[6] Therefore, the extent to which an economy is export-oriented is becoming a more important determinant of its ability to attract FDI than it was in the past.[7]

Moreover, the links between enterprises in different economies have been growing at an accelerating pace. These links include long-term subcontracting arrangements, cross-investments, minority equity shares, licensing agreements, etc. The growing importance of FDI and non-equity links between enterprises in different countries implies that production and distribution are increasingly being carried out within worldwide networks of firms. All of these factors have contributed to the widening of the spread between the growth of world trade and world output (see Table 1.2).

The internationalization of finance has also been a driving force behind the process of globalization. Since the deregulation of international financial transactions began in the 1970s in the major international financial centres, the growth of financial transactions with international characteristics[8] has far outstripped the growth of purely domestic transactions. As can be seen in Table 1.3, international finance has tended to grow relative to world output, world trade, and

Table 1.2   The growth of world trade and output, 1970–89 (average annual rates of growth, percentages)

	1970–80	1980–3	1983–9
World trade	5	0	6
World GDP	4	2	3.5

Source: Based on data of UNCTAD and GATT.

Table 1.3   International financial deepening: international banking in relation to world output, trade and investment, selected years

	1964	1972	1980	1983	1985	1987
As % of world output[a]						
Net international bank loans[b]	0.7	3.7	8.0	12.0	13.2	14.8
Gross size of international banking market[c]	1.2	6.3	15.5	21.8a	25.3	27.9
As % of world trade[a]						
Net international bank loans[b]	6.4	25.7	35.2	57.3	63.9	72.9
Gross size of international banking market[c]	10.6	43.8	67.8	104.0	122.2	137.2
As % of world gross fixed investment[a]						
Net international bank loans[b]	4.0	18.0	39.2	66.3	72.4	78.2
Gross size of international banking market[c]	6.7	30.6	75.4	120.5	138.7	147.3

Notes: The table relates the stock of bank loans outstanding at the end of the year to world output, trade and gross fixed investment in current dollars during the year.
[a] Excluding Eastern European countries.
[b] Claims of banks in the BIS reporting area, excluding inter-bank redepositing.
[c] Claims of banks in nearly all European countries, the Bahamas, Bahrain, Canada, Cayman Islands, Hong Kong, Japan, Netherlands Antilles, Panama, Singapore and the United States, including inter-bank redepositing.
Source: Akyüz (1992).

world gross fixed investment. Moreover, the internationalization of finance is making it increasingly difficult to distinguish between national and international markets (Akyüz, 1992).

Two factors have accelerated the trend towards increasing internationalization. The first of these is technology and the second is financial deregulation; they act in tandem as enabling factors and driving forces. To this tandem we now turn.

The revolution in communications has broadened international contacts by leaps and bounds and has facilitated the integration of national markets. One immediate impact has been to diminish the economic distance between countries, and this undoubtedly has been a force for rapid expansion in world trade. Moreover, the advent of new information and telecommunications technologies has had direct implications for the organization of production worldwide. The global reach of multinational companies means that different countries become close locational substitutes. The ability of global companies to transfer and diversify production regionally as part of their worldwide activities has brought about increasing locational competition between countries. In this new environment, hitherto unnoticed differences in institutional practices and relatively small shifts in relative competitiveness can have significant effects on international trade and investment flows. In an era of man-made comparative advantages, locational competition between countries has emerged as a new and increasingly more contentious form of competition.

In addition, new information technologies have had a formidable impact on global financial flows. By making it increasingly difficult for governments to control cross-border financial information and capital flows, information technology has contributed to the internationalization of finance. As some governments have lifted or relaxed restrictions on financial activities, the movement of funds across national borders has increased; and as finance has become increasingly adept at functioning globally, governmental restrictions on international financial flows have further become less effective. At the same time, technology has allowed financial services to become more tradeable across borders; as already noted, such trade has grown exponentially, far exceeding the expansion of production, trade in goods, or FDI. Exchange rates and domestic interest rates have become progressively more sensitive to fluctuations in international financial flows. Thus the process of the growing interrelationship of financial markets has made trade (and hence production, investment and employment) more directly exposed to fluctuations in the international financial environment (Akyüz, 1992).

The process of financial deregulation and internationalization remains incomplete as regards the developing countries. A number of developing countries have not been fully drawn into liberalizing their international capital movements and, notwithstanding the growth of transborder transactions, they retain restrictions on the rights of establishment of foreign banks and on their activities. In other words, foreign banks are not automatically granted national treatment and the right of establishment. These restrictions to financial openness have been a bone of contention in the course of the Uruguay Round, since banks and other financial agents have been actively pursuing an increased presence and participation in financial markets and, more generally, a liberalized regime for international banking services.

For developing countries, this is perhaps one of the most important issues under negotiation in the Uruguay Round, since it poses particular problems for them, with direct implications for their policy autonomy. Liberalization of cross-border transactions in financial services entails a commitment to lift exchange controls, thus restricting the ability of governments to control capital movements, to manage the exchange rate and to conduct monetary and financial policies that are independent of the vagaries of international financial markets. Moreover, unless subject to appropriate controls, the activities of international banks could complicate further the conduct of autonomous macroeconomic management, since these banks are able to move funds in and out of the domestic economy.

Some Policy Consequences of Globalization

Globalization has been fostered partly by economic forces and partly by government deregulation of international trade, finance and foreign investment. On the other hand, globalization itself puts increasing pressures on national governments to liberalize further their policies towards international transactions and to align their policies and regulatory regimes in an increasing number of areas, some of them quite removed from trade concerns, with those prevailing in the main trading nations. To these pressures we now turn.

Globalization is having a profound impact on the international trading system and on developing country policies. Two chapters in this volume address this set of issues. While Lawrence (Chapter 2) looks at the impact of globalization on the policy options of countries, Tussie (Chapter 3) examines the implications of the Uruguay Round (where the pressures arising from globalization have been clearly in evidence) for developing countries' room for manoeuvre in formulating policy.

As discussed in Chapter 2, the underpinnings of the trading system have hitherto been based on the principle of 'shallow integration': the reciprocal freeing of trade was pursued primarily by dealing with instruments and issues as they were reflected at the border and, once beyond the border, there was a simple commitment to guarantee goods the right to national treatment. Under a system of shallow integration, different national practices with effects on trade are tolerated; domestic policy goals are not a subject of contention, so long as national treatment is provided at home and no serious injury is caused to other countries abroad.[9] In fact, the GATT was constructed as a regime for enabling countries to tolerate each others' differences and to trade despite such differences. The GATT, as it has existed up to now, is not unlike the principle of equal treatment before the law, which does not require that all people become identical; on the contrary, equal treatment before the law is based on the opposite proposition, that differences between people are so many and various that criteria for harmonization can never be universally agreed upon (Wolf, 1984). As regards GATT, its basic requirement is a minimum standard of international discipline on narrowly defined commercial policies.

With globalization and more complex forms of economic interpenetration of markets, the problems associated with different practices that affect the competitive environment have become a source of potential friction. As Tussie indicates in Chapter 3, the era of simple multilateral GATT tariff rounds has come to an end. The agenda of international negotiations is at a turning point whereby negotiations are shifting from the treatment of products to the treatment of policies. Increasingly, the new content of multilateral and regional negotiations includes negotiations over policies.

One type of response to this new environment is to proceed from 'shallow' towards 'deep integration', whereby countries smooth out such differences. This route poses risks for the system as a whole and for developing countries in particular. At the level of the system, it is obviously an unmanageable option. The pursuit of structural economic harmonization in wholly new and rather disparate areas, such as workers' rights, environmental policies, the incidence of savings rates, land costs and shopping habits, is essentially positing that *everything* has trade effects and must therefore be the object of international scrutiny. The search for a wider mandate for GATT in the direction of assessing policy and institutional differences as sources of 'distortion' is a straightjacket, essentially caught in the notion that every policy (or, for that matter, absence of policy) can have an impact on competitiveness and must be subjected to international scrutiny.

This has crucial implications for developing countries. As pointed out in Chapters 2 and 3, international trade negotiations in the era of globalization are important for the trade policies of developing countries because, as a precondition for improved market access, they set limits to the policy options open to them. This is reflected in the incorporation into the GATT's agenda – and, therefore, into the realm of international scrutiny – of services, intellectual property rights and the regulation of foreign investment. And the pressures on developing countries to align their policies and practices to those of their main trading partners has already gone beyond the so-called "new issues' in GATT. Questions such as environmental policies and wage levels and their incidence on international competitiveness have already been put on the agenda of multilateral and regional trade negotiations.

According to Tussie, the pressures on developing countries to give up a significant amount of trade policy discretion have been clearly in evidence during the Uruguay Round and could be incorporated into its results, as can be gleaned from an examination of the Draft Final Act of December 1991.[10] If adopted in anything close to its present form, the Final Act would severely limit the autonomy of developing countries in trade policy matters in several crucial respects. For example, they would have to adopt the entire package and would not have the freedom not to sign some of its provisions, as was the case with the Tokyo Round Codes; with few exceptions, developing countries would have to accept the same subsidy disciplines as the developed countries and would have to restrict severely their right to use QRs for balance of payments purposes; credit for past trade liberalizations would depend partially on whether liberalizing countries were willing to bind their lower tariffs; and developing countries would have to enact intellectual property legislation similar to that prevailing in developed countries. On the other hand, developing countries are likely to benefit from the strengthening of the multilateral system resulting from some of the provisions of the Final Act, such as the disciplining of antidumping actions, the phasing out of the Multifibre Arrangement and the creation of a Multilateral Trade Organization that would follow the conclusion of the Uruguay Round. Whether these provisions will be sufficient to provide significantly enhanced market access to developing countries, and whether they will be able to discipline unilateral action by the most powerful trading nations, still remains to be seen.

In the era of globalization, differences in national regulations can be seen as sources of competitive advantages and disadvantages in international markets. Thus global competitive advantages arise not only from attributes that are inherent to firms and to particular locations, but also as a result of measures taken by governments. In this context, a number of critical issues have emerged, some of which are leading to policy initiatives at both the global and regional levels. For example, many governments are inclined to conduct deliberate industrial policies to lend direction and support to firms in order to improve international competitiveness. Such policies of 'industrial targeting', or 'picking winners', which are being increasingly applied in various guises by developed and developing countries, have become a source of friction. This has been reflected in disputes over the legitimacy of any kind of government support that might have an impact on competitiveness, including production, investment and research and development subsidies. The implications for developing countries (at least those that have already succeeded in penetrating developed country markets for manufactures) are clear: henceforth, trade negotiations may well involve their right to conduct active industrial policies.

For developing countries, the *quid pro quo* of accepting increasingly severe restrictions on their policy autonomy is the promise of significantly enhanced market access. Yet such improvements do not seem to be forthcoming, regardless of the commitments made. The balanced incorporation of developing countries into the system requires, therefore, not only what they have already shown an increasing disposition to do (i.e. to give up their acquired rights to derogations from GATT rules on development grounds). It also requires that the goods they export or could potentially export be incorporated fully into the system of reciprocal bargaining.

The New Regional Alternatives

Paradoxically, at the same time that the number of parties to the GATT is expanding as is its prospective competence over issues, so are the number of trading arrangements at the sub-global level. Regional and sub-regional trading arrangements are not new, but they have undoubtedly acquired new dimensions and features in recent years, with the EC's programmes to create a Single European Market and to achieve Economic and Monetary Union by the end of the century; the possible expansion of integration arrangements in Europe to encompass the EC, EFTA and parts of Eastern Europe; the coming into force of the Canada–United States Free Trade Agreement; the recently concluded North American Free Trade Agreement (NAFTA) between the United States, Canada and Mexico; and the flurry of bilateral and plurilateral agreements in Latin America in response to the so-called Bush Initiative.

The regional initiatives have emerged for a variety of reasons. In the first place, the policy convergence that the new trade agenda requires is certainly easier to achieve in smaller and more homogeneous groups of countries than among the entire GATT membership. This has clearly been an incentive to deepening European integration. Secondly, the United States appears to have embraced the regional route out of dissatisfaction with the slowness of the GATT process and as a strategic response to the possibility that deeper European integration may turn out to be protectionist toward non-participants. Finally, it would appear that dealing with market access issues of interest to developing countries is more easily done in the context of regional arrangements which require the major trading powers to open up their markets *selectively* than in the multilateral framework of GATT (see Chapter 3). Thus while the United States may well relax its NTBs in favour of Latin American countries in the context of its integration initiatives with them, it is likely that the EC will follow a similar path with respect to those countries with which it maintains preferential trade agreements (e.g. the ACP countries, some Mediterranean countries and, especially, Eastern Europe).

Of course, the regional option does entail serious risks. Recent estimates of the impact of proposed regional arrangements show that they could have significant trade diversion effects on non-members, even if trade barriers towards non-members are kept unchanged.[11] Moreover, the temptation to shift restrictions from members to third parties will be high.

As regards the trade policies of developing countries, the regional initiatives have consequences that are similar to those of the transformed trade agenda at the multilateral level. Developing countries wishing to participate in regional groupings will have to surrender significant portions of their policy autonomy not only in the traditional trade area (for example, by lowering tariffs and disciplining subsidies) but also in other realms of policy and particularly in services and intellectual property protection. On the other hand, they may be able to obtain more by way of market access through the regional route than they would via multilateral negotiations.

For developing countries as a whole, the regional alternative could turn out to be distinctly inferior to multilateral liberalization, particularly if the improved market access conditions for one group of countries is accompanied by more stringent restrictions on the exports of others. In this latter case, the multilateral system would be well advanced towards a final break-up, with unforeseeable consequences for developing countries. Impartial and multilaterally agreed rules would be replaced with permanent negotiations where considerations of political gain would predominate and where the weak would have scant chances of protecting their interests. In such a scenario, it would be necessary for developing countries to reassess their strategies of unilateral trade liberalization on a multilateral basis.

Of course, as Robert Lawrence points out in Chapter 2, this is not the only possible scenario. Rather than 'stumbling blocks' to freer trade system-wide, the emerging regional groupings could be 'building blocks' to an improved multilateral system. In this scenario, the regional groupings could serve as a kind of 'dry run' for broader trade liberalization and harmonization of policies on a system-wide basis. Tussie argues that, in the best of circumstances, the regional agreements could provide meaningful precedents for multilateral negotiations to follow, the Single European Market in policy harmonization and eventual free trade agreements in the Americas in reducing non-tariff barriers in favour of developing countries. For this scenario to materialize, the emergence of regional groupings would have to be accompanied by significant trade liberalization towards non-members, and this can only be accomplished by continued progress in the negotiations at the multilateral level. In the case of the negotiations in the Americas, the first to include both developed and developing countries, meaningful free trade agreements must lead to a relaxation of current trade restrictions in the United States and Canada.

If these conditions were met, the participation of developing countries in the regional groupings would clearly be in their interest, even if it did mean that they would have to surrender certain degrees of policy autonomy. However, it may be considerably more difficult for them to negotiate, on development grounds, temporary exemptions from some disciplines when dealing with a large regional trading partner than on a multilateral basis, where coalitions of large numbers of countries with common interests are possible. For these and other reasons, multilateral liberalization remains the most desirable option for developing countries.

While the movement towards greater liberalization and policy convergence entails increasing pressures on governments' policy autonomy, the need of developing countries to conduct active industrial and trade policies in order to build competitive supply capabilities remains undisputed by evidence. The challenge to the social scientist interested in policy is to come up with recommendations for policy-makers whose actions are constrained in various ways. In this context, what policies can governments implement to maximize the probability of positive outcomes? This question has two aspects: (a)

What trade policy tools must be retained in the domestic domain if developing countries are to succeed in industrializing with an outward orientation? and (b) In what ways should national development needs be taken into account in international trade negotiations, and how can the process of policy convergence be tailored to accommodate developing countries' needs? We now turn to the first issue. The second one will be tackled in the conclusions to this introductory essay.

II NEW APPROACHES TO TRADE POLICY

Policy Implications of the New Trade Theories

In recent years, a whole body of literature on the theory of international trade has appeared whose main policy message has been to challenge the policy conclusion of traditional trade theory based on static comparative advantage that the optimal policy is one of neutrality of incentives and non-intervention in international trade (e.g. Krugman, 1987 and Krugman, 1990). According to traditional analysis, this is achieved through the abolition of all interferences with 'free trade' (e.g. tariffs, QRs, export subsidies, foreign exchange allocation schemes, preferential interest rates for some tradeables and not for others, etc.). As we shall see, while the new trade theories do not lend support to a return to the high levels of protectionism that were common in developing countries in the past, they do arrive at policy conclusions that are quite different from those of conventional trade theory. In general, it can be said that the main policy implication of the new trade theories is to rescue the validity of a degree of trade policy selectivity.

The results of the standard neo-classical model of international trade which underpins the preference for the neutrality of incentives depend on a number of critical assumptions (revolving around the model of a perfectly competitive economy with perfect information) which, more than a mere simplification of reality, do not accord with the way real economies operate. By way of contrast, the new trade literature stresses three basic ideas which lend this theorizing a greater degree of realism: the pervasiveness of learning effects and external economies in all economic development processes; the widespread presence of economies of scale in the manufacturing sector; and the imperfect nature of most markets, be it in the form of product differentiation, oligopoly, barriers to entry, or costly information about technologies or market conditions. Once the assumptions of conventional trade theory are relaxed to incorporate one or more of these notions, the presumption in favour of incentive neutrality falls apart. Ocampo's essay (Chapter 5 in this volume) discusses the policy implications of this literature for developing countries.

While the kinds of imperfect markets that give rise to international oligopoly are not relevant to most developing countries, there are other types of market imperfections, particularly those associated with product differentiation, which must be taken into account in designing an export-oriented strategy. Product differentiation is a widespread characteristic of most manufactures (differences in design of the same good, in quality, in brand name, in packaging, etc.) and even of a number of agricultural goods (out-of-season fruits and vegetables, for example). The recently adopted export strategy of many developing countries of positioning themselves in specific market 'niches' is based on taking advantage of possibilities for product differentiation. This can be greatly facilitated by an active government role in the identification of such niches and in export promotion, something that is recognized even by the most pro-market governments. Government intervention is needed because these activities have significant spillover effects in the form of creating a market for the country's products or establishing a reputation for its suppliers which private entrepreneurs would not be able to appropriate for themselves and, therefore, would under-invest in the activities giving rise to them.

If economies of scale are important in an activity, a temporary phase of import substitution behind protective barriers may well be justified. This kind of policy has been labelled 'import substitution as export promotion'. Temporary protection would allow firms to expand production and lower costs, eventually enabling them to export to international markets.

More generally, in the presence of widespread economies of scale, the benefits of trade liberalization will depend critically on which sectors contract and which ones expand as a result of the trade liberalization. If contracting sectors are those where the economies of scale are located, the benefits that can be expected from trade liberalization will be considerably reduced.

Learning effects are pervasive in all economies, developed or developing. In fact, self-sustained development can be considered to arise from a 'virtuous cycle' in which increased production leads to greater learning, and learning enhances productivity and output further. Technologies are not 'things' that can be purchased in the market. The mastery of new (and usually foreign) technology and its adaptation to local conditions has significant learning effects which eventually lower costs. In addition, the positive externalities through the migration of trained labour or through the impact on suppliers and customers can be quite important.

Learning processes are cumulative and their speed depends on the rate of growth of the economy, not necessarily of exports. The importance of exports is that they permit a growth of output which is not limited by the size of the domestic market, they allow for sustained growth unhindered by foreign exchange availability, and they make it possible to import capital goods, which are the largest source of imported technology in developing countries.

By the same token, processes of contraction are also cumulative. Wholesale trade liberalization can lead to losses of production and employment which go well beyond the contraction of firms initially affected by the removal of import barriers. Therefore, even sound firms which are not dependent on protection but which provide inputs to protected sectors, or which depend on the markets created by employment in the protected sector, can be adversely affected by poorly designed programmes of trade liberalization. Moreover, in contractionary processes, long spells of unemployment can lead to the loss of human skills acquired at great cost. This is an important reason to design trade policy reforms with great care.

All of these arguments support selective trade policies and selective trade liberalization. They clearly do not argue for import substitution as practised in most of the developing world until recently. For most countries, export expansion and diversification are the surest road to sustained growth. But this is unlikely to be achieved through sheer incentive neutrality. In some cases, import substitution may clearly be desirable (for example, in the case, already noted, of 'import substitution as export promotion'). In others, various forms of temporary export subsidy may be the best policy. Perhaps the most important policy conclusion of the new theories is that it is impossible to make generalizations as to the optimal trade policy and that knowledge of the particular conditions prevailing in each country at the sectoral level is necessary before any conclusion with regard to policy can be reached.

The Sequencing-of-Reform Debate

A closely related issue discussed in the literature is the one of sequencing of policy reforms (for opposing views, see Choksi and

Papageorgiou, 1986; and Fanelli and Frenkel, 1992). As regards trade policy reform, it is argued that it is better to first 'tariffy' QRs and other foreign exchange controls having effects similar to QRs and then proceed to reduce tariffs to a low level (Thomas, Matin and Nash, 1990; and Michaely, 1986). The elimination of QRs would, then, be the first and indispensable step towards a liberal trade policy.

QRs are clearly a poor way of controlling imports with adverse impacts on resource allocation. But in fragile economies like those of developing countries, where external shocks tend to produce large swings in the trade balance and in economic activity, the temporary use of QRs may well be justified as a first and most effective expedient to deal with adverse external shocks (see Ocampo, 1990). As demonstrated by the Chilean experience during the debt crisis, renouncing the use of QRs can be very costly in times of emergency (see Chapter 7 in this volume). It is fairly easy to prohibit the importation of certain consumer (particularly luxury) goods for the duration of a crisis, and the impact of such measures is likely to be considerably less disruptive than the price changes that would ensue if resort is not had to QRs. For example, a deterioration in the terms of trade, even if temporary, will put downward pressures on the exchange rate which can be avoided with a judicious use of QRs.

Moreover, QRs and foreign exchange allocations can be used for socially productive purposes, for example if they are tied to export performance, as the Koreans did in order to launch their export drive (see Chapter 8 in this volume). In fact, in economies with small industrial sectors and which are not responsive to price changes, these sorts of crude incentives work better than incentive neutrality, if the objective is to launch a sustained export drive. Of course, such expedients must be considered transitional and must be abandoned as an articulated industrial sector that is more responsive to price signals is built. This is the path that has been adopted by South Korea.

Trade Policy and Performance: Empirical Evidence

If one examines the record of the post-war period, the evidence is unkind to the hypothesis that incentive neutrality or import liberalization has led to faster economic growth. As pointed out in Chapter 4 in this volume, cross-section analysis for the 1980s reveals that higher rates of growth of manufactured exports were indeed statistically associated with higher rates of economic growth, particularly in those countries where genuine processes of economic opening took place (as measured by the *joint* increase in the ratios of exports *and* imports to GDP). However, there was no statistical relationship between the rates of growth of manufactured exports or GDP, on the one hand, and available measures of the restrictiveness of the trade regime (the average level of tariffs and the incidence of non-tariff barriers), on the other.

Clearly, the historical record seems to favour selectivity. With very few exceptions, countries that have succeeded in promoting long-term export-oriented growth have relied on selective trade and industrialization policies. Conversely, there are few examples of developing countries achieving fast growth through purely market-oriented policies and incentive neutrality.

The historical record also shows that the management of the exchange rate is considerably more important than import policy for successful exporting and for sustained growth generally. All countries that have succeeded in generating a sustained growth of their exports, leading to high rates of growth of output over the long term, have also been able to maintain exchange rates that are attractive to exporters over long periods of time. The exchange rate in such countries has also tended to be fairly stable, enabling producers of tradeables to make long-term investment plans.

The ability to manage the real exchange rate appears to be closely correlated to the prior achievement of rough price stability. Thus countries that succeeded in setting in motion a process of export-oriented growth did not fall into the temptation of using the nominal exchange rate as a substitute for sound monetary and fiscal policies. This should be a clear warning to policy-makers in a number of Latin American countries who insist in using the exchange rate as a nominal anchor for domestic prices.

Trade Impact of External Financial Variables

Hence control over macroeconomic variables, particularly fiscal and monetary, is essential for successful exchange rate management. As Akyüz (see Chapter 6) points out, control over capital flows is just as important. Many developing countries have recently liberalized their external financial sector, for a variety of reasons. Experience so far shows that financial liberalization leaves the real exchange rate at the mercy of fickle short-term capital movements in search of interest-arbitrage opportunities. The foreign exchange markets of most developing countries are small and highly susceptible to small swings in capital flows (or in the terms of trade). Therefore, even small changes in the direction of trade and capital flows can produce large swings in the real exchange rate.

Thus countries that have not yet embarked on external financial liberalization would be well advised not to do so and to establish strict supervision and control of short-term capital outflows and inflows. In countries where international financial flows have already been liberalized, unwanted capital inflows that put upward pressures on the real exchange rate must be discouraged. This can be accomplished with the use of a tax on short-term capital movements, the imposition of higher reserve requirements on banks' foreign exchange liabilities than on their domestic currency liabilities, by requiring banks to match the size and maturity of foreign exchange assets and liabilities, and through moral suasion or administrative guidance.[12] It may even be appropriate to design some queuing mechanism for FDI, whenever very large flows of the latter threaten to disrupt exchange markets or cannot be absorbed by the domestic economy without an inflationary impact. Disruptive capital outflows that threaten major devaluations may necessitate the temporary reimposition of exchange controls, particularly on the ability of nationals to hold foreign assets or assets denominated in foreign currencies.

In addition, financial liberalization increases the difficulties of implementing selective industrial policies, since policy makers lose control over the interest rate. External financial liberalization means that domestic financial assets must compete with international assets, which tends to tie domestic interest rates to those prevailing in international capital markets. In fact, given the greater uncertainties attached to domestic assets, yields must usually be higher than those on international assets. This gives an upward push to domestic interest rates generally and impairs the competitiveness of domestic producers in international markets.

External financial liberalization is usually accompanied by liberalization of internal financial transactions. The latter involves the elimination of subsidized credits for activities which are not currently profitable. The banking sectors of developing countries tend to be notoriously myopic, and other financial intermediaries are usually nonexistent. This means that governments must normally take the place of venture capitalists. Moreover, the ability of government to allocate financial resources to priority activities is an indispensable element of active industrial policies. Leaving the allocation of such resources entirely to the market will place severe limits on the capacity of policy-makers to influence the long-term decisions of the private sector.

III   WHAT THE CASE STUDIES REVEAL

The objective of Part III is to carry out a comparative analysis of the various topics discussed in Part II using case studies of countries in Asia and Latin America that have had particularly relevant experiences with the management of processes of trade policy reform. Case studies conducted along a common pattern of enquiry yield generalizations in two ways. First, each country study itself suggests possible inferences; and these, looked at in the aggregate, may yield certain patterns that are not visible without a comparative approach. In this section, we attempt to draw the various conclusions for the relationship between trade policy and economic performance that we see arising from the country studies.

The Asian case studies (South Korea and Turkey) are illustrative of the policies followed by two countries that have been successful (in different degrees and in very different contexts) in encouraging a sustained increase in their exports of manufactures and in diversifying their export structures. On the other hand, the Latin American case studies (Chile, Argentina and Mexico) are interesting because it is in this region that the most wide-ranging shift towards trade liberalization is now taking place, and these three countries are in the vanguard of the process.

One of these countries – Chile – has a long track record with trade liberalization. In many ways, other liberalizing countries in Latin America are consciously attempting to emulate the Chilean experience and, therefore, a careful reading of what Chile's trade liberalization did and did not accomplish is a very timely exercise. Moreover, its experience provides a useful contrast with that of South Korea, since trade policy reforms have been quite different in these two countries, and so have been the results obtained.

Trade policy reform is a necessity in the developing world, particularly in middle-income countries that have long relied on an import-substitution pattern of industrial development. The old model of import substitution has lost dynamism, and currently there are very few countries that practise it in its pure form. The drawbacks of protracted protection have been amply chronicled and do not need to be repeated here. Most of the arguments against import substitution rely on static considerations about the inefficiencies of deviating from a Pareto-optimal allocation of resources. More recently, the literature on rent-seeking has emphasized the losses that result from the utilization of resources in unproductive activities (Bhagwati, 1982). Other critiques have also stressed dynamic aspects: in comparison with export orientation, protectionist policies are likely to lead to lower rates of growth of total factor productivity and fewer economies of scale (for greater elaboration, see Chapter 4 in this volume).

Therefore, greater export orientation is more suited to current circumstances than out-and-out protection. There is, however, considerable controversy on how to attain it. The analysis in this section will be organized along a broad set of issues. In the first place, should liberalization be selective or wholesale? Second, should import liberalization be postponed until the structure of the economy has been permanently altered towards export orientation? Third, what is the role of the exchange rate in achieving export orientation? Finally, should policies designed to effect a shift from import substitution to export orientation be postponed until after the economy has been stabilized?

Selective or Wholesale Trade Liberalization?

A selective trade liberalization begins with a clear notion of what its objectives are. If it is desired to expose certain sectors that have been protected for too long to greater import competition, protective barriers in those sectors can be gradually brought down, retaining protection for those sectors where the discounted social benefits are deemed to be higher than the social costs of protection. Or if policy objectives shift to export orientation, liberalization could begin with imported inputs used in the production of exports. At the same time, a selective approach would emphasize a variety of measures to ensure that resources are reallocated towards export industries. Such incentives could take the form of an adequate exchange rate, temporary export subsidies and the provision of credit at preferential interest rates.

Wholesale liberalization is an entirely different kettle of fish. Its basic philosophical premises are that *no protection is the best protection and that all economic decisions are best left to the market*. This approach would tie the hands of government with regard to trade policy and would make it impossible for policy makers to exert a direct influence on the sectoral allocation of resources. This view is the one that the major trading powers are pressing on developing countries (one which, it should be remarked, they do not themselves follow in practice). It is also in line with the international pressures on developing countries to abandon discretionary trade and industrial policies, discussed in Part I. As regards concrete trade policy action, this approach would have governments eliminate all QRs and reduce tariffs to a minimum and uniform level.

The problem is that there are no examples of countries that have achieved strong growth rates of output and exports following whole-sale liberalization policies. Both South Korea and Taiwan, the paradigmatic outward-oriented industrializers, used highly selective trade policies (see Chapter 8 in this volume; and Wade, 1990a, Chapter 5). As Amsden points out in Chapter 8, when South Korea launched its outward-oriented industrialization drive, it did not begin by liberal-izing its imports. In fact, import liberalization did not figure as an important part in implementing the Korean strategy. On the contrary, it left the protective structures it had erected earlier relatively untouched and superimposed on them a layer of strong export incentives, including tariff drawback mechanisms, allocation of scarce foreign exchange and import quotas to exporters, subsidized credits, and tax breaks. Moral suasion, the tying of governmental benefits to specific export goals and the granting of high protection at home in exchange for the attainment of export targets were all part of a complete strategy to induce the private sector to industrialize on an outward-oriented pattern.

By contrast, as already noted, Chile and Mexico did follow a policy of wholesale liberalization rather than export-oriented growth using selective policy instruments. Over the period 1974–9, Chile attempted a thorough-going trade policy reform which eliminated all non-tariff restrictions and reduced tariffs from peaks exceeding 1000 per cent and varying enormously from one tariff line to another to a uniform tariff of 10 per cent (see Chapter 7 in this volume). Likewise, between 1985 and 1988 Mexico eliminated all non-tariff barriers, swept away the system of customs valuation which served as an important, and variable, surcharge to tariffs, and brought down tariffs to an average of about 12 per cent (see Chapter 10 in this volume). Much like the Chilean and Mexican liberalizations, the one undertaken by Argentina in 1991 was also quite unselective (see Chapter 11 in this volume).

So far, across-the-board liberalization does not seem to have yielded the results in terms of resource reallocation and growth that had been expected by its adherents. Trade liberalization is, in essence, a negative impulse designed to force resources out of sectors that are deemed to be inefficient. Developing economies respond very slowly to such negative incentives. If the policy is maintained even in the face of unemployment and depression, as was the case in Chile, exports of goods with obvious comparative advantages eventually do increase, but at tremendous social costs. Ffrench-Davis, Leiva and Madrid argue that (see Chapter 7), in the design of Chile's trade liberalization, more selective policies with regard to tariff reductions and a more activist support for non-traditional exports would have led to a more dynamic performance of the economy as a whole. The way things turned out, between 1973 and 1989 the Chilean economy grew at less than 1 per cent per annum in per capita terms. Instead of modernizing, an important proportion of the industrial sector that had grown under the import substitution regime disappeared. The emergence of a vigorous modernized sector of the economy was insufficient for value added *per capita* in the manufacturing sector to recover the levels it had reached in the early 1970s. Many of the firms that were bankrupted under the joint impact of import liberalization and exchange rate overvaluation (a topic that is discussed below) were potentially strong and, with adequate policies of industrial conversion, they could have contributed to a more dynamic expansion of the economy under an outward-oriented model of development. Thus most of the export expansion that did eventually result from the reorientation of incentives came from new investments in the primary sector.

Neither has Mexican growth responded very strongly to the wholesale import liberalization to which the economy was subjected. Until 1988, the economy remained depressed and GDP was below its pre-reform level; more recent rates of growth have been in the order of 3.5 per cent per annum. While non-oil exports have indeed grown rapidly, such growth can hardly be ascribed to the trade liberalization programme. Exports began rising strongly in 1983, well before the initiation of the trade policy reform and as a consequence mainly of the steep depreciation of the peso, which was expected to remain depressed owing to the debt crisis. Much of Mexico's original export spurt came from affiliates of United States companies which had originally invested in the country to take advantage of protectionist policies. The depression of the domestic market and the fall in the value of the Mexican currency brought about by the debt crisis induced several of these affiliates to export to their home market. More recently, export growth has become more broad-based and investment has recovered.

The Chilean experience does not augur well for the unselective liberalizations undertaken recently by several other Latin American countries, including Argentina. Like Chile, Argentina has an important manufacturing sector which could be adversely affected by the combination of wholesale import liberalization and exchange rate appreciation. Therefore, Argentina could be in danger of experiencing a 'reprimarization' of its exports and a severe loss of the relative importance of manufacturing in its economy, and of the accompanying know-how, much as took place in Chile.

Some Real Sequencing Issues: Liberalization Before or After Export Growth?

The question arises as to whether import liberalization, by itself, will produce a reallocation of resources away from previously protected activities towards the export sector. If this were the case, it would be advisable to liberalize imports and wait for the positive effect in terms of export growth and the greater efficiency that is implicit in the reallocation of resources away from less efficient activities. Alternatively, if import liberalization elicits weak allocative responses from producers, the most appropriate policy would be to secure strong and sustained export growth first and then seek the greater efficiency promised by liberalization.

As indicated by Amsden in Chapter 8, South Korea followed this latter path. Korea did adopt an import liberalization programme in the early 1980s, and it is still pursuing it. The reasons have been many. At this stage of Korean development, the ability to innovate and to continue to upgrade the export mix has become crucial to sustained high growth, and this is best done in a more market-oriented environment. Moreover, it is not as easy as it once was to identify and create winners. Finally, Korea's major trading partners, and particularly the United States, have been putting intense pressure on the country to liberalize its imports. Similar policies have been followed by Taiwan (see Noland, 1990, chapter 2; and Wade, 1990b).

The only examples of economies that have succeeded in industrializing for world markets following liberal import policies from the start are Hong Kong and Singapore, and even the case of the latter is in question in this respect, because Singapore went through a short-lived period of import substitution in the 1960s. At any rate, these city states are not really comparable with most other developing countries. It is as if one were to discuss the advantages of a free import policy for the economy of New York, London or Bombay.

More recently, some of the newcomers to international markets for manufactures in South and East Asia have also followed trade policy patterns similar to those of South Korea and Taiwan. Although at the beginning their trade barriers were considerably lower than those of other developing countries, when in the second half of the 1970s export expansion superseded import substitution as the centrepiece of their development strategy, they did not proceed to dismantle existing protection. Instead, they instituted strong export support mechanisms *while at the same time maintaining significant levels of effective protection to import-substituting activities.* The trade liberalizations that have taken place since the second half of the 1980s have been cautious and came after the economy had been restructured and oriented towards international markets (Noland, 1990).

In Turkey, also, the spectacular success of non-traditional exports beginning in 1980 was not the result of a presumed prior import liberalization, which got under way in earnest only towards the end of the decade and still remains very incomplete. Turkey's export drive did not rely on import liberalization but on the introduction or strengthening of existing export incentives. While there was a significant relaxation of QRs (in particular, the abolition of licensing for most goods), tariffs were in fact raised. Another important characteristic of the Turkish experience is that the export surge took place in industries that had been established during the long import substitution phase of industrialization which had preceded the policy shift of 1980 (see Chapter 9 in this volume).

As already noted, Chile's import liberalization in the second half of the 1970s was premised on the kinds of thinking described above, i.e. that exports would pick up spontaneously as a result of the changed pattern of incentives that would follow the import liberalization.[13] This did not happen, and the positive impulses to the production of exportables were considerably weaker than the negative impulses on industries producing import substitutes. The strong real devaluations of the period 1982–7 corrected this picture and permitted a vigorous increase in exports that has lasted up to the present.[14]

In most of the liberalizations that have recently been put into effect in Latin America, including the Argentinian programme, the option of first stimulating export growth and then gradually liberalizing imports no longer exists: liberalization had already taken place and it was undertaken in a context in which the economy as a whole and the export sector in particular were far from exhibiting a dynamic behaviour. The conclusions that can be drawn are that these liberalization exercises will not be the *deus ex machina* construed by their supporters and that their probabilities of success are exceedingly low.

Since these experiences are taking place in conjunction with a return
to democracy and greater social pluralism, their political viability can
also be seriously questioned. Therefore, a return to a greater
pragmatism may be imposed on policy makers by both economic
and political realities.

The Role of the Exchange Rate

As already noted in the preceding section, the management of the
exchange rate is a more fundamental determinant of trade performance
than import policies. This is one of the lessons that emerges from the
studies prepared for this work; this finding is also in line with the long
experience of developing countries generally. The avoidance of
currency overvaluation is a *sine qua non* condition for the success of
any trade policy reform, be it wholesale liberalization or a controlled
and gradual shift towards export orientation. Once again, the Chilean
experience – as well as that of other Southern Cone countries during
the second half of the 1970s – highlights how damaging real exchange
rate appreciation can be. During the period 1977–82, the exchange rate
was targeted increasingly at slowing down inflation. In 1979 the
nominal exchange rate was actually fixed. The real exchange rate
appreciation that ensued (because prices for non-tradeables continued
to rise strongly) was facilitated by the huge capital inflow that followed
the liberalization of the capital account of the balance of payments in
1977. The exchange rate appreciation came at a time when the trade
regime was being drastically liberalized and standard trade policy
advice would have called for a large real devaluation. As already noted,
there were widespread bankruptcies, including firms that might have
survived the trade liberalization under a different exchange rate policy.

The more recent trade liberalizations in Latin America are also being
implemented together with external financial liberalizations and at a
time when there has been a sudden and sharp reversal in the direction
of capital flows. Large capital inflows and the ensuing appreciation of
national currencies have been widespread throughout the region. In
effect, some of the countries where import liberalization has been most
thorough-going (e.g. Argentina, Colombia and Peru) have also
experienced pronounced appreciation in their real exchange rates. As
the experiences of the Southern Cone countries during the 1970s show,
the consequences for economic growth of rapid tariff reductions and
exchange rate appreciation can be devastating (Díaz-Alejandro, 1981;
Díaz-Alejandro, 1985; Dornbusch and de Pablo, 1989).

A corollary of the above is that, in situations of abundance of foreign exchange, it is essential to develop mechanisms to prevent excessive capital inflows from wrecking the country's long-term growth strategy. This will be all the more important in countries such as those of Latin America which have undergone capital account liberalizations which can be reversed only at the cost of very hard-won credibility.

There are important lessons to be learned from the exchange rate experience of the economies of East Asia and of Turkey which today's candidates to export-oriented growth would do well to heed. As Amsden points out in Chapter 8, South Korea was able to achieve remarkable real exchange rate stability. This was a common feature of the successful export-oriented economies of the region (see Chapter 4 in this volume). Real exchange rate stability served as a background against which export incentives could be effective. In the case of Turkey, while the battery of incentives thrown at exporters as part of the structural adjustment programme of 1980 appears to have been crucial in helping producers to break into export markets, it was an exchange rate policy favourable to exports that kept them growing throughout most of the decade. When policy-makers, in the late 1980s, began to use the exchange rate as an anti-inflationary tool, the momentum of export growth declined (see Chapter 9 in this volume).

The importance of a crawling peg exchange rate regime in Brazil's and Colombia's successful record of export diversification in the long period that runs from the 1960s up to the early 1990s also lends support to the contention that the exchange rate is fundamental for the success of export-oriented growth. The recent abandonment of the crawling peg by both countries could result in a significant deceleration of export growth (Ocampo and Villar, 1992; and Fritsch and Franco, 1992).

Trade Policy Reform and Price Stability

The changes in relative prices that are sought with trade policy reform are difficult to bring about in an environment of high and variable inflation. Moreover, in economies with high inflation, prices lose their information content for making investment decisions. The experiences of countries such as South Korea and Taiwan indicate that price stability was achieved before the economy was oriented towards world markets and much before imports were liberalized.

One of the most striking characteristics of the trade liberalizations that have been carried out in Latin America has been the fact that they have been implemented in a setting of high inflation. It would seem that the rationale for the inclusion of drastic measures of trade liberalization in a package of policies geared mainly towards price disinflation is the assignment of a rather unconventional role to trade policy reform, which is to give greater credibility to the package as a whole. This was certainly the case with Mexico's reforms; Rodrik (1990) sees a general trend in this rather peculiar use of trade policy.

The joint pursuit of stabilization and greater trade openness involves obvious dangers. If price stability were to be an elusive goal, this could destroy confidence in the ability of the government to stick to the entire package, including the trade policy component. And a failed reform would have very adverse effects on credibility and on the investments that are necessary for the success of any trade policy reform effort in the future.

Policy management is very different when the objective is price stability than when it is greater openness. In several respects, certain contradictions could arise if both objectives are pursued at the same time. As already noted, the management of the exchange rate is quite different when the objective is to stabilize than when it is to liberalize trade. The need to stabilize an economy prone to high inflation can also induce the authorities to use instruments of trade policy for anti-inflationary objectives which detract from their effectiveness and endanger the credibility of trade policy reforms. In Argentina (as well as in other Latin American countries), difficulties in bringing down inflation through fiscal and monetary policies have induced the authorities to use unconventional means, including tariff reductions (see Chapter 11 in this volume). This has undermined the capacity of the economy to recover its growth momentum and has diminished the credibility of trade policy announcements.

IV SOME POLICY IMPLICATIONS

We now re-examine some of the earlier strands of this introduction with the question we asked at the end of section I: In what ways can development needs be taken into account in the new international trade order that is emerging and which is almost certain to involve the setting up of an all-encompassing multilateral trade organization that will increasingly limit the policy autonomy of member states? On the one hand, in a globalizing world economy, integration into international markets has become a principal source of growth and, therefore, developing countries cannot afford to stay on the sidelines. On the other, it is becoming increasingly clear that there is a tension between the development needs of developing countries and the demands for policy conformity arising from globalization.

At the same time, a shift has taken place in attitudes towards trade liberalization. While the doctrine of liberalization is gaining widespread acceptance in developing countries, trade relations between developed and developing countries are undergoing more change than at any other time in the post-war period. Developing countries have drastically altered their approach both to their own trade policies and to participation in GATT negotiations. This shift coincides, however, with a growing ambivalence by key developed countries with regard to the principles of ruled-based multilateralism.

Until the 1980s, developed countries did not find that the self-exclusion of developing countries was something to be concerned about. It was inconsequential to their own trading interests. A turning point, however, seems to have been reached in this respect. On the one hand, the markets of developing countries are of growing importance to the industrialized countries and, for this reason, the demands on the former to assume greater responsibilities within the system have become more insistent. On the other hand, the turn by the developed countries to more aggressive demands for reciprocity is not being matched by a willingness to open up their markets to developing countries. This contradiction is an element undermining the success of trade liberalization in developing countries.

The new ideas that have emerged in the theory of international trade, as well as the case studies that have been examined, suggest some clear conclusions for national policy which may be at variance both with the liberalizing trend that one can observe in developing countries and with the pressures towards policy convergence and surrender of policy autonomy.

In the first place, as has already been argued, exchange rate management is crucial to the success of trade policy reform. For this reason, it is essential that policy-makers retain control over international capital flows. This requirement must be taken into account in the design of an international agreement on trade in banking sevices, which undoubtedly will deal with the setting up of affiliates of international banks in developing countries and may curtail the discretion of host governments to limit the freedom of international banks to move foreign exchange across national boundaries.

Secondly, governments must retain the right to apply selective trade and industrial policies. This is not an argument for continued import substitution in the old style. The proper use of selectivity lies in identifying sectors with potential comparative advantage and gearing policies towards their acquisition. Neutral policies do not serve these objectives well. Neither is the extreme and arbitrary distortion of incentives through tariffs, QRs or subsidies a good prescription for building dynamic comparative advantage. Co-operation between the private and public sectors for the achievement of clearly specified and understood social goals seems to have been the main trait of those economies that have been able to generate long-term, outward-oriented growth processes.

Import substitution is not, *per se*, an inferior policy option, particularly at incipient levels of industrialization. But the lessons of experience show that it should be pursued with moderate and temporary protection, with extreme selectivity, and in exchange for tangible standards of performance. At the international level, it is important that the need of developing countries for greater flexibility in the application of tariffs be recognized.

Export subsidization has been characteristic of most developing countries that have succeeded in penetrating international markets and in launching a sustained growth process based on exports. As with the case of import substitution, subsidies need to be moderate and to decrease over time. They can take a variety of forms. One form that is not in contradiction with GATT norms is the setting up of a system of tariff and indirect taxation drawbacks for direct and indirect exporters so as to put exporters on the same footing as their international competitors. But other more direct subsidies, which may give rise to international frictions unless their economic rationale is accepted, will surely be necessary if self-sustained export-oriented growth is to get underway. The justification for subsidies to non-traditional exports is not difficult to find: the start-up costs of export promotion (e.g. the gathering of information about foreign markets, changes in product design, marketing efforts, etc.) are large and usually beyond the capabilities of most enterprises in developing countries. Moreover, there are significant benefits to these activities which cannot be appropriated privately. Breaking into export markets makes it easier for imitators and followers.

There are other activities that the government should undertake on behalf of exporters of new products, also on the grounds that they have large externalities. These have to do with the factors making the exports of the country as a whole more attractive in foreign markets and export market research. All of these activities presuppose an active industrial policy and selectivity in trade policy.

Therefore, a solid argument can be built for the retention of a degree of selectivity in trade policy. The drift of trade policies in the developed countries towards managed trade and regional preferential agreements and the gradual *de facto* abandonment of multilateralism reinforce the desirability of selectivity. Individual developing countries must now engage increasingly in identifying what they can produce and sell and in what markets. In addition, international negotiations over market access for individual products have become increasingly important.

Developing countries have participated actively in the Uruguay Round, and their stance has changed significantly since the initiation of the Round. As the trade policies of many developing countries (particularly large countries such as India, Brazil, Mexico and Argentina) began to shift in a more liberal direction, developing countries have come to understand that, in exchange for market access, they will have to accept greater international obligations with regard to their trade policies and even other policies that are perceived as having an impact on international competitiveness (see Tussie and Glover, 1993a). At the present time, in view of the trends towards unilateral action and politically motivated preferences on the part of the major trading powers, the costs of exclusion are likely to be higher than the costs of being part of any eventual new global trade compact.

One interesting option for developing countries would be to bargain for the retention of 'development clauses' in the global and regional rules that are now being negotiated. These could involve temporary and internationally agreed derogations from the rules which would be subject to a periodic review mechanism (say, every ten years). These development clauses would have some crucial differences from the current Generalized System of Preferences (GSP) schemes operated by most developed countries. Under the GSP, each national scheme is 'autonomous'. In other words, it is a concession that can be withdrawn by a donor country without negotiation or compensation, and the list of beneficiaries, product coverage, tariff reductions, etc. are determined unilaterally by the donors. On the other hand, the condition of 'developing country', which makes a country nominally eligible for

GSP benefits, is a matter of self-election, and this renders the question of 'graduation' an internationally contentious one. The 'development clause' notion advocated here would be binding on all participants; it would deal with all trade issues and not just tariffs; it would involve the adoption of commonly agreed criteria to accede to the benefits of derogation, it would set (renewable) time limits to those benefits; and it would establish a system of international review to determine graduation. As a *quid pro quo*, developing countries could accept to bind their tariff schedules, perhaps in the form of establishing a ceiling to their tariffs which is somewhat above the level of actual tariffs.

As has already been noted, the incorporation of the developing countries to the system *as it now exists* is far from having been completed. Now that a growing number of countries are willing to accept fuller GATT disciplines, the main reason for their exclusion is the non-applicability of GATT principles to a significant share of their exports by the major importing countries. If the developed countries are serious about bringing the developing countries into the system as full partners, they should show their good faith by eliminating the asymmetry that exists between their demands on developing countries and what they are willing to offer the latter in terms of market access. The success of the efforts of developing countries to open up their economies to international trade rests, in the aggregate, on effective market openings in developed countries.

The rapid spread in the number of developing countries embracing more liberal trade policies is opening up new and previously unsuspected bargaining possibilities for groups of developing countries. In the recent past, liberalizations have occurred unilaterally. While most individual countries taken in isolation are unlikely to have much bargaining strength, collectively they may be able to extract meaningful concessions as a *quid pro quo* for past and prospective liberalizations. Thus flexible coalitions of countries around specific interests may prove to be an avenue worth exploring.

Notes

1. We wish to thank Yilmaz Akyüz, Andrew Cornford, José María Fanelli, Gerry Helleiner and Ian Kinniburgh for generous comments on earlier drafts of this chapter. The usual caveats apply.
2. As an example of the cumbersome process of permanent bargaining for market access, the experience of the newly industrializing Asian countries is relevant (Glover, 1993).

3. As of early 1992, 63 developing countries had liberalized their trade since the start of the Uruguay Round (GATT/1538, Geneva, 12 March 1992).
4. A similar model is developed by Cline (1984). However, in Cline's model, intra-industry trade is not used as a variable explaining protection.
5. The proper comparison is, of course, between stocks of FDI and domestic capital stocks, both for the countries where FDI originates and for recipient countries. However, domestic capital stock figures are available for very few countries.
6. It should be noted, however, that a good portion of FDI is now going into the services sector (UNCTC, 1988, part five). Since most services are non-tradeables, a large share of FDI is still oriented to the domestic markets of the recipient countries.
7. It should also be noted that export orientation provides some guarantee to prospective investors that there will be foreign exchange available with which to remit their earnings abroad, and this provides an additional rationale for their interest in countries with export-oriented policies (we owe this point to Gerry Helleiner).
8. These transactions involve either residents and non-residents or the use by residents of a foreign currency.
9. The principle of shallow integration (i.e. the acceptance of different approaches to domestic policy-making) is not altogether obsolete. It is applied by Jackson (1990) in his proposal for reforming the international trading system.
10. At the time of writing (end-1992), it was unclear whether the Uruguay Round would conclude with positive results and whether the Draft Final Act presented by the Director-General of GATT to the Contracting Parties would be approved and in what form. Regardless of the outcome, however, the notions contained in it represent the summary statement of the Round's negotiating achievements and give a good indication of what developing countries can expect, and what is expected of them, in today's international climate.
11. For some estimates of the impact of EC 1992 on developing countries, see Alizadeh and Griffith-Jones, with Agosin (1992) and Davenport, with Page (1991). Erzan and Yeats (1991) make some estimates of the trade creation and trade diversion of a free-trade agreement between the United States and Mexico and under various options of the Enterprise for the Americas Initiative.
12. It sould be noted that the route of imposing high reserve requirements on the foreign exchange liabilities of banks has been followed in Chile since mid-1991, with considerable success in staving off unwanted speculative flows.
13. In fairness to the policy-makers of the time, the import liberalization package was expected to be accompanied by a strong real devaluation, which was judged necessary to the attainment of reallocating resources from inefficient import substitutes and non-traded goods to the export sector. The devaluations of the early years of the regime were more than compensated for by strong real exchange rate appreciation 1977–82, as exchange rate policy shifted from the support of structural adjustment to the control of inflation.

14. Real devaluation also gave renewed impulses to import substituting
     activities which counteracted to some extent the disincentive of import
     liberalization.

References

Akyüz, Y, (1992), 'Financial Globalization and Instability', in United Nations
     Development Programme, *Change: Threat or Opportunity?* (New York).
Alizadeh, P., and S. Griffith-Jones, with M. R. Agosin (1992), 'La Integración
     Europea y Sus Consequencias para los Países en Desarrollo', *Pensamiento
     Iberoamericano* (Madrid), No. 20, July–December.
Bergsten, C. F. and W. R. Cline (1982), *Trade Policy in the 1980s* (Washington,
     DC: Institute for International Economics).
Bhagwati, J. (1982), 'Directly-Unproductive, Profit-seeking (DUP) Activities',
     Journal of Political Economy, Vol. 5, October, pp. 988–1002.
Bhagwati, J. (1987), 'Outward Orientation: Trade Issues' in V. Corbo, M.
     Goldstein and M. Khan, eds, *Growth-Oriented Adjustment Programs*
     (Washington, DC: International Monetary Fund and World Bank).
Choksi, A. M., and D. Papageorgiou, eds (1986), *Economic Liberalization in
     Developing Countries* (Oxford: Basil Blackwell).
Cline, W. R. (1982), 'Can the East Asian Model of Development be General-
     ized?', *World Development*, Vol. 10, No. 2.
Cline, W. R. (1984), *Exports of Manufactures from Developing Countries*
     (Washington, DC: The Brookings Institution).
Davenport, M., with S. Page (1991), *Europe: 1992 and the Developing Countries*
     (London: Overseas Development Institute).
De Castro, J. A. (1989), 'Determinants of Protection and Evolving Forms of
     North–South Trade', *UNCTAD Review* (Geneva), Vol. 1, No. 2.
Díaz-Alejandro, C. F. (1981), 'Southern Cone Stabilization Plans', in W. R.
     Cline and S. Weintraub, eds, *Economic Stabilization in Developing Countries*
     (Washington, DC: The Brookings Institution).
Díaz-Alejandro, C. F. (1985), 'Good-bye Financial Repression, Hello Financial
     Crash', *Journal of Development Economics*, Vol. 19, No. 1–2.
Dornbusch, R., and J. C. De Pablo (1989), 'Debt and Macroeconomic Stability
     in Argentina', in J. D. Sachs, ed., *Developing Country Debt and the World
     Economy* (Chicago and London: University of Chicago Press, for National
     Bureau of Economic Research).
Erzan, R., and A. Yeats (1991), 'Prospects for United States–Latin America
     Free Trade Areas: Empirical Evidence Concerning the View from the South',
     Washington, DC, World Bank, October (processed).
Fanelli, J. M., and R. Frenkel (1992), 'On Gradualism, Shock and Sequencing
     in Economic Adjustment', Documento CEDES/81, Buenos Aires.
Fritsch, W., and G. Franco (1992), 'Política Comercial no Brasil: Passado e
     Presente', *Pensamiento Iberoamericano* (Madrid), No. 21, January–June.
Glover, D. (1993), 'Bypassing the Barriers: Lessons from the Asian NICs', in
     Tussie and Glover (1993b).
Jackson, J. (1990), *Restructuring the GATT System* (London: Royal Institute of
     International Affairs, Pinter Publishers).

Julius, D. A. (1990), *Global Companies and Public Policy: The Growing Challenge of FDI* (London: Royal Institute of International Affairs, Pinter Publishers).

Krugman, P. R. (1987), 'Is Free Trade Passé', *The Journal of Economic Perspectives*, Vol. 1, No. 2 (Fall).

Krugman, P. R. (1990), *Rethinking International Trade* (Cambridge, Mass., and London: MIT Press).

Michaely, M. (1986), 'The Timing and Sequencing of a Trade Liberalization Policy', in Choksi and Papageorgiou (1986).

Noland, M. (1990), *Pacific Basin Developing Countries – Prospects for the Future* (Washington, DC: Institute for International Economics).

Ocampo, J. A. (1990), 'La Apertura Externa en Perspectiva', in F. Gomez, ed., *Apertura Económica y Sistema Financiero* (Bogota: Asociacion Bancaria de Colombia).

Ocampo, J. A., and L. Villar (1992), 'Trayectoria y Vicisitudes de la Apertura Económica Colombiana', *Pensamiento Iberoamericano*, No. 21, January–June.

Rodrik, D. (1990), 'Trade Policies and Development: Some New Issues', Discussion Paper Series No. 447, Centre for Economic Policy Research, London, August.

Thomas, V., K. Matin and J. Nash (1990), 'Lessons in Trade Policy Reform', Policy and Research Series No.10, World Bank, Washington, DC.

Tussie, D. (1989), *The Less Developed Countries and the World Trading System: A Challenge to the GATT* (London and New York: Pinter Publishers).

Tussie, D., and D. Glover, (1993a), 'Developing Countries in World Trade: Implications for Bargaining', in Tussie and Glover (1993b).

Tussie, D., and D. Glover, eds. (1993b), *Developing Countries in World Trade: Policies and Bargaining Strategies* (Boulder: Lynne Rienner).

UNCTC (1988) (United Nations Centre on Transnational Corporations), *Transnational Corporations in World Development: Fourth Survey* (New York: United Nations).

UNCTC (1991), *World Investment Report 1991*.

UNCTC (1992), 'Trends in Foreign Direct Investment', E/C.10/1992/3, New York, 20 January.

Wade, R. (1990a), *Governing the Market – Economic Theory and the Role of Government in East Asian Industrialization* (Princeton: Princeton University Press).

Wade, R. (1990b), 'Industrial Policy in East Asia: Does it Lead or Follow the Market?', in G. Gereffi and D. Wyman, eds, *Manufacturing Miracles – Paths of Industrialization in Latin America and East Asia* (Princeton: Princeton University Press).

Wolf, M. (1984), 'Two-Edged Sword: Demands of Developing Countries and the Trading System', in J. N. Bhagwati and J. G. Ruggie, eds, *Power, Passions and Purpose* (Cambridge, Mass.: MIT Press).

Part I

Developing Countries in the International Trading System

2 Futures for the World Trading System and their Implications for Developing Countries

Robert Z. Lawrence

The world economy has become increasingly globalized. Declining transportation and communications costs, the international convergence of technological capabilities among developed economies and the spread of multinational companies with global reach have made many countries fairly close locational substitutes. In such an environment, relatively small differences in institutional practices and shifts in relative competitiveness can have large effects on international trade and investment flows.

Globalization has generated at least two quite different policy responses in the trading system. For those whose politics follow logically from underlying economic trends, the answer is to harmonize national differences; if economic trends are leading to integration, then so should institutions and laws. Of course, in a world of diverse institutional practices, achieving such harmonization can be extremely difficult. Traditionally, therefore, international trading rules have emphasized 'shallow integration', i.e. the removal of border barriers and the elimination of policies that intentionally discriminate against foreign products and firms. Increasingly, however, there are calls for 'deep integration' which seek to reconcile even those policies and practices that may inadvertently discriminate against outsiders.[1] This deeper integration, of course, implies a curtailment of national sovereignty.

The alternative response to increasing globalization is to resist or channel market pressures to ensure 'equitable results'. This generally involves efforts to manage trade (through quotas) and investment (through local content provisions and performance requirements). The

43

prime example at the global level is the extensive system of managed trade in textiles in the Multifibre Arrangement (MFA).

But harmonization or management at the global level is particularly cumbersome. As a result, many of the institutional responses to globalization have taken place at a sub-global level. In the 1980s, some of these efforts have also aimed at harmonization, most notably the EC92 initiative and the MOSS (Market-Opening Sector Specific) and SII (Structural Impediments Initiative) talks between the United States and Japan.

On the other hand, there have also been new, sub-global initiatives aimed at managing trade: in particular, the 'voluntary restraint arrangements' and orderly marketing agreements that have proliferated against Japanese and other Asian exporters, and the arrangements that seek quotas and regulate prices in the semiconductor trade.

These responses to globalization suggest a matrix. As indicated in Figure 2.1, one axis is distinguished by the mode of operation – with 'deep integration' or harmonization of domestic practices on the one hand, to managed trade on the other, and the removal of border trade barriers and other explicitly discriminatory practices (shallow integration) occupying a middle ground. A second axis is defined by the scope of membership. Bilateral arrangements occupy one end of this spectrum and global arrangements the other, with regional and plurilateral arrangements occupying a middle ground.

Figure 2.1   Trade policy matrix

Participation

	Managed trade	Shallow integration	Deep integration
Unilateral	Quantitative Restrictions	CVDs 1980s Chile	Super 301
Bilateral	US–Japan Semiconductor Arrangement	FTAs	US–Japan SII
Regional/ Plurilateral	COMECON	FTAs	EC 92
Global	MFA	GATT	OECD 2000?

Policy Mechanism

From a systemic perspective, the sum total of global trading relations will be affected by developments in each of these cells, but the question to be explored here is the direction in which developments will predominate. In this chapter I will emphasize developments in four of these cells to outline scenarios for the global trading system in the 1990s. I will then consider their implications for developing countries. I discuss in this chapter four major scenarios:

(i)   further development of a GATT-based trading regime;
(ii)   development of a world of regional trading blocs;
(iii) evolution towards a managed trade system; and
(iv)   development of a 'GATT-plus' system of deeper economic integration.

Which of these scenarios will predominate? The answer to this question has become increasingly important to the developing countries. The "demonstration" effect of the successful outward orientation of the East Asian economies has persuaded many developing countries that trade can indeed be an engine of growth. Debt problems have made the attraction of direct foreign investment a critically important source of new capital while programmes adopted at the behest of organizations such as the World Bank and the IMF have made trade liberalization an essential component of adjustment. The success of such policies will depend critically not only on the domestic economic responses but also on a hospitable international environment.

The international environment is important for developing countries both because of the market access it provides and because of the reciprocal demands it makes on developing country policies. My analysis suggests that access for developing countries will differ under the various scenarios and countries will be affected differently. As will be discussed in greater detail below, regional location and commodity patterns of specialization play an important role in affecting access.

Developing country concerns relate also to the obligations countries have to meet to obtain that access. Indeed, the most important conclusion I have reached is that whichever of the scenarios for the world trading system prevails, the pressures on developing countries for increased global integration – and the associated reductions in national sovereignty and control – are likely to increase. Regardless of the regime that will dominate, developing countries seeking to increase trade and attract investment will experience greater pressures to open their economies and to bring their practices more closely in line with those in developed countries. In each of the scenarios, preferential treatment for developing countries is likely to be weakened.

All four scenarios require increased obligations by developing countries. The *GATT system* is evolving in the direction of increased participation by developing countries as full members. In particular the rights afforded by new codes are conditional on accepting increased obligations. *Regional initiatives* will increasingly include developing countries, individually or in groups, but participation will entail providing reciprocal access for developed countries' goods, services and investment, moving more closely towards developed country regulatory standards and reducing government industrial policies. *Managed trade arrangements* could well be selective and more onerous on countries perceived as relatively closed or different. Again the pressures will be to conform to international norms. Finally, to participate in *deep integration* arrangements, developing countries will be required not only to remove trade barriers but also to submit to international norms.

These trends mark a major change. Over the years, developing countries have claimed and received exemptions from GATT rules. In regional arrangements and in GSP they were granted access – albeit limited – but without reciprocal obligations. The major challenge in the future will be reconciling the increased requirements of 'deeper' integration with the use of infant-industry development strategies. Let us turn now to the four scenarios and then consider their implications for developing countries.

I MORE OF GATT

The GATT has been instrumental in facilitating freer trade. Since the end of the Second World War, tariff rates around the world have plummeted. Among the major industrialized countries, weighted-average tariff levels have been lowered to below 5 per cent.[2] Despite these achievements, there is considerable dissatisfaction with the GATT which the current Uruguay Round of trade negotiations is, in principle, addressing. Its 15 working groups are divided into three broad subject matters: *increased market access,* including more open trade in agriculture, textiles and natural resources and removal or reduction of remaining tariff and non-tariff measures; *extension of the GATT to new areas,* principally trade in services, standards and enforcement of intellectual property rights, and trade-related investment requirements imposed by governments; and *strengthening of*

GATT rules, especially those covering antidumping, subsidization, product standards, import licensing, 'safeguards' (temporary import protection), and dispute settlement. In short, the Uruguay Round is covering a broad, ambitious agenda.

Even at this late date it is impossible to know how successful the Round will be (Schott, 1990). Clearly, if the Round fails or, just as significant, is perceived to be a failure, evolution of the world trading system under a GATT-based regime will be unlikely. While in principle the previous achievements of the GATT would be unaffected, with tariffs and trading rules remaining as they were prior to the round, in practice, failure would encourage the negative implications of numerous centrifugal trends operating on the current system – such as grey-area measures, managed trade and regional trading blocs. However, even if the Round is perceived to be successful – that is, if major progress is made toward liberalization in many of the areas currently being negotiated, the GATT, as presently structured, could play a diminishing, albeit still important, role in governing economic relationships between countries.

The original conception of the GATT was based on the MFN removal of tariffs as the principal means of achieving free trade. While its scope has broadened, the GATT remains essentially based on the principle of 'shallow integration', i.e. that international trade can be regulated primarily by dealing with problems as they appear at the border or where they involve explicit measures that discriminate against foreigners.[3] On this view, different national practices that *affect* trade should be tolerated, as long as actors operating within each economy are granted national treatment and not discriminated against and/or as long as they do not cause injury to other nations. For this reason, it is doubtful whether, at least for some significant period of time the current GATT will provide the forum for negotiating deep world economic integration. Instead, as I outline further in connection with the next scenario, it is much more probable that deep integration will be accomplished at regional levels, or between developed countries first, before seriously being negotiated (let alone accomplished) at such a broad level as the GATT.

II REGIONAL BLOCS

The spectre of global fragmentation is haunting the global trading system. The fear is that progress towards global integration over the past four decades will be reversed as the world economy splits up into three regional trading blocs, each centred on a major currency, each closed to outsiders.[4]

Outsiders have fears about each of the regional initiatives currently underway.[5] EC92 is viewed with concern because of fears that (a) this initiative will divert more trade than it creates; (b) as its membership grows, the EC will become increasingly preoccupied with internal concerns and thus neglect its external relations; and (c) a more centralized European Community would be dominated by the preferences of its more protectionist members and erect new external barriers.

A second concern is that Japan will spearhead a South-east Asian bloc, principally by moving its manufacturing industry off-shore. A third concern relates to US initiatives in the Western Hemisphere. One fear is that such an agreement could have substantial trade-diversion effects. A second is that, like the EC, the United States would be diverted from global initiatives, which, given the major leadership role it has played in the post-war trading system, would be a major blow to liberalization. A third fear is that Asian nations will respond to the US and European initiatives with a protectionist response of their own. Clearly, any turn inwards by the EC or the United States could have domino effects. A Fortress Europe would encourage non-European countries shut out of European markets to think about forming their own closed blocs among their neighbours. An Asian bloc run by Japan could topple the global trading system by increasing demands for managed trade.

But these concerns could be misplaced. Stronger regional integration need not be associated with higher external barriers. Indeed, as the GATT itself recognizes, such a trend could have positive effects on the rest of the world provided the emerging regional blocs are 'open' to trade from outside.

External Barriers

Open regional blocs can actually promote and facilitate external liberalization, that is, trade with parties outside blocs. With the noteworthy exception of agriculture (an exception for which the EC was not solely to blame), increased regional integration among the original six members of the EC was associated with extensive participation in multilateral tariff reductions. Indeed the formation of the EEC was an important impulse for the Kennedy Round.

The European experience also demonstrates that excluded countries may have stronger incentives to liberalize in a system with emerging regional arrangements. The EEC's formation, for example, set in motion a cumulative regional liberalization process in which the United Kingdom was initially induced to join EFTA and later the EC itself. Similar pressures are now operating with EC 92 in which the EFTA nations, East Europeans and others such as Turkey are clamouring for inclusion.

As was the case with the EC, the North American FTA also is not developing as an exclusive process. Indeed, as Mexico has moved into the FTA negotiations with the United States, it has simultaneously sought to counterbalance this growing dependence on its more powerful partners with new initiatives towards the Pacific, Central and South America. Mexico is seeking, for example, to join the OECD, is negotiating another FTA with Venezuela and Chile, and has signed agreements to achieve freer trade with several Central American countries.

The United States has also not been able to confine its attention to Mexico. President Bush has invited other Western Hemisphere nations to sign FTAs with the United States separately or as groups in his Enterprise for the Americas Initiative. This US invitation to Latin America has also stimulated increased interest in regional initiatives throughout Latin America. For example, the five Andean nations – Bolivia, Colombia, Peru, Ecuador and Venezuela – have signed an accord to lift all barriers to intra-regional trade by 1991, while Brazil, Argentina, Paraguay and Uruguay have agreed to form the Mercosur common market by the end of 1995.

It remains to be seen, however, if the United States will be able to confine its free-trade area initiatives to the Western Hemisphere (and Israel). Far more likely will be pressures on the United States to extend its invitation to willing Asian and other economies. The result could be an open agreement which will then be readily linked in a global arrangement.

The Asian bloc allegedly emerging around Japan is the least likely to develop into a formal protectionist arrangement. This region is particularly dependent on extra-regional trade (see Table 2.1). It is also particularly heterogeneous politically. To be sure, Japan's influence in the East Asian area is likely to increase, but precisely because other Asian nations are reluctant to submit to an arrangement with a single dominant economy, progress towards a single regional arrangement centred solely on Japan is likely to be slow. Moreover, the United States will be unwilling to concede Asia to Japan and is likely to use its influence to prevent a formal Pacific arrangement from which it is excluded. For a time, the United States could well be caught in the hypocritical position of promoting Western Hemisphere integration while resisting an Asian arrangement. Eventually, therefore, it will be forced to extend its invitation to form FTAs to willing Asian nations. Two, rather than three major regional arrangements could emerge (Krause, 1991).

The Importance of Extra-Bloc Trade

Current trade patterns and trends suggest that extra-bloc trade is vital for each of the current or prospective regional arrangements. While each of the major players may benefit from regional arrangements none can afford to ignore its extra-regional relations. The United States, Europe and Japan are all global rather than regional traders.

Tables 2.1 to 2.3 provide trade data for three major regions and Japan for selected years from 1973 through to 1988. Each of the tables breaks down both the total dollar volume and percentage of exports sold from a specific region to other countries within the same region as well as to nations in other major regions around the world.

Taken together, the tables on trade illustrate the importance of extra-regional trade as a share of total trade. Over half of the Western Hemisphere's exports and two-thirds of Asian exports are outside these regions. Only for Europe are extra-regional exports less than a third of trade. But the share of intra-regional trade in total trade is not the most relevant measure of dependence on extra-regional trade. The importance of extra-regional trade is more usefully measured by the ratio of total extra-regional trade – exports plus imports – to GNP. Table 2.4 reports these ratios for major trading regions. The table illustrates that measured as a share of GDP, extra-regional trade is actually more important to Europe than to North America. None the less, extra-regional trade remains very significant to North America and to the United States in particular. Since goods are roughly 45 per cent of North American GNP, this implies that about 25 per cent of all American transactions in goods involve an extra-regional buyer or seller. Clearly, efforts to liberalize at the global level through the GATT remain of vital importance.

Table 2.1   Japan and South-east Asia: total exports, by region of destination (billions of dollars and percentages)

	1973	1980	1985	1988
Japan and South-east Asia	19	64	85	160
	30.5%	27.4%	25.8%	28.8%
Western Hemisphere	20	76	134	197
	31.7%	32.5%	40.6%	35.4%
Western Europe	11	45	48	109
	17.5%	14.2%	14.5%	19.6%
Other	13	49	63	91
(Africa, Middle East, South Asia)	20.3%	20.9%	19.1%	16.3%
Total	63	234	330	557

Notes: 'Western Hemisphere' is composed of the USA, Canada and all of Latin America.
'South-east Asia' is composed of Korea, Taiwan, Hong Kong, Singapore, Malaysia, Thailand, Indonesia and the Philippines.
'Western Europe' is composed of the EC plus EFTA.
Sources: General Agreement on Tariffs and Trade, *International Trade 1988-89*, volume II.
Figures for South-east Asia from IMF, *Direction of Trade*, various issues.

Table 2.2   Western Hemisphere: total exports, by region of destination (billions of dollars and percentages)

	1973	1980	1985	1988
Western Hemisphere	61	189	222	269
	47.3%	46.7%	52.7%	48.1%
Japan and South-east Asia	18	54	60	103
	14.0%	13.3%	14.3%	18.4%
Western Europe	35	105	85	119
	27.1%	25.9%	20.2%	21.3%
Other	15	57	54	68
(Africa, Middle East, South Asia)	11.6%	14.1%	12.8%	12.2%
Total	129	405	421	559

Notes: 'Western Hemisphere' is composed of the USA, Canada and all of Latin America.
'South-east Asia' is composed of Korea, Taiwan, Hong Kong, Singapore, Malaysia, Thailand, Indonesia and the Philippines.
'Western Europe' is composed of the EC plus EFTA.
Sources: See Table 2.1.

Table 2.3   Western Europe: total exports, by region of destination (billions of dollars and percentages)

	1973	1980	1985	1988
Western Europe	178	551	508	904
	68.5%	67.5%	65.2%	71.3%
Western Hemisphere	31	75	101	137
	11.9%	9.2%	13.0%	10.8%
Japan and South-east Asia	10	30	34	69
	3.7%	3.7%	4.4%	5.4%
Other	42	160	136	158
(Africa, Middle East, South Asia)	16.0%	19.6%	17.5%	12.5%
Total	260	816	779	1268

Notes: 'Western Hemisphere' is composed of the USA, Canada and all of Latin America.
'South-east Asia' is composed of Korea, Taiwan, Hong Kong, Singapore, Malaysia, Thailand, Indonesia and the Philippines.
'Western Europe' is composed of the EC plus EFTA.
Sources: See Table 2.1.

Table 2.4   Extra-regional trade as percentage of GDP in 1987 (all figures in billions of dollars)

Region	GDP	Total trade	Extra-regional trade	As % of total trade	As % of GDP
North America	4.910	815	560	68.7	11.4
Western Hemisphere	5.675	1.025	665	64.9	11.7
Japan and South-east Asia[a]	2.910	960	635	66.1	21.8
Western Europe	4.925	2.245	640	28.5	13.0

Notes: See Table 2.1 for country groupings.
Total trade equals exports plus imports.
[a]Japan and South-east Asia figures for 1988.
Sources: GDP figures from *GATT International Trade, 88–89* for the Western Hemisphere and Europe. GDP figures for Japan and South-east Asia from IMF, *IFS Annual 1989*.
Total trade from *GATT International Trade, 87–88* for Western Hemisphere and Europe. Total trade for Asia from IMF, *Direction of Trade*.

Motivation

The forces driving nations into regional arrangements are dramatically different from those that drove them into preferential trading blocs in the inter-war period. The motive for completing the internal market is not to secure the European market for European producers by providing them with preferential access, but instead to facilitate the free movement of goods, services, labour and capital throughout the Community.

This deeper integration within Europe will facilitate trade with the rest of the world. A common set of standards, for example, makes it easier for *all* who wish to sell in Europe – not just insiders. A tough set of rules which prevents governments from subsidizing domestic firms aids all their competitors, not only those located in the European Community. To be sure, some European countries will continue to implement industrial policies, but the restraints on these initiatives will be greater than in the absence of EC92. Once the larger European economies are committed to allow the free flow of resources within Europe, they will no longer be able to ensure each has a national champion in every industry located within its territories. This under-mining of the nationalist sentiments that drives much of the protection-ism in the larger European countries will benefit outsiders. In addition, some of the mechanisms developed by the EC to deal with national diversity could serve as a model for further integration between the EC and its trading partners.

Likewise, Mexico is not seeking an FTA with the United States to avoid liberalization with the rest of the world. On the contrary, since the mid-1980s, Mexico has engaged in an extensive unilateral reduction in external restrictions accompanied by internal liberalization. Instead, much of the appeal of an FTA is that it provides credibility and permanence to Mexico's liberalization measures. A second rationale is that an export-oriented Mexico requires secure access to its major trading partner. The FTA is thus an important complement to an outward oriented policy which is based on attracting foreign invest-ment.

The key point here is that once Mexico accepts obligations *vis-à-vis* the United States to permit foreign investment, to enforce intellectual property rights, to unwind its elaborate protectionist programmes for motor vehicles and electronics, then these changes will provide benefits for all its trading partners – not just the United States. US involvement in particular would dramatically enhance the credibility of intra-Latin

American regional liberalization arrangements by making the costs particularly high of violating the agreement for any individual Latin American country.

Again the context and motivation for these efforts in Latin America must be appreciated. In addition to Mexico, over the past three years Brazil, Argentina and Colombia have all significantly reduced tariff levels as well as the dispersion of tariff levels, while Chilean liberalization has been in place even longer (see Part III in this volume).

Remaining problems

This optimistic viewpoint needs to be qualified. While overt protectionist barriers are unlikely, each of the regional arrangements might well resort to more subtle protectionist measures, particularly if the Uruguay Round should fail.

In the case of the United States, these typically involve so-called voluntary restraint arrangements (VRAs) and harassment through the use of antidumping actions. In the case of Europe, protection could be applied through the strict and less than transparent application of antidumping rules;[6] increased application of safeguards measures; efforts to nurture European firms (through implicit subsidies, selective government procurement and consortia excluding non-European firms); and the promulgation of standards purportedly addressing environmental and safety concerns that have the effect (if not the purpose) of discriminating against extra-bloc trade. In the case of Asia, protection might be applied through actions taken by Japanese companies, implicitly sanctioned by the Japanese government.

These concerns highlight the importance of disciplines on these practices at the global level through the GATT. In particular, the Uruguay Round contains measures to limit some of these practices. A successful round, which is in the interests of each of the regions, would enhance the prospects that protectionist responses will be limited. Failure of the Uruguay Round, or just as important a *perception* of failure, would increase the chances of more closed blocs. In such an event, protectionist forces around the world may then gain sufficient ammunition not only to turn their countries towards managed trade (the third scenario), but to deflect any movement towards open blocs as a response into a closed bloc regime. While dramatic overt protectionist measures are unlikely, there are reasons for concerns about more subtle measures that might respond to particular industry pressures and could be accomplished through any number of less-than-transparent devices.

III MANAGED TRADE

The third scenario for the future development of the world trading system – more 'managed trade' – is favoured by some academics and politicians in the United States who have grown increasingly frustrated with the apparent stubbornness of the bilateral US trade balances with a number of this country's trading partners, most importantly Japan. Managed trade proponents are of course not confined to the United States, however. Proposals come in various forms, but all share the common feature of attempting to specify *outcomes* rather than *rules*.

The broadest managed trade proposal, or 'macro trade management', would have countries set bilateral trade balances with others (ideally after negotiation, but, if that fails, then unilaterally) (Kissinger and Vance, 1988, pp. 899–921). Less sweeping would be overall bilateral export targets and (their counterpart) import targets for trading partners (Dornbusch, Krugman and Park, 1989).

Alternatively, trade could be 'micro-managed', with targets set for individual products or industry sectors, such as the quantitative import restrictions (quotas or VERs) that now govern trade in cars, semiconductors, steel and textiles. In the past, many managed trade arrangements were the response to the adjustment problems of declining industries. Increasingly, however, they reflect concerns about industries of the future.[7] Global competition, according to proponents of this view, is a zero sum game, in which nations that fail to adopt the correct strategic trade policies lose out to those that do. Since agreements over international rules for the conduct of such policies are unlikely, numerical targets should be set for trade in key sectors.

Whether or not the Uruguay Round is perceived to be successful, the world trading system in the future is likely to see more efforts at micro, or sectoral, management in particular, largely because this is the way many trade disputes have been resolved in the past. The outcome of the Uruguay Round also may not have as much effect on the prospects for managed trade at the 'macro' level – targets for bilateral trade balances and/or import/export levels – as some may believe. The key factor will be whether current trade frictions between Japan and its trading partners subside or intensify.

IV 'SUPER-GATT'

I argued earlier that globalization has induced major pressures towards deep integration that have been seen in efforts to broaden the scope of the GATT and to increase harmonization of practices at the regional level. The final scenario, therefore, involves a 'Super-GATT' liberalization among participating countries, which would be more revolutionary than any of the trade policy measures that have thus far been debated in the political arena. The principal argument for such an arrangement among like-minded countries, whether developed or developing, is that any progress towards liberalization made in the Uruguay Round will be about as much as one can reasonably expect from the more than one hundred highly diverse economies such as those that now belong to the GATT. In addition, the internal and external barriers that remain will be even tougher to negotiate away in the future. Only those countries truly interested in further liberalization and harmonization of their economies will be able to participate.

An arrangement for deep integration clearly requires much more extensive political commitments than the more conventional GATT-type arrangement. Accordingly these arrangements could only be made on a selective basis. One approach might be sectoral rather than plurilateral. It may be easier to obtain agreement for common standards for capital requirements for banks than it is to obtain agreement on common safety standards for drugs. Another would begin with a small group of countries. Some industrialized countries in particular might join together with any like-minded advanced developing countries to begin negotiations for achieving a single, unified market for goods, services and capital by the year 2000 – an arrangement Hufbauer has termed an OECD Free Trade and Investment Area (FTIA).[8] The Organization for Economic Cooperation and Development (OECD) might be given the task of formulating measures to create such an integrated market, modelled most likely on the EC 1992 initiative.

A GATT-plus arrangement also need not produce identical economic and regulatory systems in all participating countries. Indeed, some competition among regulatory regimes could be beneficial. The difficult task would be to determine those issues on which harmonization will be essential and those in which differences must be tolerated (while guaranteeing national treatment and mutual recognition of technical standards). Ideally, however, participating countries would agree to common procedures for handling unfair trade allegations and safeguards measures, to rules encouraging innovation, and for provisions for non-discriminatory government procurement; and also, to a supra-national entity to supplement national anti-trust policies.

V IMPLICATIONS FOR DEVELOPING COUNTRIES

GATT System

What would a continuation of the GATT regime imply for developing countries? If it operated according to the principles enshrined in its original Articles, and the pious statements contained in more recent declarations, the GATT system would provide a favourable environment for trade with developed countries, both for developing countries that followed liberal trade policies and for developing countries that did not.

The essence of the GATT is non-discrimination achieved through Most Favoured Nation (MFN) treatment. The strategy is to leverage the bargaining power of the strong into an open system for all. Over all, the developing countries have been beneficiaries of the liberalization of global markets in which the GATT has played a major role. In particular, the MFN provisions have lowered barriers for their goods in major markets, making possible several spectacular success stories based on export-led growth.

Moreover, over the years, developing countries have claimed and received exemptions from GATT rules (Whalley, 1990). By invoking Article XII or Article XVIIb to safeguard their balance of payments and Part IV of the Agreement, which exempts them from the need to make reciprocal concessions in trade negotiations, developing countries can, for the most part, permanently escape GATT disciplines. Thus the typical developing country is able to follow whatever trade policies it chooses at home while benefiting from liberalization in developed countries. In principle, developing countries are given a free ride.

Over the years developing countries have, in some cases, actually obtained better than MFN treatment through GSP arrangements, and from both the EC and the United States, through regional schemes such as the Lomé Convention and the Caribbean Basin Initiative. But these arrangements have been limited in scope. Indeed in several cases, developing countries have not received preferential treatment for a number of reasons: (a) The GATT itself explicitly enshrined negative discrimination against developing countries in the Multifibre Arrangement; (b) Article XXIV of the GATT, which allows customs unions and free-trade areas, has been used mainly by developed countries – among OECD countries only Japan is not part of a free-trade area; (c) in the Codes of the Tokyo Round, the GATT shifted towards conditional MFN. Only signatories to the Codes, rather than all GATT members, benefit from its rights; (d) the full array of GATT rules has not been extended to sectors such as agriculture which are vital to many developing countries; (e) tariff reductions have tended to be much lower in specific categories that are important to developing countries (hence the inclusion of tropical products as a distinct area in the Uruguay Round); and (f) the special treatment of developing countries has also meant much less progress in reducing developing country tariffs. The result has been less expansion in South–South trade particularly in regions in which many developing countries are to be found.

Success in the Uruguay Round could offer important opportunities for developing country exports, particularly in vital areas such as agriculture, tropical products and textiles.[9] There has been a noteworthy shift in developing-country negotiating strategy away from the earlier North–South schism aimed at achieving Special and Differential Treatment (Whalley, 1990). In numerous cases developing countries have increasingly taken positions reflecting their commodity interests rather than their developing-country status. Indeed, the importance of progress in agriculture to the developing countries has been reflected in the major role played by developing countries in the negotiations. The breakdown in the talks was attributable to the unwillingness of agricultural exporters, particularly from Latin America, to agree to concessions in other areas without compensation in agriculture. Success in reining in agricultural support programmes in the EC, the United States and Japan could offer major benefits for developing country exporters, although it could also mean higher costs for some importers. Progress in unravelling the Multifibre Arrangement would also bring major benefits, particularly to new entrants into textiles and clothing – although here too some countries might lose rents. Improved disciplines on grey-area activities and a better safeguards code would also be important.

At the same time, the Round is not expected to increase the preferential treatment of developing countries – if anything, it could weaken it, particularly in new areas, if the practice of providing conditional MFN treatment is applied. Moreover, in a successful round developing countries will be obliged to agree to increased inhibitions on national sovereignty in intellectual-property, services and trade-related investment measures. They could also face tougher anti-circumvention measures and national rules of origin in the dumping area.

Conversely, developing countries would lose important opportunities if the Round failed. The potential benefits outlined above would be lost. These would be particularly serious in agriculture, in which the global nature of the problem makes regional solutions relatively ineffective. Canada and the United States, for example, could not make much progress in restraining agricultural subsidies in the context of the US–Canada Free Trade Agreement, because other major exporters were not in the talks.

Developing countries would also be adversely affected by the increased use of unilateral and bilateral pressures that would emanate particularly from the United States in the event of a GATT failure.

It is ironic that as developing countries have increasingly shifted towards more liberal trading regimes, the differential treatment accorded them by the GATT has actually become a hindrance rather than a benefit. A major motive behind liberalization has been the attraction of foreign capital. However, pledges to maintain open markets made at the GATT have not been particularly credible, in part because of the weakness of the disciplines imposed on developing countries. By contrast, as I discuss below, commitments in regional FTAs with developed countries are likely to be much more credible.

Regionalism

Developing countries are not all affected in the same way by either the open or the closed versions of these regional scenarios.[10] One important distinction is between those that join these groups and those that do not. For countries in Latin America and those with European associations participation entails trading off increased and more secure access to foreign markets in return for reductions in national economic sovereignty. Inevitably, particularly for developing countries, participation in a regional arrangement will require increased conformity to the rules and norms of developed country partners. Some are sceptical whether this trade-off will be worth it. They argue, for example, that products from Mexico are still likely to be harassed by US fair-trade rules, while on the other hand, Americans are likely to dominate the Mexican economy. None the less, in principle this is a trade-off that will be particularly attractive for countries with the capacity to attract foreign investment, particularly in manufacturing.

As the regions broaden their scope, the value of access is likely to erode. Spain and Portugal for example, will find increased competition from Eastern Europe as the European Economic Area is extended. Similarly, Mexico will experience increased competition from the rest of Latin America in the North American market. For countries that currently enjoy special access to regions under schemes such as GSP, the Caribbean Basin Initiative and the Lomé Convention, the value of these privileges are likely to erode as the regions broaden participation. If the regions become protectionist and already include some developing countries, the trade diversion could be significant. Particularly if the GATT Round fails to deal with textiles, for example, it would become extremely attractive for the United States to divert, implicitly or explicitly, to Mexico its quotas within the Multifibre Arrangement that it currently provides to China. The countries least affected by the direct impact of these developments would probably be those producing raw materials which are not at present typically subject to high levels of tariff or non-tariff protection. However, a trade war that had serious macroeconomic effects could indirectly harm such exporters.

In sum therefore, for developing countries who become members of blocks, considerable adjustment will be required. In particular, industries that have been protected will be forced to compete with those from developed country partners. And countries will be required to assume increased obligations in sectors such as services and in practices relating to industrial policies and intellectual property rights. Specialization along free-trade lines will be encouraged. On the other hand, for those excluded, the closed regional scenario provides significant dangers of trade diversion, particularly from other developing country competitors who produce substitute products. The open scenario, however, could increase the opportunities. If the regional arrangements such as those for Latin American countries are successful in making the current shifts towards multilateral liberalization permanent, they will open up increased opportunities for South–South trade. If they succeed in stimulating overall growth for their members, again those outside these regions will find increased export opportunities.

Managed Trade

If managed trade is systemic and comprehensive, smaller participants without political clout will be adversely affected. If it is selective and partial, however, opportunities for unconstrained smaller newcomers could actually improve. Comprehensive managed trade arrangements subject trade to political influences and are inherently discriminatory against newcomers since quotas are generally distributed on the basis of historical market share. Some more powerful and more developed countries may manage to secure their trade but many small developing countries would undoubtedly be hurt. However, where managed trade has been selective, it has provided opportunities to newcomers either directly to penetrate markets in which one country has been constrained, or to attract investment from the constrained country with a view to providing an export platform. Thus, for example, in the late 1950s, US imports from Hong Kong surged once Japanese textiles had been subject to a VRA. Similarly, US imports of televisions from Taiwan and Korea – typically by Japanese-affiliated companies – surged when televisions from Japan were subject to an orderly marketing agreement in the late 1970s. None the less, restraints were later placed on televisions from these countries as well.

This does not mean, of course, that managed trade is not harmful to developing countries that are affected by it. The experience in textiles and footwear is illustrative. Two major conclusions emerge from studies of developing-country experience under the Multifibre Arrangement. The first is that developing countries are hurt by the MFA. The MFA has recently been analysed extensively in a new study (Hamilton, 1990). In their editors' introduction, Hamilton and Martin report on some major results (Hamilton, 1990, pp. 1–5). According to Trela and Whalley, gains for developing countries as a whole from the removal of the MFA would be $8 billion and almost all developing countries, including major exporters, would gain from the liberalization. Martin and Supachalasai point out that although the MFA yields higher prices in protected markets, these are offset by lower prices in the residual market. Erzan, Goto and Homes show that the MFA effectively restricts exports from developing countries as a group, and that the gains of the unconstrained exporters from trade diversion are relatively small. They also find that over time quotas have become increasingly restrictive.

The second conclusion, though, is that despite these restrictions, considerable export growth has been possible. In their study of Korea, in the same volume, for example, Hamilton and Kim find that in spite of the binding MFA restrictions, from the early 1980s to mid 1986–7, the volume of Korean exports almost trebled and the value of exports grew even faster because of rapidly rising prices of exports to the US market (Hamilton, 1990, p. 178). They argue, 'The case of Korea during the 1980s illustrates that it has been possible for a country to expand – and expand rapidly – in spite of increasingly binding MFA restrictions in major markets' (Hamilton, 1990, p. 171).

Studies of the experience in the footwear industry reach similar conclusions. VRAs reduced welfare in both importing and exporting countries despite the transfer of rents from importing to exporting countries (de Melo *et al.*, 1990). But again, the non-tariff barriers in footwear do not appear to have prevented export growth. As Hamilton points out, they have been relatively porous and some have not been permanent (Hamilton, 1989).

Nevertheless, a world of managed trade is not the most likely outcome for the trading system. At best, the world should see only some movement in this direction as trade in various products that are subject to trade disputes becomes micro-managed. But the dangers that micro-management will be upstaged by macro-management are very real and, if this occurs, so are the dangers that the liberalized multilateral trading system as we know it today could disappear. Under these circumstances the benefits of regional shelters from these arrangements could become particularly attractive.

If managed trade were to be applied at an aggregate level, it would probably also be applied selectively – i.e. against countries such as Japan and perhaps other Asians that are perceived to be too different to play by normal trading rules. Frequently proponents of these approaches argue that there is no reason to apply managed trade to economies with similar institutional practices. To avoid being subjected to such arrangements, these countries will be subject to increased pressure to conform more closely to international norms. Therefore, even under a managed trade system, Asian countries will experience considerable pressure to harmonize or reconcile their institutional practices to avoid such treatment.

Deep Integration

If the movement towards deep integration was confined to a rich man's club, it could prove detrimental to developing countries that were excluded. In particular, if such an arrangement made transactions within the club much easier than outside it, trade diversion could outweigh trade creation.

However, much would depend on the precise form of deep integration. Harmonization of regulatory and environmental standards – the 'social dimension' – could well raise production costs in some developed countries and thereby create new opportunities for countries where such regulations are more lenient. On the other hand, efficiency-promoting harmonization might create new forms of competition.

If it were operated as an open arrangement, however, a deep integration arrangement would be unlikely to provide access on a preferential basis. i.e. developing countries seeking to join would be obligated to meet the same conditions as other participants. Indeed, the essence of deep integration is precisely that major differences in institutional practices be reconciled. Thus movement towards this type of regime initiates strong pressures in developing countries to meet international norms.

As the discussion on US–Mexico free trade has indicated, demands could well be placed on developing countries to raise safety, occupational and environmental standards. In addition, developing countries could find themselves subject to increasing constraints on the use of infant-industry protection, subsidies, and other forms of industrial policy. In both the regulatory and industrial policy areas, there are dangers that the legitimate need for differentiated treatment could be undermined.

VI CONCLUDING COMMENTS

A successful completion of the Uruguay Round is a necessary, but not sufficient, condition for evolution of the system based on GATT. If the current Round succeeds, it will represent considerable progress towards removing border barriers and some progress towards deeper integration. None the less, it is doubtful that at least for some time the GATT can meet the need for deep integration that globalization requires. The GATT's scope is simply too confined and its membership too diverse and there will be pressures to deal with integration through other fora and means.

Accordingly, at least in the near future – a decade, if not longer – increased regional integration is inevitable. The critical question, though, is whether the regional arrangements will become 'building blocks' in a more integrated global system or 'stumbling blocks' that cause the system to fragment. There are reasons for believing in the 'building blocks' view. In particular, both EC92 and the North America Free Trade Area represent initiatives to enhance the role of market forces and are, therefore, radically different in purpose from the blocs formed in the 1930s or earlier regional arrangements in Latin America. With the noteworthy exception of agriculture, the experience of the EC in general also leaves room for optimism: increased European integration was compatible with sustained progress in liberalizing extra-EC trade. Moreover, the extent to which each potential regional bloc continues to rely on extra-regional trade reinforces the conclusion about building blocks: none of the regions can afford to neglect their extra-regional trade links. None the less, while overall the regional measures are unlikely to result in trade wars, they could pose new challenges and introduce or spread more subtle forms of protection and trade diversion, particularly if the GATT system is weakened.

The third scenario – increased management of trade through quotas and local content rules – currently applies to global trade in sectors such as textiles and steel. Invariably, such arrangements have grown out of the friction between the United States and the EC, on the one hand, and Japan and the exporters of manufactures from developing countries, on the other. Additional sectoral problems could increase the use of managed trade, perhaps leading to efforts to manage aggregate trade flows and balances. Continued trade friction between Japan and its developed-country trading partners increases the likelihood of this scenario. Under these arrangements political forces will dominate the outcomes.

The most ambitious direction for the world trading system is represented by the last scenario, or movement beyond the GATT toward deeper global harmonization: 'GATT-plus', or perhaps 'OECD-2000'. Patterned perhaps on the EC 1992 programme (with the exception of provisions for free-labour migration), this would entail increased efforts to harmonize global rules and reconcile practices in areas such as competition policy, standards, regulatory practices and technology policies. For this scenario to come to pass, of course, both the initial membership of the negotiating group and its institutional setting must be resolved. It is conceivable that further development of 'open' regional blocs could evolve into a GATT-plus arrangement. Alternatively, the industrialized countries might pursue such an option immediately with conditional MFN treatment accorded to developing countries seeking to join.

In sum, much uncertainty surrounds the development of the trading system during the 1990s. Nevertheless, it appears clear that the major challenge facing the system will be dealing with the pressures induced by globalization that have made shallow integration arrangements inadequate. The response could take place through open regional blocs or in GATT-plus arrangements. However, these outcomes will require two conditions. First, that the conclusion of the Uruguay Round will be perceived to be at least moderately successful and, second, that macroeconomic events will not trigger protectionist counter-reactions. If either of these assumptions proves to be unwarranted, the trading system could easily turn towards managed trade and/or closed blocs.

It is striking, however, that under each of the likely scenarios, the freedom of developing countries to enjoy special and differential treatment is likely to be eroded. To participate in new arrangements for a wider GATT, regional integration schemes or deep integration arrangements, developing countries will inevitably have to conform increasingly to practices prevalent in developed countries. In some cases, meeting these requirements could aid their development and assist in attracting foreign investment and technology. In other cases, for example, the imposition of social and regulatory standards and constraints on infant-industry policies, these requirements will be particularly controversial.

Overall, however, the likely systemic developments will leave various countries with different opportunities. One key distinguishing feature is location. For countries with opportunities to join new regional groupings, market access could become more secure. For those currently participating in regions, preferences could be eroded. For those outside regions, trade and investment diversion could become a threat, particularly if the GATT is weakened and if the closed regional scenario occurs. A second feature is the pattern of commodity specialization. Agricultural exporters could be particularly damaged by closed regional arrangements. They clearly have a strong interest in GATT-imposed disciplines on agricultural subsidies and protection. Producers of other primary commodities that are generally not subject to high tariffs or non-tariff barriers, are unlikely to be heavily affected by these developments. Producers of manufactured goods, particularly those seeking to attract foreign investment, will be the most heavily impacted.

Do these scenarios imply that developing countries should not try to rely on export-led strategies? Clearly the answer is no. These alternative scenarios will affect countries differently. In addition, however, the experience of the past two decades should be taken into account. Simply because the terms of trade may worsen, and some markets may be protected, it does not imply that inward-oriented strategies are superior. Developing-country manufactured-goods exports have been able to grow rapidly over the past two decades despite a decline in global growth and the rise in protectionist actions. Developing-country exports of textiles and footwear have grown rapidly despite quota protection against them. Moreover, developing countries remain small participants in developed-country markets and low-wage countries generally constitute a smaller share of the world economy than they did three decades ago.

Notes

1. The measures for EC92 and the Structural Impediments Initiative between Japan and the United States are examples of where the goal is deeper integration.
2. See the *Economic Report of the President, 1989*, p. 151.
3. This would also be true of a restructured GATT system as envisaged by Jackson. See Jackson (1990).
4. For a historical account, see Kindleberger (1986), p. 280.
5. For a discussion of the trading bloc issue, see Bhagwati (1991), pp. 58–80; Stoeckel, Pearce and Banks (1990); Schott (1989); and Belous and Hartley (1990). See also Dornbusch (1991).
6. See, for example, Messerlin (1990).
7. See, for example, Tyson (1990).
8. Such a proposal has been advanced by Gary Clyde Hufbauer in *The Free Trade Debate*, background paper for a report of the Twentieth Century Fund Task Force on the Future of American Trade Policy (New York: Priority Press, 1980). For an excellent discussion of these issues, see also Ostry (1990).
9. See Tussie, in Chapter 3 of this volume.
10. For discussion of the impact of the EC on developing countries, see Griffith-Jones and Alizadeh, with Agosin (1991). See also Davenport with Page (1991), and papers prepared for the project on Globalization and Regionalization by the OECD Development Centre in 1990 by Michel Foquin, 'The Impact of European Integration on International Trade and Specialization'; Winston Fritsch, 'EC92 and Latin America'; and Sheila Page, 'Implications of EC92 for Developing Countries'.

References

Belous, R. S., and R. S. Hartley, eds (1990), *The Growth of Regional Trading Blocs in the Global Economy* (Washington, DC: National Planning Association).

Bhagwati, J. (1991), *The World Trading System at Risk* (Princeton: Princeton University Press).

Davenport, M., with O. Page (1991), *Europe 1992 and the Developing World* (London: Overseas Development Institute).

de Melo, J., C. B. Hamilton and L. A. Winters (1990), 'Voluntary Export Restraints: A Case Study Focussing on Effects in Exporting Countries', paper no. 464 (Stockholm: Institute for International Economic Studies).

Dornbusch, R. (1991), 'Policy Options for Freer Trade: The Case for Bilateralism', in Lawrence and Schultze (1990).

Dornbusch, R., P. Krugman and Y. C. Park (1989), *Meeting World Challenges: US Manufacturing in the 1990s* (Rochester, NY: Eastman Kodak Company).

Griffith-Jones, S., and P. Alizadeh, with M. R. Agosin (1991), 'La Integración Europea y sus Consecuencias para los Países en Desarrolo. Algunas Sugerencias de Respuestas Estratégicas', *Pensamiento Iberoamericano* (Madrid), No. 20, July–December.

Hamilton, C. B. (1989), 'The Political Economy of Transient "New" Protectionism', *Weltwirschattliches Archiv*, Vol. 125, No. 3, pp. 522–46.

Hamilton, C. B. (1990), *Textiles Trade and the Developing Countries: Eliminating the Multi-Fiber Arrangement in the 1990s* (Washington, DC: World Bank).

Jackson, J. H. (1990), *Restructuring the GATT System* (New York: Council on Foreign Relations Press, Royal Institute of International Affairs).

Kindleburger, C. (1986), *The World in Depression 1929–1939* (University of California Press).

Kissinger, H., and C. Vance (1988), 'Bipartisan Objectives for American Foreign Policy', *Foreign Affairs*, Vol. 66, No. 5 (Summer).

Krause, L. (1991), 'Can the Pacific Save US–Japanese Economic Relations?' (San Diego: University of California), mimeo.

Lawrence, R. and C. L. Schultze, eds (1991), *An American Trade Strategy: Options for the 1990s* (Washington, DC: The Brookings Institution).

Messerlin, P. A. (1990), 'The Antidumping Regulations of the European Community: The "Privatization" of the Administered Protection', paper presented at the colloquium on 'Reforming Trade Remedy Laws' at the University of Toronto, May.

Ostry, S. (1990), *Governments and Corporations in a Shrinking World* (New York: Council on Foreign Relations Press).

Schott, J. J., ed. (1989), *Free Trade Areas and US Trade Policy* (Washington, DC: Institute for International Economics).

Schott, J. J. (1990), *The Global Trade Negotiations: What Can be Achieved?* (Washington, DC: Institute for International Economics, September).

Stoeckel, A., D. Pearce and G. Banks (1990), *Western Trade Blocs: Game, Set or Match for Asia Pacific and the World Economy* (Canberra: Centre for International Economics).

Tyson, L. (1990), 'Managed Trade: Making the Best of Second Best', in Lawrence and Schultze (1991), pp. 142–94.

Whalley, J. (1990) 'Non-Discriminatory Discrimination: Special and Differential Treatment Under the GATT for Developing Countries', *Economic Journal 100* (December), pp. 1318–28.

3 The Uruguay Round and the Trading System in the Balance: Dilemmas for Developing Countries

Diana Tussie[1]

I INTRODUCTION

The multilateral negotiations in the GATT have always been the bedrock of world trade policy. The Uruguay Round is a milestone in international trade policy; irrespective of the particular stitching involved in the production of the final outcome, it provides a glimpse into the international trading system that is likely to emerge in an increasingly globalized world economy.

The essential features of the Uruguay Round differ from its predecessors in a very substantial way. Previous rounds (with the partial exception of the Tokyo Round) have sought trade liberalization on the basis of reciprocal tariff concessions. The Uruguay Round has involved discussions over domestic policies, institutional practices and regulations to an unprecedented extent. A shift of this nature in the trading system is in essence a constitutional labour. For the first time, harmonization of domestic practices has become an internationally negotiable proposition. Such a route could eventually lead to a truly globalized world economy whereby a set of norms, rules and economic policies must be accepted by every party as a 'price' to be paid for access to markets.

For developing countries the new constituent elements of the trading system represent both dilemmas and challenges. Simultaneous to the Uruguay Round, an ever-growing list of developing countries have liberalized their trade regimes. In Latin America, in particular, almost all countries have cut back tariff rates and simplified tariff structures, besides reducing non-tariff barriers.[2] Alongside such dismantling of traditional protection, developing countries are experiencing growing pressures to accept more and more responsibilities in the system, including a curtailment of their prerogatives under special and differential treatment (S&D) and the acceptance of greater disciplines in services, intellectual property rights and foreign investment regimes, issues that hitherto had not been under the GATT purview. This entails moving nearer to the regulatory regimes preferred and applied by the main trade deman-deur, the United States. In these circumstances the capacity of developing countries to exercise an active commercial policy will be severely curtailed. A key challenge that these countries now confront is how to redefine the content and direction of industrial policies. How can they retain their prerogatives to 'create winners' (see Chapter 5 in this volume) in a system that demands that they surrender growing portions of their autonomy to design and imple-ment economic policy-making?

Moreover, there is a persistingly disturbing conflict between the muscle that developed countries have applied to incorporate the new issues into the Round and their reluctance to eliminate their own protectionist devices. These conflicting policies introduce elements of tension and selectivity into the process of globalization that may undermine the efforts of many developing countries to sustain outward-oriented growth. Domestic policy reform is a necessary but insufficient condition to sustain outward oriented growth (see Chapter 4 in this volume).

The purpose of this chapter is to examine the Uruguay Round with a view to evaluating its implications for developing countries. How much would the commitments required of developing countries inhibit or constrain the adoption of appropriate growth and industrialization policies? The experience of the newly industrializing countries suggests that the ability to replicate their path should not be dismissed lightly by any country.

The outline of the chapter is as follows. There is first an analysis of the emerging trade agenda, its contents and direction. This is followed by an overview of what is in store as a result of the Uruguay Round for industrial policy in developing countries. Lastly, the chapter concludes with a discussion of the regional trade negotiations that have been mushrooming in parallel to the Uruguay Round.

II THE NEW AGENDA

The agenda of the Uruguay Round was ambitious and complex; moreover, it evolved over a period of profound upheaval and economic restructuring marked, on one hand, by the collapse of the communist states, and on the other, by the severe balance of payments problems and the ensuing adjustment policies in many developing countries. With regard to many issues, positions and principles were reversed quite dramatically as the Round evolved. Superimposed on these changes and indeed perhaps motivated by them, trade policy came to be discussed increasingly in regional fora. The GATT-centred system of multilateral trade relations came under considerable strain.

GATT agreements set precedents and are points of departure for national trade policies as well as for regional integration. In the early post-war years, trade policy was confined to deal only with policies that directly affected trade in goods. Tariffs and quantitative restrictions (QRs) were then the main impediments to trade. So at inception the GATT was conceived as an instrument for the removal of tariffs on an MFN basis and the virtual proscription of QRs. This was seen to be the principal way of achieving free trade.

As GATT rounds proceeded they removed a significant layer of tariffs applied by developed countries. When the full extent of the Tokyo Round tariff reductions became effective in 1987, import weighted average tariff rates reached about 4.3 per cent for the United States and 6 per cent for the nine countries in the EC. For Japan, which had brought forward the full implementation of its cuts by March 1983, the equivalent figure is 2.9 per cent. The tariff has thus lost much of its traditional significance as an effective means of protection. For almost two-thirds of world trade the incidence of tariff costs are less or as important as transport costs.

There are, of course, some significant exceptions to this general trend. At the sectoral and product level, in particular, tariff peaks and tariff escalation according to the degree of processing for goods of export interest to developing countries are notorious. At the same time that tariffs in developed countries have come down to very low levels, non-tariff barriers have been increasing, particularly in the EC and the United States. Non-tariff measures – and more importantly, their incidence – are difficult to quantify. Therefore, it is not clear that such measures are now a more important impediment to trade than they were in the past.[3] But there can be little doubt that they are significant. Moreover, they affect disproportionately the exports of manufactures of developing countries, which concentrate on labour-intensive goods in which developed countries are losing competitiveness. In short, large segments of international trade have been partially excluded from the trend towards trade liberalization, which has been centred on trade among developed countries and in manufactured goods for which trade tends to be of an intra-industry kind.

In other words, the trade that has been liberalized is largely of a two-way nature in goods where both partners have production capacity and are at roughly equivalent levels of development. By contrast, one-way exports from developing to developed countries are subject to restrictions of both a tariff and a non-tariff nature[4]. This implies that, so far, the incorporation of developing countries into the international trading system has been far from complete, not merely because they have insisted in derogations from GATT rules for development reasons; but mainly because the goods they export – or could potentially export – have been increasingly excluded from GATT disciplines by the importers themselves. This, as we shall see, has important implications for the prospects for harmonizing trade and trade-related policies on a global scale.

With this important caveat, the reduction in border protection in the developed countries on imports of manufactures implies a major change in the workings of the system. The unilateral liberalization of an increasing number of developing countries has operated in the same fashion. The first 'peel of protection' of most economies has been shed. Thus, with border measures receding, non-border measures applied by governments to shape competition have by force become more visible. They are now a negotiating matter.

The complexity and importance of this development is patently illustrated by the growing scope of GATT rounds. The Tokyo Round, for example, over and above the conventional tariff reductions, delivered six codes on non-tariff barriers (government procurement, import licensing, subsidies and countervailing duties, dumping, technical standards and customs valuations). With the exception of the code on government procurement, these codes focused on border measures which were seen as capable of offsetting the effects of disappearing tariffs. The mandate for the Uruguay Round was a further step in this direction going, however, much beyond border measures with the inclusion of intellectual property rights, measures affecting foreign investors, and services. The aim of going down this road is not merely to prevent the left hand from undoing what is achieved with the right hand, but to broaden the scope of competence of the GATT.

The conventional concept of protection has become more far-reaching and encompassing; it has been widened to include a host of measures and policy tools that hitherto were out of the bounds of international concern. The accountability of governments for their trade and trade-related actions has increased with their shedding of the outer layer of protection. A panoply of measures that were traditionally seen to have only indirect links with trade policy are now found to have 'trade-interfering effects'. To quote from the World Bank's handbook, non-tariff barriers are considered to be 'all public regulations and government practices that introduce unequal treatment for domestic and foreign goods of the same or similar production'. Under such an extended net, they naturally 'constitute the single most important obstacle to the growth of international trade' (Olechowski, 1987, p. 121).

A wider net has been cast over economic policy, the implication being that the dividing line between trade and other policies has become increasingly blurred; the distinction between border and non-border measures seems largely artificial. Robert Lawrence (see Chapter 2 in this volume) has distinguished the integration achieved so far via the traditional tariff mechanism as 'shallow integration'. Freeing of trade was pursued by dealing with measures as they were reflected at the border. Yet the Uruguay Round has closed the era of shallow integration and has given way to a new policy arena 'beyond the border' (Ostry, 1990).

An illustrative case showing the new realms is the argument that has been raised in the context of the dispute between the United States and four EC countries over the jet airliner industry. While the United States alleged that the financial subsidies granted to Airbus Industries were unfair competition, the Europeans counter-argued that the US industry is hardly a model of perfect competition. In particular, the airline industry has not been immune to subsidies in albeit somewhat more covert ways – in so far as the cream of defence expenditure has provided the industry with a captive market. Government contracts cannot be distinguished from subsidies to R&D costs. Thus a subject usually unrelated to trade, such as the destination of the defence budget and the role of the military industrial complex in shaping the conditions of competition, can turn into a bone of contention in an international trade dispute.

Similarly, in the EC the disparate treatment of inward foreign investment across countries overspilt on to the trade agenda raising serious controversies over the practice of mutual recognition of rules of origin. The Treaty of Rome does not require that all members apply the same rules of origin on goods which, when treated as European would be entitled to zero tariff rates. Instead, it was accepted that each country was free to set the rules that best served its interests with the proviso that they would be mutually recognized by other members. With the upsurge of non-tariff-jumping Japanese investment into the EC and the different treatment accorded to it among members, the principle of mutual recognition has come under fire. Taking an unprecedented course of action, in 1988 France refused to consider as 'made in the EC' cars exported from Britain but manufactured by Nissan. The justification was that Nissan cars did not meet the minimum European content rules demanded by France despite meeting the laxer British requirements.

Thus, the treatment accorded to foreign investment, as well as broader matters of industrial policies, have become a legitimate subject for discussion at the bargaining table. Previously accepted simple expedients as mutual recognition of rules of origin become a matter of conflict when governments insist on discriminatory polices in conditions of increased integration. It is natural that this should eventually lead to drafting a standard system for determining rules of origin. Inroads into harmonizing a host of rules such as these was the difficult task at hand for participants in the Uruguay Round.

In this sense the GATT is confronted with the obstacle created by its own success in significantly lowering the tariff barriers of developed countries. *Ceteris paribus*, it is now close to the political limit of what it can do. A crisis is inevitable as the thrust of its business, if it is not to die of atrophy, shifts from tariff liberalization to rule-making for progressive harmonization. There is a fundamental difference between these two types of activities. They point to deepening degrees of international integration, the progressive shift from separate national economies to global markets.

Put simply, liberalization had hitherto been enacted on the basis of a calculation of concrete and immediate economic benefit. When bargaining is essentially restricted to tariff items, behaviour at home is not significantly constrained so long as national treatment is ensured. Interested parties exchange concessions over products, a deal from which they expect to extract returns in the short run. Here bargaining occurs over products; it takes an essentially item-by-item approach. This means that the decision to liberalize remains mainly a domestic issue. True, tariff rates are negotiable, but they are set according to domestic preferences.

As the content of multilateralism shifts from negotiations over products for which national treatment was appropriate to negotiations over the policies that shape the conditions of competition, new principles are required. A first step may be mutual recognition of regulations, but the road is paved for convergence or harmonization of laws over and above tariff law. A new phase of international negotiations has been opened.[5]

If tariff removal involves striking a deal, rule-making entails reaching an agreement over a framework of principles, norms, rules and decision-making procedures for transactions that will be spread over time. The trade-off is a difficult one for most governments, but more so for weaker countries without the muscle or clout to dictate terms. If rule-making leads to placing limits on the discretion of governments, commitments to a framework of principles are undertaken in so far as the absence of an agreement might result in unilateral sanctions.

Once national regulatory regimes become negotiable, the legitimacy of autonomous national economic management is gradually undermined. The various national economic policies are first exposed to one another; they will then tend to become intertwined and, lastly, there will be pressures towards harmonization or convergence. For the countries with weakest bargaining strength – e.g. the developing countries – 'harmonization' implies moving closer to the policies, institutions and practices of the major trading powers. In place of domestic policies with international implications, there will be the integration of various domestic policies into an international one (Meyer, 1978).

The Uruguay Round was confronted with uncharted territory. At the same time more and more members joined the GATT and placed further strains on the system. The difficult task for the Uruguay Round has been one of demarcation; that is, to determine those issues for which harmonization can be achieved and those for which national treatment or mutual recognition suffices. The really serious hurdle of harmonization is that it involves difficult choices between liberalisation and national autonomy. The problems are such that previous well-established procedures for international negotiations may be inadequate and even obsolete. The Uruguay Round has become stuck precisely over these questions, although the apparent problem was disagreement over agriculture. Agriculture, in many ways, was the syndrome in which myriad complex factors converged. But even taken in isolation, inherent to the problem of agricultural negotiations is the question of what changes or alignments must be made in other policies in order to facilitate the freeing of trade. The question that has been raised in the context of agriculture, just as in the Round more generally, is how much freedom of choice must governments sacrifice, and how much are foreign governments entitled to demand, to seek the benefits of specialization. What is at stake is a delimitation of government intervention in the competitive allocation of resources on an extensive scale.

Approaches to Policy Harmonization

The road of policy harmonization opens up a multitude of further questions. A central point to be elucidated is how far this should go. One way of looking at the problem might be to view harmonization as a mere corrective. Harmonization in this case is meant as a preventive action which should lead to a commitment not to use policy tools to offset the effect of liberalisation. It is undertaken as an obligation insofar as the freeing of trade from customs duties risks being nullified by such non-tariff barriers as technical or health standards, customs laws or procedures. In this vein participants in the Uruguay Round have drafted agreements on preshipment inspection and rules of origin and have tried to provide tighter definitions of the circumstances under which countervailing and anti-dumping duties can be imposed. The point of such negotiations is to determine to what extent such resorts involve evasion of free trade commitments via tariff substitutes.

More far-reaching pressures for policy harmonization hold that it must be structural. It ought to go beyond the tidying up of administrative procedures and must be undertaken in order to extend the free trade principle. Under this approach what ought to be harmonised are rules relating to the conditions of production. The question is then which policies are negotiable, how much harmonisation is necessary, and whether it is a requirement for freeing trade or the end-result of a process. This is the type of problem that must be sorted out in the definition and categorization of subsidies, trade-related investment measures (TRIMs) and the enforcement of patent rights. It also underlies the US zero-for-zero proposal under which tariffs, non-tariff barriers and subsidies on a broad range of manufactured goods could be completely eliminated on a reciprocal sector-by-sector basis. Similarly, the European textile lobby has demanded harmonization of tariff levels across countries as a pre-condition to the phasing out of the Multifibre Arrangement (MFA).

The first road towards harmonization would provide for negative harmonization: it would aim to ensure that governments honour agreed-upon market access commitments. It would serve to lay the ground for tariff reductions to operate more effectively. Yet border measures are seen here to be the ultimate trade policy tool. The second road would provide for positive harmonization: it would aim to enforce specific common rules to prescribe how exactly economic affairs are to be conducted, operating much in the same way as conditionality now does for borrowing countries.

In considering the problem of such positive or structural harmonization, it is important to note some of the logical and procedural limits it confronts. Although most of these are problems of degree rather than of kind, the contention that structural harmonization must be exacted as a precondition for freer trade has a rather obvious logical flaw. Indeed, if the creation of a 'level playing field' is carried to the extreme of establishing uniformity for its own sake, the implication is that if economies are dissimilar they ought not to engage in trade with one another. A *modus operandi* such as this bears close intellectual affinity to the idea of 'market disruption', the make-shift concept on the basis of which, first the Long Term Cotton Arrangement and then the MFA, were seen to be justified (see Tussie, 1989, especially chapter 4). The notion is dangerous enough, as the experience of the MFA has shown. The line between a 'competitive advantage' and a 'distortion' is one that is very difficult to draw.

The pressure for harmonization of policies could risk the impression that all theoretically desirable measures of harmonization are of equal importance, both absolutely and relatively, to sustain trade. If all regulations are seen as arbitrary 'distortions', the corollary will be drawn that all such 'distortions' ought to be eliminated in the interests of economic efficiency, an implication that automatically asserts priority for harmonization of policy over other goals or autonomous national economic management. Carried to the extreme it would lead to investigation of the overall impact of all relevant government policies on the competitive situation of particular industries and sectors of the economy, in order to assess the incidence of 'distortions' of competition associated with domestic policies, rules or practices. This trade route, as Bhagwati (1990, p. 22) has pointed out, may be 'unwise'. Furthermore, it may turn out to be quite unmanageable.

The pursuit of structural harmonization in wholly new and rather disparate areas, such as intellectual property regimes, workers' rights, the environment, etc., is essentially saying that *everything* affects trade and must therefore come under international scrutiny. A still more fundamental problem remains. Governments in developed countries are themselves responsible for creating market distortions under pressure from threatened lobbies. Both the United States and the EC have compelled competitive suppliers abroad to accept voluntary export restraints and orderly market agreements (the so-called 'grey-area' measures) which in essence amount to officially sanctioned cartels.

In sum, a great deal of research, assessment and negotiation is required before an international consensus can be built on issues such as these. There are at the very least three layers to this discussion: what are the desirable lines of harmonization, what targets may be reasonably set, and what methods may be legitimately used to implement them. These questions raise thorny political issues because they bring to the fore 'distortions' that may be the deliberate choice of governmental policies designed for priorities other than trade. Generally, they are inspired in considerations of the social welfare; at other times they are engrained in local values and local culture, rather elusive non-tariff barriers. Not surprisingly, there is much unresolved controversy about how legitimate harmonization is, how far it should be taken and what policies must be incorporated. Moreover, for developing countries 'harmonization' could well become a quasi-conditionality for them to accede to their full GATT rights. The road ahead is fraught with a morass of political, legal and economic difficulties.

III   THE URUGUAY ROUND: A WATERSHED FOR DEVELOPING COUNTRIES

The full effects of the Uruguay Round on developing countries will only be clarified at the close of negotiations. On the one hand, market access negotiations had not been finalized at the time of writing. Market access (and, particularly, many aspects of the negotiations on agriculture) is pivotal to countries that have embarked on radical unilateral liberalization. On the other, it is still unclear whether the 436 pages of the Draft Final Act submitted by Arthur Dunkel, the Director General of GATT, in December 1991 will be approved without modification. None the less, the Dunkel Draft sets the framework within which developing countries must gradually expect to design their industrial policies in the foreseeable future.[6]

The Round was a major challenge to developing countries. The campaign of the US administration to foist its own model of economic policy-making on other countries was evident, in particular, in the pressures to enforce an international regime for trade-related intellectual property rights (TRIPs). The effort to curtail the use of subsidies was also among one of the most important issues whereby the United States hoped to transform the GATT into a more active and in many ways more intrusive arrangement.

Moreover, the United States was bent on redefining the overall participation of developing countries within the system. Special and differential treatment (S&D), embodied in Part IV of the General Agreement in 1964, was viewed as a mechanism whereby developing countries had been 'free riding' on multilateralism. Thus the call for 'fuller participation' was a move to withdraw S&D treatment and compel developing countries to accept the same disciplines as developed ones.

Developing countries have been unprecedentedly active in the negotiations. Far from abiding by S&D or 'free riding', they have offered major concessions in market access negotiations with the hope of gaining some credit for unilateral liberalization initiatives. Moreover, the spirit and the letter of the Dunkel Draft requires them to share nearly all the obligations of developed countries. However, the commitments that developed countries are expected to make to redress the biases in their trade policies described above and genuinely to incorporate developing countries into the system are far from being thorough; they contain many safeguards (even the use of QRs targeted at individual suppliers, in the case of textiles), and they would be implemented only towards the end of a lengthy transitional period (see Ocampo, 1992; and UNCTAD, 1992).

The Dunkel Draft suggests that S&D has been drastically revised; it is merely addressed by allowing developing countries longer periods of adjustment or some technical assistance to comply with the same obligations as the developed countries. There is no financial commitment to offset any higher costs of food or technology imports resulting from agreements in these areas.[7]

The preferential treatment that remains is marginal. As an indication, safeguard action under Article XIX stipulates a *de minimis* exemption by which it will not be implemented on countries with market shares below 3 per cent – unless, as a whole, they share more than 9 per cent of the import market of the country resorting to the safeguard.

The agreement on safeguards is important for more fundamental reasons. The consistent violation of Article XIX is perhaps the GATT's biggest loophole. It is here that the greatest disparities between principle and practice as applied to developing countries can be seen at work. Avoidance of legal non-discriminatory safeguards has riddled the system; 'grey-area' measures have mushroomed and anti-dumping and countervailing duties have been abused. Two ways have been discussed to deal with the discrepancy between principle and practice. One is to stick to the principle of non-discrimination as originally drafted in the General Agreement. A second option is to legally allow selectivity under strictly predetermined circumstances so as to induce greater respect for accepted rules. Critics of this option argue that this would blatantly undermine the GATT; it would be equivalent to legalizing crime because it cannot be combated. Defenders uphold that the system can be strengthened only by injecting some realism and pragmatism into it and that is by allowing further, but well-defined departures from a principle to which only lip-service is being paid (see Nicolaides, 1990).

An examination of these options began even before the launching of the Tokyo Round in 1973. The industrial countries have consistently made the return to GATT disciplines conditional on selective treatment. Selectivity would amount to legalizing existing 'grey area' restrictions. Developing countries, on the other hand, have consistently resisted this alternative, fearing a re-edition of the MFA, which gave legal sanction to the violation of their right to MFN treatment.

The Dunkel Draft has opted for pragmatism and legitimized selectivity. Developed countries will have to remove illegal 'grey area' measures over four years in exchange for which they will be allowed to implement quantitative controls, and target countries with more rapid export growth under the new agreement. Yet the same leniency is not allowed to developing countries. Safeguards used for balance of payments disequilibria under Article XVII will have to avoid QRs and give priority to temporary tariffs. Taken together, these new safeguard provisions have 'turned upside down the principle of special and differential treatment' in the critical area of quantitative import restrictions (Ocampo, 1992). Hopefully, the price paid in terms of selectivity will contribute towards increasing certainty and security of market access.

Over and above the undermining of S&D, there are two central areas in which the Uruguay Round outcome may restrict specific policies designed to encourage activities with important externalities in the early stages of industrialization (see Chapter 4 in this volume). These are tighter provisions for industrial subsidies and the new intellectual property regime.

The new agreement on subsidies establishes important precedents for the industrial policies of developing countries. On the one hand, it undermines the acceptability of subsidization as an integral part of economic development programmes which was included in Article 14 of the Tokyo Round Subsidies Code (UNCTAD, 1992). On the other, it legitimizes in a multilateral context the concept of 'graduation' according to level of development and general economic indicators such as GNP per capita. Although there is some degree of flexibility and grace periods, the graduation rule is explicit and very stringent. Countries with a per capita GDP over $1,000 will be subject to the same disciplines as industrialized countries.[8] Developing countries as well as least developed ones, will also be required to graduate in those sectors in which they have reached export competitiveness, measured as a world market share above 3.25 per cent for two consecutive years. Lastly, the injury test to which exporters accused of receiving subsidies have a right before countervailing action has also been curtailed. Serious injury to the interests of local producers will automatically be presumed when subsidies exceed 5 per cent *ad valorem*.

Only 11 developing countries are parties to the existing Tokyo Round Code on Subsidies. Such reluctance to join the Code lies in the fact that, despite accepting subsidization as an integral part of development needs, countries were required to commit themselves to a gradual phase out. But they were free to sign any, all or none of the six codes negotiated during the Round. Contrary to that practice, the Uruguay Round agreements are 'a single undertaking' and will be incorporated into a single legal instrument. Countries are, therefore, not free to bargain on which parts of the whole they will accept. A Multilateral Trade Organization will supervise all agreements in the three areas of goods, services and intellectual property. Thus, the final balance of the Round for developing countries hinges crucially on the balance of market access achieved in exchange for the increased commitments in respect of their industrial policies.

The Case of Intellectual Property

Copyright, patent and other intellectual property issues have been a divisive North–South issue. For net importers of technology the traditional choice has been to offer immediate protection and buy technology abroad, or to obtain technology through diffusion (including copying and the hiring of foreign experts, as all previous industrializing countries have done) and minimize current import costs. The case of pharmaceuticals has been among the most contentious of all because it is at once a sector with very high research and development (R&D) costs, potentially accessible process technology, and has a direct bearing on health costs and health policies more generally. The countries most frequently targeted as 'violating' property rights include not only the fastest growing economies but also the most important recipients of foreign investment: Brazil, Singapore, South Korea, Taiwan and Thailand.

The introduction of an intellectual property regime into the GATT system is a considerable extension of its scope; it epitomizes the dilemmas inherent in the convergence of national regulatory regimes described above. It, moreover, throws light on the hard choices confronted by countries in need of securing market access, which is gradually less contingent on reciprocal liberalization than on policy conditionality. By laying down 'minimum conditions' instead of national treatment as the required behaviour, it is a landmark agreement that could be used as a precedent in other areas where the matter of debate hinges on the conditions of competition.

Hitherto almost all national laws dealing with the protection of patents and trademarks had been shaped by the Paris Convention for the Protection of Industrial Property of 1883. The Paris Convention guaranteed national treatment: countries were obliged to follow disciplines on the form of protection but were allowed freedom on the level of protection (Maskus, 1990). National treatment established a commitment to a minimum common denominator from which standards were supposed to be built upwards through an evolutionary process. It was thus unsuitable to obtain the immediate international enforcement of rights held at the highest level of protection demanded by technology exporters.

The US agenda, driven mainly by the pharmaceutical lobby, aimed to obtain: (a) upward harmonization of intellectual property protection without sectoral exceptions (and thus to include pharmaceuticals, the most controversial sector); (b) revision of the concept of 'effective exploitation' of a patent so as to remove the obligation to produce locally and allow it to mean merely supplying the local market; (c) the provision of administrative and judicial procedures under national laws to enforce the harmonized protection standards; and (d) dispute settlement mechanisms to allow 'cross retaliation' between non-compliance with intellectual property rights and market access in goods.

Most of these demands have been met in the Draft Final Act of the Uruguay Round. The draft agreement on TRIPs aims to set harmonized standards for copyright, trademarks, geographical indications, industrial designs, patents, lay-out designs of integrated circuits and trade secrets, as well as the obligations of governments for enforcing those rights.

The most controversial of all these is patents, which grants the patent-holders rights for a 20-year term (Article 33) with no explicit obligation to work the patent locally (Article 31). Moreover, the patent-holder is also granted exclusive rights of importation (Article 28). In other words, shipments of identical goods from lower-price countries, outside manufacturers' official distribution channels, or 'parallel imports', are banned, thus eliminating competition from wholesalers. Patentability is applied to all fields of technology (Article 27); it is extended to micro-organisms, food, chemicals and pharmaceuticals and the processes to produce them. However, animals and plants that provide the raw materials for biotechnology (many of which are abundant in developing countries) have been excepted.

Dispute settlement procedures tighten further these concessions. The burden of the proof is reversed should there be a dispute over patented processes (Article 34).[9] Since the agreement will be part of a Multilateral Trade Organization which will implement an integrated dispute settlement mechanism, in the future 'cross retaliation' between non-compliance in this area and market access in goods will be possible. The possibility of trade sanctions (transferring a principle of US trade law to the GATT) may further hinder the diffusion of technology.

Only two considerations advanced by developing countries were incorporated into the draft agreement. First, compulsory licences are allowed under Article 31 although under very strictly defined circumstances. They cannot be established for a particular field of technology and can only be applied to supply the local market for reasons related to public health, nutrition or other public interests in national emergencies, public non-commercial use, to correct anti-competitive practices or when the holder refuses to grant licences on reasonably commercial terms. Second, there is no 'pipeline protection' or recognition of patents on a retroactive basis.

The Dunkel Draft provides, in short, an upward 'levelling of the playing field' very much in line with US preferences and imposing restrictions on learning by doing processes in developing countries. By diluting local working obligations it may also hinder the execution of inventions and the related transfer of technology to developing countries. It will also lead to substantial increases in short-run costs in the form of large rents transferred to the foreign owners of patent rights.

Since the manner in which intellectual property has been managed up to the present was not a violation of current obligations, if accepted in its present form, the Draft implies a significant policy concession by developing countries. Not only will developing countries have to conform to US preferences, but they will also have to devote scarce engineering, governmental and entrepreneurial skills to enforce the new standards. Starting from the top downwards means that developing countries will need to enforce uniform intellectual property standards without equivalent scientific, education and health systems.

IV THE MULTILATERAL SYSTEM AND REGIONAL INITIATIVES: A PIECEMEAL EXPEDIENT

The analysis of an emerging trade agenda 'beyond the border' should help to explain the paradox posed at the beginning of this chapter. The Uruguay Round is a milestone for world trade policy irrespective of its outcome. Innovative principles, techniques and procedures must be devised as the thrust of the negotiations shift from bargaining over products to bargaining over policies. Hard bargaining is inevitable until core issues are mapped out and broken down and a consensus gradually evolves on the precise new content to be given to multilateralism, as applied to policies. The predicament of the Uruguay Round was in direct relation to the practical problems inherent in developing rules of international co-operation on non-trade issues and practices. The problem has been one of laying the conceptual underpinnings for the task at hand, including the liberalization of agriculture.

Progress along this trade route requires that growing portions of government autonomy be surrendered. It involves, moreover, a constitutional labour, as illustrated by the process of building a truly single market in Europe, in many respects a trade-policy laboratory. The resolution of the many issues posed by the 1985 White Paper, or by the Maastricht Treaty of 1990, is difficult even among a group of countries such as those in the EC.

The GATT may have reached a political limit with the transformation of the trade agenda and its virtual unmanageableness, partly because of growing membership from developing and former communist countries. This no doubt is a factor adding further complications. The GATT now confronts the reluctance of countries to cede growing portions of sovereignty to a global multilateral organization. So, alongside the changing nature of the agenda, the locus of negotiations has also begun to shift. The regional initiatives that are gathering momentum do not necessarily indicate a retreat from the GATT – although they have created a certain disquiet that the multilateral system will slide into re-trenchment within blocs, unravelling the integration achieved so far.

However, if more than a minimum common denominator is desired, smaller units may provide an answer. Given both the growing number of parties and policies under international scrutiny and given the inherent sensitivity of many issues now on the bargaining table, regional negotiations are more than simple trading arrangements. They are perhaps best described as policy blocs in which issue by issue can be tackled in piecemeal fashion. On the one hand, among fewer participants the adjustment required to dismantle remaining tariffs and NTBs in hard-core sectors may be easier to manage; on the other hand, discussions over harmonization of trade-related policies can be taken up less reluctantly among a smaller and less dispersed number of countries. These are the sort of issues that in a variety of ways both the North American Free Trade Area (NAFTA) and the creation of the Single European Market are now trying to come to grips with. If Europe shows the way but also the obstacles in respect of policy convergence, NAFTA may be a guide for tackling hard core neo-protectionism and for the adoption of multinational procedures for dispute settlement.

This is said to put the upsurge of regional negotiations in their appropriate perspective. The extent to which these piecemeal initiatives short-circuit or distract attention from the GATT is still an open question. So long as they do not raise additional barriers to outsiders, and so long as they serve to lay the necessary ground on which to build the new trade agenda, the GATT option may receive fresh impetus at the end of the road when the bilateral consensus is sewn up. After all the Anglo-American negotiations leading to Bretton Woods provide an historical precedent of the bilateral road to multilateralism.

V   SOME CONCLUSIONS

The precedent, as is obvious, also illustrates the costs of exclusion. The strategic challenge for developing countries will be to keep the spirit of multilateralism alive and continue to demand a broad-based management of the world economy. The attitude of many developing countries (including Eastern Europe) that took unilateral steps to reduce trade barriers must be contrasted to that of big trading powers that have held back concessions as bargaining chips for the last stage of the Round. Such readiness of developing countries to take the initiative has produced a mirror image of their traditional passivity in the GATT. Their present expectation of reciprocal market access cannot be reduced to a mere question of principle: the cost of unreciprocated liberalizations in a large number of developing countries would be steeper devaluations and/or lower export prices than with improved market access.

The final balance of the Round (as well as of regional negotiations) will depend less on the increasing commitments that they seem ready to make than on the balance of market access negotiations as a *quid pro quo*. In sum, if developed countries persist in their disinclination to tackle the backlog of unresolved market access issues that affect developing countries, the Round will have provided few benefits. The by-now-historical dilemma whereby countries enjoying access do not have supply and those that have supply are not granted access (Abreu, 1989) will have been given a further twist. So far the greatest attraction is centred in the phasing out of the MFA. Over all, however, the litmus test is the extent to which market access has been effectively improved in exchange for surrendering the layers of national autonomy in policy-making that are inherent to the new commitments.

There is little doubt that the interests of developing countries are best served by strengthening multilateralism. Partly as a result of changing convictions, developing countries now have a greater stake in an open trading system. They have been more engaged in the Uruguay Round than in preceding GATT rounds. Instead of their traditional role as by-standers, they have been active negotiators. But extreme care is needed. There is a sea-change in the workings of the system. At the same time that the number of parties to the GATT is expanding, as is its prospective competence over issues, so are the number of trading arrangements at the sub-global level. As the regulatory regimes and domestic policies of developing countries gradually come under pressure to conform to those of developed countries, either at the global or sub-global levels, institutional practices with a bearing on competitiveness will be targeted.

It follows from this that the available range of trade and industrial policy options of developing countries is becoming more limited. Developing countries will have to tie their hands progressively if they wish to participate more actively in the international division of labour. The Draft Final Act of the Uruguay Round crystallizes these pressures in a number of ways, all of which add up to the virtual abrogation of S&D. Furthermore, it would involve the acceptance by developing countries of an international regime for intellectual property akin to those prevailing in developed countries. Under such conditions, the room to employ active trade, industrial or investment policies would be severely curtailed. The challenge for the most industrialized developing countries will be to reconcile these exigencies with national economic management and development concerns.

Notes

1. The author wishes to acknowledge generous comments from Manuel Agosin and Andrew Cornford. The usual caveats apply.
2. UNCTAD (1991) provides a list of countries in the process of trade liberalization as well as measures undertaken.
3. For many years UNCTAD has been calculating the share of imports into developed countries that is affected by non-tariff measures. As regards imports from all origins, the share of imports covered by non-tariff measures rose somewhat between 1981 and 1990, but the increase was modest (from around 16 to 17.5 per cent). The trade coverage ratio for imports from developing countries was considerably higher in both years, although the increase from 22.5 to 23 per cent was less significant (UNCTAD, 1991, p. 59).
4. This hypothesis is spelt out in Tussie (1989). Empirical verification can be found in de Castro (1989).
5. These issues have been raised in the context of freeing trade within a customs union in Johnson, Wonnacott and Shibata (1968). The question there was how far harmonization ought to be sought as a prerequisite for freer trade. The present chapter is inspired by that work, but raises the issue of harmonization from a different perspective, i.e. as the process unfolding as a result of lowered barriers at the border.

6. Sheila Page *et al.* (1991) provide preliminary quantitative estimates of the impact of the Uruguay Round on developing countries.
7. Extending patent rights and curbs on compulsory licensing will raise the import bill of many developing countries.
8. There are only a total of 21 countries with a per capita GDP below $1,000, 13 in Africa, 3 in Latin America and 5 in Asia.
9. Before, it was customary for intellectual property right holders to prove their case against presumed violators. Under the text on TRIPs of the Draft Final Act, the burden of proof falls on the accused.

References

Abreu, M. de Paiva (1989), 'Developing Countries and the Uruguay Round', *Proceedings of the World Bank Annual Conference on Development Economics* (Washington, DC).

Bhagwati, J. (1990), *The World Trading System at Risk* (Princeton: Princeton University Press).

De Castro, J. (1989), 'Determinants of Protection and Evolving Forms of North–South Trade', *UNCTAD Review*, (Geneva), Vol. 1, No. 2.

Johnson, H., P. Wonnacott and H. Shibata (1968), *Harmonization of National Economic Policies under Free Trade* (Toronto: University of Toronto Press).

Maskus, K. (1990), 'Intellectual Property', in Jeffrey Schott, ed., *Completing the Uruguay Round* (Washington, DC: Institute for International Economics).

Meyer, F.V. (1978), *International Trade Policy* (London: Croom Helm).

Nicolaides, P. (1990), 'Safeguards and the Problem of VERs', *Intereconomics*, January–February.

Ocampo, J.A. (1992), 'Developing Countries and the GATT Uruguay Round: A Preliminary Balance', in UNCTAD, *International Monetary and Financial Issues for the 1990s*, Research Papers for the Group of 24, Volume I, United Nations, New York, 1992.

Olechowski, A. (1987), 'Non-Tariff Barriers to Trade', in Michael J. Finger, and A. Olechowski, eds., *A Handbook on the Multilateral Trade Negotiations* (Washington, DC: World Bank).

Ostry, S. (1990), *Governments and Corporations in a Shrinking World* (New York: Council on Foreign Relations Press).

Page, S., with M. Davenport and A. Hewitt (1991), *The GATT Uruguay Round: Effects on Developing Countries*, (London: Overseas Development Institute).

Tussie, D. (1989), *The Less Developed Countries and the World Trading System: A Challenge to the GATT* (London and New York: Pinter Publishers).

UNCTAD (1991), *Trade and Development Report 1991*, Geneva.

UNCTAD (1992), 'Preliminary Comments on the Draft Final Act Embodying the Results of the Uruguay Round of Multilateral Trade Negotiations', Geneva.

Part II
New Approaches and Policy Options

4 Trade Policy Reform and Economic Performance: Empirical Experience

Manuel R. Agosin[1]

In the course of the 1980s, an increasing number of developing countries came to recognize the need to achieve a greater degree of economic openness and to give greater priority to increasing and diversifying exports. This was the result of a number of factors. Undoubtedly, the dynamism of the export-oriented Asian economies had a demonstration effect on many other developing countries. In many countries, particularly those in Latin America, it was felt that import substitution, initially adopted as a policy response to specific conditions prevailing in the international economy, had been continued far too long. Another important influence was the need to stimulate exports in order to overcome the effects on economic growth of the debt crisis. Several countries also came under pressure from the multilateral financial institutions to liberalize their economies, including their trade policies. As a result, the climate of opinion among policy-makers in a large number of developing countries shifted away from an emphasis on import-substituting industrialization and towards greater reliance on export expansion and liberalization of the trade regime.

The objective of this chapter is to contribute to the elucidation of the major issues involved in trade policy reform and to provide some empirical evidence on them drawn from the experience of developing countries. Section I discusses the issues. Section II examines statistical data from the 1980s, and Section III provides qualitative evidence on the relationship between trade and exchange rate regimes, on the one hand, and economic growth, on the other. Section IV summarizes the results.

I   A REVIEW OF THE ISSUES[2]

Trade policy reform has given rise to a number of debates. This chapter will review some of the most important ones, including the measurement of the degree of openness of the trade regime, the relationship between outward orientation and growth, the question of whether import substitution is necessarily the first stage of industrialization; the extent to which import liberalization is needed to encourage export growth; the role of the exchange rate in export performance, and whether stabilization must be achieved before trade policy reform can be successfully implemented.

The Problem of Measuring Policy Orientation

Measuring policy orientation is intrinsically difficult, because trade policies in most countries, particularly developing countries, are exceedingly complex, not always transparent, and not easily described in terms of a few dimensions that are amenable to quantification. In addition, one must distinguish between the export orientation of an economy and the extent to which it relies on market forces or on government intervention. In principle, a country can achieve a high degree of export orientation through government intervention and without recourse to liberal trade policies. This appears to have been the case in the Republic of Korea and, to a lesser extent, in Taiwan. Admittedly, this is not easy to achieve for most developing countries, since it requires the heavy use of export subsidies and intervention in the process of credit allocation.

Generally, one can typify a country's trade regime by the extent to which the incentive structure deviates from neutrality as between exporting and producing for domestic markets and as between different activities. For this purpose, ideally one would calculate for each tradeable activity two effective exchange rates, one for exports and one for imports, each incorporating the effect of all appropriate tariffs, tariff equivalents of non-tariff barriers (NTBs), and subsidies.[3]

For each tradeable activity, then, one would have to calculate two sets of effective exchange rates, EERM and EERX. In a world of perfect neutrality, all effective exchange rates would be equal. In reality, they are likely to differ as between different activities and, within each activity, as between exports and imports. The coefficients of variation of EERX and EERM would be a fairly accurate measure of the extent to which the trade regime diverges from neutrality. The difficulty with such an approach, however appealing it may be from an analytical point of view, is that its information requirements are likely to be formidable. In most studies on the subject, certain shortcuts are sought. Some of these are discussed below.

The degree of outward or inward orientation is usually measured by examining either trade outcomes or broad indicators of policy incidence (see Pritchett, 1991). A third approach can be categorized as subjective: countries are classified broadly as being outward or inward oriented after an examination of their entire trade policy apparatus (UNCTAD, 1989; and World Bank, 1987). Among the first group of measures, the most commonly used are the ratios of imports or exports to GDP (or the ratio of exports plus imports to GDP). The problem that arises is that these unadjusted ratios are influenced by the structural characteristics of the economy at least as much as by the nature of the policy regime. Therefore, several authors have sought to adjust them by such structural characteristics as population, per capita income, distance to markets, availability of natural resources, etc. This can be readily done by cross-country regression analysis, where the dependent variables are the trade ratios and the independent variables are the structural characteristics one wishes to adjust for. The residuals of such regression analyses represent the adjusted measures of trade orientation. While interesting, such adjusted ratios tend to yield rather idiosyncratic results which, in many instances, do not accord with *a priori* expectations or with available qualitative information.

Policy incidence measures include average tariff levels, the dispersion of tariff rates, effective rates of protection (ERPs), the frequency of NTBs, the share of subsidies in goods' prices, and the like. All of these measures have their problems: in some cases, particularly those where they are very high, tariffs contain 'water' and, thus, may over-estimate the extent to which they grant protection to domestic industry; under the best of circumstances, ERPs are available only for one point in time, and their calculation requires a prodigious amount of information; the frequency of NTBs says nothing about their stringency; subsidies are notoriously difficult to track, and their incidence on price levels is even more difficult to estimate.

It is interesting to note that Pritchett (1991) found that country rankings by outcome measures were uncorrelated with rankings by policy incidence measures. This absence of correlation may arise because such simple indicators are by nature one-dimensional and, therefore, are unable to capture the complexity of trade policy regimes.

The difficulties involved with the subjective approach are illustrated by the problems with the classification used by the World Bank (1987, p. 83) to argue in favour of outward orientation in its *World Development Report, 1987*. In that exercise, countries were classified into four groups (strongly outward oriented, moderately outward oriented, moderately inward oriented, and strongly inward oriented) according to the nature of their trade policies during the periods 1963–73 and 1973–85. It appears that the criteria used in characterizing countries' trade regimes were rather subjective and designed to prove the superiority of outward orientation. For example, only three economies in the sample were included in the 'strongly outward oriented' group in both periods (Hong Kong, Republic of Korea and Singapore). Although these economies have pursued unambiguous outward-oriented policies and have recorded high rates of economic growth, it would be hazardous to generalize as to the virtues of outward orientation on the basis of such a small sample and, moreover, one that contains such 'special cases' as Hong Kong and Singapore. On the other hand, Chile is described as having switched from a 'strongly inward oriented' to a 'moderately outward oriented' regime. Given the fact that, in the second period, the Chilean economy underwent what must be the most extensive and consistent trade liberalization exercise in the developing world (see Chapter 7), its categorization as 'moderately outward oriented' comes as a surprise. Since Chile's economic growth record during the period was poor, one suspects that the authors were influenced in their classification by a desire not to spoil the 'finding' of a positive relationship between outward orientation and economic performance.

The issue is clearly not settled. For purposes of broad categorization of trade regimes, the subjective approach seems unavoidable (for another use of this approach, see UNCTAD, 1989). However, care must be taken not to overlay the exercise with preconceptions as to the relationship between trade regimes and growth. For purposes of statistical analysis of the record of the 1980s, section II of this chapter uses a simple measure of policy-induced incremental openness: the rate of growth in the volume of manufactured exports. It is argued that this variable is not as affected by structural variables as total exports and that it is a relatively robust indicator of the extent to which countries have succeeded in achieving greater integration into the international economy.

Export Orientation and Economic Growth

The advocates of export-oriented trade strategies have argued that export orientation is more conducive to rapid overall growth than import-substituting industrialization. Simple correlations between export and GDP growth are insufficient to settle the issue, since exports are a part of GDP – in some countries quite a considerable part.

Export growth, by easing the foreign exchange constraint, is bound to have a positive effect on growth. But so would successful import substitution. The argument for exports must surely rest on the fact that import substitution is limited by the size of the domestic market, while export growth is not bound by such limits.[4]

Several arguments have been deployed in favour of export orientation. It is claimed that exports allow the manufacturing sector to reap economies of scale to a greater extent than import substitution. Moreover, since production for export markets has exacting cost and quality control requirements and brings producers in contact with new technologies and business practices, it is thought to be more conducive than import substitution to innovation and to the lowering of costs. Both of these factors – larger scope for economies of scale and greater inducements to innovation – would result in faster total factor productivity growth (TFPG) under export-oriented policies than under an import-substituting regime. An econometric investigation of the issue would appear to lend support to this hypothesis. Using cross-section analysis for the industrial sectors of Turkey, the Republic of Korea, Yugoslavia and Japan, Nishimizu and Robinson (1984) found that TFPG was positively and significantly correlated with the share of the growth of output that can be attributed to export growth.[5]

The link that some observers posit between outward orientation and growth has recently been contested by Rodrik (1991). He points out that the validity of the argument in favour of outward orientation that relies on economies of scale depends crucially on the assumption that such economies are more prevalent in the production of exportables than in activities oriented to the domestic market. He also argues that a positive association between outward orientation and TFPG depends largely on the assumption that there are significant gains to be made from increasing X-efficiency. If, however, entrepreneurs are optimizers rather than 'satisficers', he goes on to show that innovation can be quite substantial in protected markets, since the larger market provided by protection increases the benefits to be derived from cost improvements.

The inconclusive nature of the evidence advanced in the recent literature on the subject suggests that the extent to which growth is correlated positively to outward orientation will vary from country to country. There is no reason to expect on *a priori* grounds that import substitution must be in all cases an inferior option. However, the statistical evidence for the 1980s examined in section II shows a positive relationship between incremental outward orientation and economic growth. This could be due to the particular characteristics of the period: severe external shocks and almost ubiquitous foreign exchange constaints to growth. It may also be related to the fact that those countries that succeeded in penetrating foreign markets for manufactures were also able to achieve high rates of absorption and adaptation of foreign technology and high rates of growth in manufacturing, a sector with strong externalities for the entire economy.

Import Substitution and Industrialization

An important issue for the developing countries which are at an incipient level of industrialization is whether they must necessarily pass through a stage of import substitution before they can begin to penetrate international markets for manufactures. The expansion of manufacturing production in developing countries has been overwhelmingly based on import substitution. In most of the current exporters of manufactures among developing countries (e.g. Republic of Korea, Taiwan Province of China, Brazil, Mexico or Turkey), the supply capabilities created through import substitution policies proved to be the foundation of their export drives.[6] In low-income countries, a stage of import substitution is likely to be inescapable, given the lack of knowledge of foreign markets, the stringent quality requirements of international markets, and the paucity of indigenous skills. Most manufacturing activities have steep learning curves and external economies in the form of labour skills useful to other firms and even in other sectors of the economy. Therefore, once industrialization has gotten underway, the efficiency of the manufacturing sector can be expected to rise and costs are bound to decline, eventually enabling the country to penetrate foreign markets in some lines of production. Bruton (1989) argues that import substitution should be considered as the effort to build supply capabilities which will eventually give a country a greater degree of autonomy in pursuing its goals. The resulting inefficiencies, in his view, should be considered as the cost to be paid for acquiring such capabilities.

Obviously, this argument is not meant to justify all programmes of import substitution undertaken in the developing world in the post-war period. The inefficiencies of indiscriminate protection are well known and do not need to be repeated here. The test of success for an import substitution programme is whether it renders the country adopting it capable of producing the protected manufactures competitively and without the need for protection in a reasonable period of time.

The issue of whether, for most bar the smallest of countries, import substitution is a necessary first stage of industrialization is still open. Several African countries with undeveloped manufacturing sectors embraced drastic trade liberalization policies during the 1980s. The degree of success that these programmes will eventually prove to have will be a good empirical test of the need – or lack thereof – for an initial import-substituting industrialization process.

Is Import Liberalization Needed to Achieve Export Growth?

According to some analysts, as long as there are large profits to be reaped in import-replacing industries, new investments will not be made in industries producing for export markets (Michalopoulos, 1987). Therefore, import liberalization is viewed as essential to export growth. The implicit premises of this position are that resources can be transferred costlessly between sectors and that producers respond to the *lowering* of incentives in one sector or type of activity by investing in others where incentives remain unchanged. The normal sequence recommended for import liberalization is to begin by converting NTBs to their tariff-equivalents, then to lower the highest tariffs, and to proceed further by lowering all tariffs together so as to achieve eventually a uniform and 'low' rate of protection.[7]

Undoubtedly, exports are unlikely to show much dynamism in economies with very high and variable rates of effective protection, because not even export subsidies of various kinds can possibly counteract the severe anti-export bias that such a system of incentives necessarily generates. But this is not the same thing as saying that total or substantial import liberalization is a *sine qua non* condition for export growth. In economies characterized by incomplete markets and structural rigidities, the simple removal of protection without any compensating policies is more likely to lead to the idling of resources than to their transfer to export activities. Successful structural adjustment requires investment, and entrepreneurs, particularly in a developing country, are unlikely to invest in the desired sectors unless economic signals unambiguously point them in that direction. A lowering of profits in import-substituting activities without a clear increase in the profitability of exporting – and one that is viewed as durable – is unlikely to bring forth the desired investment response.

The statistical and qualitative evidence reviewed below does not reveal any relationship between export growth, on the one hand, and the restrictiveness of import policies, on the other.

The Role of the Exchange Rate

There is little doubt that the maintenance of an adequate real exchange rate is a necessary condition for promoting exports and efficient import substitution. What is meant by 'adequate', however, is a matter of considerable debate, and there are a number of unsettled issues surrounding the exchange rate.

The tendency of the real exchange rate to become overvalued when policy-makers pursue expansionary fiscal and monetary policies in the context of a fixed nominal exchange rate has recently been analysed exhaustively by Edwards (1988 and 1989). The problem in this case is that fiscal and monetary policies are incompatible with the maintenance of a fixed nominal exchange rate. The policy solution is to devalue and to correct the underlying source of real overvaluation: excessively expansive demand management policies. While these stylized facts describe broadly the situation of several developing countries, this line of argument leads to obvious conclusions and fails to address the really interesting questions relating to the exchange rate. These have to do with how to manage the exchange rate as a tool for long-term structural change in the direction of greater openness and integration into international markets for goods and services. Another fundamental issue relates to the trade-off between using the exchange rate as a tool to encourage trade expansion and industrialization, on the one hand, and as an anchor for domestic prices, on the other.

In many developing countries it may be difficult to effect a shift in relative prices in favour of tradeables. Nominal devaluations tend to lower real wages and, in the presence of formal or informal wage indexation mechanisms, the devaluation could simply lead to a ratcheting up of domestic inflation with little change in relative prices. In countries suffering from hyper-inflation (e.g. several Latin American countries since the early 1980s), the difficulty is made more acute by the fact that all domestic prices and wages tend to be informally pegged to the exchange rate. The problem usually presents itself in terms of a policy trade-off: while a real devaluation may be needed in order to attain long-term growth objectives, the short-term anti-inflationary objective is best served by using the nominal exchange rate as an anchor for domestic prices. This latter policy is usually accompanied by substantial appreciation in the real exchange rate (as witnessed by the experiences of the Southern Cone countries in the late 1970s and early 1980s).

The exchange rate problem is often understood solely in terms of (a) determining the equilibrium real exchange rate and (b) making the actual rate converge towards the real equilibrium rate (see Edwards, 1988). At the equilibrium real exchange rate, the current account balance is compatible with expected long-term capital flows. When faced with any change in the determinants of the balance of payments, policy-makers must be able to make a judgement as to whether the change is 'temporary' or 'permanent'. Only permanent changes are said to affect the equilibrium real exchange rate. Also, in this conceptual framework, permanent changes call for changes in the exchange rate towards its new equilibrium level. For example, a deterioration in the terms of trade would require a real depreciation. Conversely, an increase in foreign direct investment viewed as permanent would necessitate a real appreciation. On the other hand, within this conceptual framework, temporary changes should not be allowed to affect the actual exchange rate, since they do not alter the equilibrium real rate.

One problem with this approach is the difficulty in determining in all instances which external shocks are temporary and which are permanent. And even if policy-makers could make accurate estimates of the real equilibrium rate, how best to ensure that the actual rate converges rapidly to its equilibrium level is still an open question. Floating exchange rates are unlikely to achieve this objective. Even in developed countries, exchange rates are very volatile. In developing countries, small changes in short-term capital flows can cause large movements in nominal exchange rates. And if the exchange rate is to be fixed by the authorities, the problems remain as to how to hit a *real* exchange rate target (as opposed to a nominal one).

A third problem, to which we now turn, is that the optimal policy, from the point of view of a country's long-term objectives, may involve engineering a departure of the actual rate from its equilibrium level.

Many developing countries have experienced significant appreciation of their real exchange rate when the prices of their primary commodity exports have risen, causing the well-known problem of

'Dutch disease' and hampering export diversification and efficient import substitution. According to Ospina Sardi (1989), much of the exchange rate instability observed in Latin American countries is a result of externally caused fluctuations in their terms of trade. If the problem is viewed as 'temporary', the solution is fairly simple: the authorities could create a fund that purchases foreign exchange during the times of foreign exchange bonanza and sells it during periods of foreign exchange scarcity. However, if the situation is viewed as 'permanent', the solutions are more difficult to envisage. It would seem that, in this case, the policy objective would be to *prevent* the actual exchange rate from appreciating towards its new, real equilibrium level.

An important policy dilemma is how to insulate the real exchange rate from the influence of short-term capital flows, which can complicate the task of exchange rate management.[8] One approach is to maintain capital controls, as the Republic of Korea and Taiwan Province of China have done until very recently. Another approach is to introduce a small tax on short-term capital flows, so as to discourage them,[9] or to impose special reserve requirements on the foreign liabilities of banks, as Chile did beginning in 1991. A third option favoured in some countries is to have dual exchange rates, with a fixed rate (or crawling peg) for commercial transactions and a parallel free-market rate for financial and tourist transactions. This approach is an attempt to insulate the exchange rate applicable to trade from the vagaries of financial flows (Solimano, 1987, pp. 228–9).

An increase in long-term capital inflows can cause similar problems to those posed by 'permanent' improvements in the terms of trade. For example, a positive change in the perceptions of foreign investors towards a particular country can lead to significant inflows of foreign direct investment over relatively long periods of time. This has apparently been the case of Chile for the last few years. These larger inflows could cause pressures for an appreciation of the real exchange rate. In the case of Chile, they have induced a slow-down in the rate at which the authorities devalue the nominal rate in response to changes in the ratio of domestic to foreign price levels. In the conceptual framework sketched above, the equilibrium real exchange rate would have appreciated, and the best policy would be to allow the real exchange rate to appreciate. However, doing so will penalize domestic producers of tradeables and may lead to under-investment in these activities. Therefore, from the point of view of the country's long-term strategy of increasing and diversifying exports, it might be best to prevent the actual exchange rate from appreciating. This will imply an accumulation of reserves, which can be used to increase domestic investment at a suitable time.

The problems facing undiversified economies are quite different. In commodity-dependent countries, the supply responses to relative price changes are likely to be very modest. In countries that export one or a few primary commodities that are not consumed domestically and where there are no close substitutes for imports (because imports are overwhelmingly intermediate or capital goods or consumer goods which cannot be easily produced domestically), the effect of a real devaluation will be small. In effect, using pooled cross-section and time series econometric analysis for 20 manufactures exporters, 11 fuel exporters and 18 primary commodity exporters over the period 1965–85, de Melo and Faini (1990) found that real devaluation was effective in improving the trade balance in the first group of countries but not in the latter two.

The small impact of real exchange rate depreciation on production and trade flows in commodity-dependent economies arises mainly because they have little or no productive capacity in place to respond to changed price signals. Generating production of exportables or importables requires investment in new sectors and non-marginal changes in the structure of production, which will not come about without a host of complementary measures to generate investment, direct investment resources to desired sectors, and create new skills.

This brief survey cannot do justice to the enormous importance of the exchange rate *problematique* for development and industrialization. This is still unexplored territory. Its importance is underscored in the empirical sections of this chapter, where it is shown that real exchange rate stability and the avoidance of exchange rate overvaluation have been much more important variables explaining long-term export success than import liberalization.

Stabilization and Trade Policy Reform

Some observers contend that trade policy reforms cannot succeed in an environment of high inflation. Sachs (1987, pp. 304–5) asserts that Republic of Korea and Taiwan Province of China did not initiate their export drives until they had achieved a reasonable degree of price stability. One important reason why trade policy reform requires an environment of relative price stability is because high rates of inflation render relative prices unstable and reduce their information content;

therefore, reforms aimed at changing the structure of incentives are likely to be ineffective in that environment.

Several Latin American countries (Argentina, Brazil and Peru) have recently introduced drastic trade liberalization programmes concurrently with policy packages designed to stop hyper-inflation. Bolivia and Mexico did something similar in 1985. Rodrik (1990) has suggested that the purpose of these liberalizations was somewhat unorthodox: the radical break with the past that they implied was used to lend credibility to the entire package of reforms. How successful these experiments are likely to be is anybody's guess. Both Bolivia and Mexico were able to bring down inflation significantly, but the success of the trade liberalization programmes in terms of increasing and diversifying exports is still by no means assured, particularly in Bolivia. It would seem that stabilization is likely to be needed before policies to re-orient the economy to foreign markets can be successful. A degree of price stability is essential if the authorities are to be able to manage the real exchange rate and use it as a signalling device for private-sector investment decisions.

II STATISTICAL EVIDENCE FROM THE 1980S

The Choice of Indicators

One main indicator has been selected to gauge inter-country differences in policy-induced trade performance: the rate of growth of manufactured exports in real terms. The growth of total exports was discarded because total exports are influenced as much by structural factors as they are by policy. A country's success in international markets for manufactures is here considered as an indicator of its ability to become competitive and achieve significant structural change. Since developing countries are small suppliers in international markets for manufactures, the rate of growth of such exports is considered to be mainly policy-induced.

Admittedly, the indicator selected is a rather imperfect one. A more precise indicator of export diversification and growth would have been the rate of growth of all non-traditional exports. Moreover, as discussed below, in some cases the growth in manufactured exports has gone hand in hand with stagnant domestic production and investment. None the less, as a first approximation, manufactured export growth appears to be a suitable proxy.

For the purposes of this analysis, then, average annual rates of growth of real manufactured exports over the 1980–8 period were calculated (using time regressions) for 35 countries whose manufactured exports exceeded 15 per cent of total exports and US$150 million in 1988. These data are shown in Table 4.1, where countries are ranked in descending order according to the rate of growth of real manufactured exports in 1980–8. The table also shows other variables related to trade and growth performance. On the other hand, Table 4.2 shows some basic trade and exchange rate policy indicators.

In order to test the adequacy of the growth of manufactured exports as a proxy for policy-induced trade outcomes, a complementary measure was also examined. Successful structural adjustment requires a rise in the share of traded goods in the economy, on the *import* as well as the export side. Since capital goods are largely imported, the rise in investment that is necessary to bring about structural adjustment will fail to take place unless import growth is significant and outpaces output growth. Therefore, simultaneous increases in both imports and exports relative to GDP can be taken to be an indication of a policy shift in favour of structural adjustment and of the ability to bring it about. In spite of significant policy reform, some countries have been unable to increase the ratios of both exports and imports to GDP. For example, the indebted countries have raised their export-GDP ratios considerably, but their import-GDP ratios have declined sharply, and this has hampered their ability to make the new investments required by successful structural adjustment.

The comparison between the two indicators is shown in Table 4.3. Countries have been classified into three groups, according to the rate of growth of manufactured exports: countries with growth rates of over 10 per cent per annum; countries with growth rates between 4 and 10 per cent; and countries with growth rates of less than 4 per cent. These countries are also arranged in Table 4.3 according to whether they experienced increases in both export and import ratios (both calculated with data in constant 1980 prices); an increase in the export ratio and a decline in the import ratio; declines in both exports and imports relative to GDP; and no change in either ratio. Growth rates of GDP are shown in parentheses.[10]

The highest GDP growth rates in the sample were recorded by the countries which met both criteria (i.e. whose manufactured exports grew rapidly and which were able, simultaneously, to increase their total exports as well as their total imports relative to GDP). These countries achieved a rapid diversification of their export base, their

Table 4.1 Export and growth performance indicators in selected developing countries, 1980–8[a] (percentages)

Country[b]	Growth of real manufactured exports	Growth of total export volumes	Change in exports/GDP	Change in imports/GDP	Growth of GDP	Growth of real manufactured value added	Share of manufactures in GDP, 1980	Investment/GDP[c] 1980	Investment/GDP[c] 1988
Indonesia	30.3	2.8	−13.5	−7.5	3.8	8.4	11.6	25.4	28.5
Turkey	23.3	14.3	19.5	11.3	5.3	7.6	22.4	22.3	19.6
Mauritius	19.8	11.4	14.3	12.5	5.9	10.8	13.0	20.9	38.1
Mexico	19.1	5.4	7.6	−3.6	0.4	0.2	23.1	28.0	17.4
Thailand	17.6	10.7	12.6	7.0	5.7	6.5	19.6	26.6	26.5
Malaysia	14.8	9.0	22.6	5.0	4.1	7.0	20.6	31.6	27.6
Sri Lanka	14.1	5.7	−11.3	−23.1	4.2	6.1	18.2	34.0	23.3
Korea, Republic of	13.7	13.7	10.7	−1.9	9.7	12.7	29.6	32.8	33.1
Taiwan, Province of	13.1	12.6	..	..	7.8	..	..	32.6	..
China	12.5	11.2	15.9	12.5	9.8	16.3	17.1	32.2	37.6
Morocco	11.3	4.8	3.7	−3.7	4.0	4.1	22.3	25.0	25.5
Hong Kong	11.2	11.6	..	..	5.8	..	14.7	36.0	27.1
Pakistan	10.1	8.1	1.8	−10.0	6.1	7.7	11.8	18.7	18.0
Tunisia	8.3	2.9	8.7	−6.5	3.1	5.8	21.4	20.3	14.6
Chile	8.1	4.4	5.2	−5.0	1.6	1.9	13.1	21.6	16.9
Egypt	7.7	6.0	2.4	−16.3	5.3	5.5	29.8	29.4	22.0
Singapore	7.3	7.0	..	..	6.8	4.7	9.8	48.1	35.3
Bangladesh	6.8	5.9	1.3	−0.5	3.5	2.4	28.5	15.0	14.5
Brazil	6.0	5.9	5.6	−3.6	2.9	4.2	11.0	23.6	17.4
Jordan	5.6	6.3	..	..	3.0	3.4	23.3	41.4	25.0
Zimbabwe	4.8	1.5	6.4	−10.9	2.5	2.0	14.7	19.1	15.2
Senegal	4.8	6.8	−3.6	−14.1	3.1	3.3	14.9	15.8	15.0
India	4.5	4.6	−0.2	0.1	5.5	7.9	18.6	22.8	21.7
Costa Rica	4.5	2.9	8.7	2.3	2.3	2.3	8.9	27.9	25.8
Trinidad and Tobago	4.1	−6.2	14.4	−27.6	−5.8	−10.0	24.4	32.2	9.7
Philippines	3.8	0.4	8.0	5.6	..	−0.3		30.7	16.9

105

Country									
Uruguay	2.0	2.0	4.8	−3.2	−0.7	−0.5	22.3	17.5	9.4
Ecuador	1.4	5.5	3.5	−10.1	1.9	0.6	17.7	27.5	16.7
Yugoslavia	0.5	0.9	4.5	−3.3	0.5	1.3	27.9	40.3	38.3
Kenya	0.3	0.1	−4.0	−16.0	3.9	4.5	11.2	31.0	19.6
Colombia	0.3	7.9	2.5	−3.7	3.0	2.9	23.3	19.1	17.9
Guatemala	0.1	−2.0	−7.2	−3.5	−0.3	1.1	16.7	11.6	10.3
Cote d'Ivoire	−1.0	1.5	−5.6	−20.5	0.4	7.5	11.2	29.8	12.9
Argentina	−1.3	0.1	4.0	−4.1	−0.3	−0.2	25.0	22.4	12.1
Peru	−2.4	−2.5	−4.9	−6.9	1.1	1.6	28.0	28.8	23.6

Notes: ^a Countries included are those whose manufactured exports were at least $150 million and whose share of manufactures in total exports exceeded 15 per cent in 1988.

^b Countries ranked according to the rate of growth of manufactured exports in 1980–8.

^c Gross fixed investment as a share of GDP. Both GDP and investment are measured in real 1980 prices.

Source: UNCTAD secretariat, based on official international sources.

Table 4.2 Manufactures-exporting developing countries: trade policy indicators, exchange rate variability and inflation rates, 1980–8 (percentages)

Country	NTB frequency ratio[a]	Total import charges[b]	Exchange rate variability[c]	Change in real exchange rate	Annual change in CPI
Indonesia	92.5	18.4	8.5	−38.0	9.0
Turkey	90.6	44.8	8.7	−25.7	42.0
Mauritius	..	13.4	10.2	−17.3	7.0
Mexico	24.1	36.9	18.6	15.7	77.7
Thailand	20.2	15.0	5.6	−6.4	4.1
Malaysia	20.2	35.4	5.6	−6.4	3.3
Sri Lanka	27.1	22.7	5.5	7.2	11.9
Korea, Republic of	14.2	32.1	7.2	11.6	6.1
China	100.0	34.6	10.4	−41.8	7.0
Morocco	39.7	2.5	2.5	−32.9	7.8
Hong Kong	14.3	68.5	5.5	−3.0	7.7
Pakistan	85.4	27.5	5.3	−23.1	6.6
Tunisia	77.6	20.2	9.3	−24.5	8.4
Chile	16.1	41.4	12.0	−49.5	20.1
Egypt	38.6	1.2	7.2	182.8	16.4
Singapore	12.9	67.1	1.5	5.4	2.1
Bangladesh	55.1	75.2	6.2	−4.9	11.1
Brazil	44.1	27.1	12.5	6.9	198.6
Jordan	16.8	20.8	8.0	−7.6	4.1
Zimbabwe	100.0	29.9	9.6	−17.1	13.6
Senegal	14.9	140.0	19.2	4.2	7.2
India	87.4	37.2	5.5	−4.2	9.2
Costa Rica	4.1		16.2	−39.6	70.1

Trinidad and Tobago	33.5	41.6	12.2	20.8	11.0
Philippines	63.6	29.8	10.6	−31.8	14.2
Uruguay	20.6	27.6	14.8	−36.6	52.9
Ecuador	51.0	39.1	13.6	−58.5	30.7
Yugoslavia	40.4	11.3	20.1	−31.6	73.5
Kenya	73.0	36.9	7.3	−22.3	10.4
Colombia	76.9	73.7	10.9	−41.5	22.7
Guatemala	13.1	17.3	13.6	−21.6	9.2
Cote d'Ivoire	20.6	22.9	9.9	−9.0	5.3
Argentina	21.2	38.6	28.3	−65.6	243.7
Peru	55.5	56.1	69.7	−84.1	132.2

Notes: [a] Mid-1980s. Trade-weighted incidence of NTBs, by tariff line, as a percentage of total imports.
[b] Mid-1980s. Trade-weighted average of all import changes, including tariffs and tariff-like charges.
[c] Standard deviation of annual change in real exchange rate. Real exchange rate estimated as units of domestic currency per US dollar deflated by the ratio of domestic consumer prices to the US wholesale price index. Real effective exchange rate as estimated by the International Monetary Fund used for Malaysia, Chile, Costa Rica, Philippines, Uruguay, Ecuador, Colombia and Cote d'Ivoire.

Source: UNCTAD secretariat, based on official international sources.

Table 4.3 Selected developing countries: changes in import-GDP and export-GDP ratios,[a] 1980–8

	Increase in exports and imports	Increase in exports and decline in imports	Decline in exports and imports	No change in exports or imports
Group I[b]	Turkey (5.3) Mauritius (5.9) Thailand (5.7) Malaysia (4.1) Rep. Korea [e](9.7) China (9.8)	Mexico (0.4) Morocco (4.0) Pakistan (6.1)	Indonesia (3.8) Sri Lanka (4.2)	
Group II[c]	Costa Rica (2.3)	Tunisia (3.1) Chile (1.6) Egypt (5.3) Bangladesh (3.5) Brazil (2.9) Zimbabwe (3.0) Trinidad and Tobago (−5.8)	Senegal (3.1)	India (5.5)
Group III[d]	Philippines (0.0)	Uruguay (−0.7) Ecuador (1.9) Yugoslavia (0.5) Colombia (3.0) Argentina (−0.3)	Kenya (3.9) Guatemala (−0.3) Cote d'Ivoire (0.4) Peru (1.1)	

Notes: Four countries have been excluded: Taiwan Province of China, because of incomplete data; and Hong Kong, Jordan and Singapore, because they have a significant amount of *entrepot* trade, which lends an upward bias to their import and export data.

[a] Figures in parentheses correspond to average annual GDP growth rates.

[b] Countries with average annual rate of growth of real manufactured exports in excess of 10 per cent.

[c] Countries with average annual rate of growth of real manufactured exports between 4 and 10 per cent.

[d] Countries with average annual rate of growth of real manufactured exports lower than 4 per cent.

[e] Republic of Korea is included in this group because of the high level of its imports-to-GDP ratio (4 per cent in 1988), in spite of the fact that it remained practically unchanged in 1980–8.

Source: Table 4.1.

export growth was concentrated in manufactures (which generally have strong external economies), and they achieved a significant increase of the overall openness of their economies.

Table 4.3 also shows that, during the 1980s, import compression, associated in most countries with the debt crisis, was an important factor explaining growth retardation and hampering successful structural adjustment. Most of the countries exhibiting increases in exports but declines in imports relative to GDP recorded relatively slow growth of GDP. An almost paradigmatic case was that of Mexico: import compression did not allow the rapid expansion of manufactured exports to translate into rising GDP. In fact, both the investment rate and per capita GDP fell sharply during the 1980s.

Slow overall growth was also associated with declining exports *and* imports relative to GDP. This was particularly the case of some commodity-dependent countries, where unfavourable trends in world demand for their exports had a detrimental influence on their trade flows and on their growth potential, sometimes in spite of significant efforts to diversify their export base and to achieve greater openness. Cases in point are Indonesia and Sri Lanka. Both countries recorded very rapid growth in their manufactured exports which, none the less, were overwhelmed by adverse price and volume trends for their main commodity exports. As a result, their overall growth rates were sluggish and their ratios of exports and imports to GDP declined.

Table 4.3 also brings out another important and often forgotten fact: in countries with large domestic markets, respectable economic growth and considerable structural change can take place even in the absence of increasing trade orientation. During the 1980s, India's rate of growth of GDP places it among the fast-growing developing countries; however, it did not experience a move towards greater openness, as measured by the ratios of exports and imports to GDP, and its rate of growth of manufactured exports was only average.

Preliminary Quantitative Results

With some caveats, then, the rate of growth of manufactured exports appears to be an adequate proxy to gauge policy-induced trade performance. Continuing with the country groupings according to this indicator, Table 4.4 shows some relationships between manufactured export growth and an assortment of other variables.[11] Simple averages of the variables for the countries in each group have been

Table 4.4 Unweighted averages of trade, growth and policy indicators for manufactures-exporting developing countries, 1980–8 (percentages)

	Group I[a]	Group II[b]	Group III[c]
Growth of manufactured exports	16.5	6.0	0.4
Growth of export volumes	9.1	4.0	1.4
Growth of real GDP	5.4[d]	2.8	1.0
Growth of real manufacturing value added	5.4[e]	2.8	1.9
Share of manufactures in GDP (1980)	19.3[d]	17.2	20.8
Ratio of investment to GDP: 1988	26.9	19.4	17.8
1980	27.8	27.3	25.9
NTB frequency (mid-1980s)	46.9[f]	41.8	43.6
Total import charges (mid-1980s)	29.5[f]	44.1	35.3
Exchange rate variability	8.0	10.0	19.9
Change in consumer prices	15.9	31.0	59.5

Notes: [a] Twelve countries with rates of growth of real manufactured exports in 1980–8 exceeding 10 per cent; Indonesia, Turkey, Mauritius, Mexico, Thailand, Malaysia, Sri Lanka, Republic of Korea, China, Morocco, Hong Kong, Pakistan.
[b] Twelve countries with rates of growth of real manufactured exports in 1980–8 between 4 and 10 per cent: Tunisia, Chile, Egypt, Singapore, Bangladesh, Brazil, Jordan, Zimbabwe, Senegal, India, Costa Rica, Trinidad and Tobago.
[c] Ten countries with rates of growth of manufactured exports in 1980–8 below 4 per cent: Philippines, Uruguay, Ecuador, Yugoslavia, Kenya, Colombia, Guatemala, Cote d'Ivoire, Argentina, Peru.
[d] Excluding Hong Kong.
[e] Excluding China.
[f] Excluding Mauritius.
Source: See Tables 4.1 and 4.2.

used. The results thus obtained can be used to derive some tentative conclusions with regard to some of the debates surrounding trade policy and economic performance discussed above.

Generally, growth in manufactured exports appears to be correlated with growth in overall exports, GDP and value added in manufacturing. Although investment ratios fell in most countries in the 1980s, countries recording rapid manufactured export growth were, on average, better able to prevent their investment rates from declining. As noted in Table 4.5, the differences in mean GDP growth rates, rates of growth of manufacturing value added and investment ratios as

Table 4.5   Statistical significance of differences in means among countries
grouped according to the rate of growth of manufactured exports
(t-statistic)

	Group I and II[a]	Group II and III[b]	Group I and III[c]
Rate of growth of GDP	2.24**	1.76*	5.00***
Rate of growth of manufacturing value added	2.82**	0.60	3.97***
Investment ratio (1988)	2.66**	0.48	2.64**
Share of manufacturing in GDP (1980)	0.80	1.24	0.60
NTB frequency	0.35	0.15	0.25
Total import changes	1.24	0.73	0.73
Exchange rate variability	1.10	1.65	1.99*
Change in consumer prices	0.87	0.99	1.76*

Notes: [a]   Degrees of freedom = 22; except for rate of growth of
          manufacturing value added, NTB frequency and total import
          changes (21).
        [b]   Degrees of freedom = 20.
        [c]   Degrees of freedom = 20, except for rate of growth of
          manufacturing value added, NTB frequency and total import
          changes (19).
        *   Means significantly different at 10 per cent level.
        **   Means significantly different at 5 per cent level.
        *** Means significantly different at 1 per cent level.
Source: See Tables 4.1 and 4.2.

between groups of countries classified according to their manufactured
export growth are (generally) statistically significant. These results
would appear to give some support to the hypothesis linking growth to
outward orientation.

In the sample chosen, there is no relationship between the share of
manufacturing in GDP at the beginning of the period and the rate of
growth of manufactured exports. At first glance, this would appear to
falsify the notion that it is necessary for countries to have a
manufacturing sector, nurtured under import substitution policies,
before they can venture into international markets. However, it should
be remembered that all the countries in the sample already had non-
negligible manufactured exports in 1980. The sample's evidence must,
therefore, be considered inconclusive. What can be said, however, is
that the simple possession of a large manufacturing sector, as for

example in Argentina or Peru, is not sufficient for a country to become an exporter of manufactures. Policies *do* matter.

Table 4.5 also shows that there is no quantitative evidence that countries with more liberal trade policies tend to have more rapid rates of growth of exports than countries with restrictive trade regimes. There is no significant difference between countries grouped according to the rate of growth of manufactured exports as regards trade-weighted average import charges or average NTB frequencies. Given the difficulties of measuring NTBs and import charges in developing countries, the lack of an association between these proxies for the degree of restrictiveness of trade policies and export growth could be the result of measurement problems. None the less, the absence of a relationship between these indicators of the trade regime and export performance is suggestive.

There does seem to be a relationship between the growth of manufactured exports, on the one hand, and low inflation and exchange rate stability (as measured by the standard deviation of annual changes in the real exchange rate),[12] on the other. Generally, countries that recorded fast rates of growth of manufactured exports had low levels of exchange rate instability and relatively low rates of inflation. The converse was also true: high price and exchange rate instability was associated with low and even negative growth in manufactured exports. However, the statistical significance of the differences in group means for both variables is not very high.

These results could be indicating that, when the real exchange rate fluctuates widely, it becomes unpredictable, and that this discourages investment in exports. However, it should be remembered that association does not necessarily imply causation: while price and exchange rate stability are likely to encourage exporting, fast-growing exports relax the foreign exchange constraint and enhance the ability of policy-makers to stabilize the exchange rate, which is often an important mechanism in the propagation of inflation. On the other hand, lower inflation makes it easier to maintain exchange rate stability.

III SOME QUALITATIVE EVIDENCE

Given the measurement difficulties already referred to and the limitations of aggregate data in shedding light on an issue as complex as the one under discussion, it is necessary to examine evidence of a less quantitative sort. For this purpose, a qualitative assessment is made of the kinds of trade regimes that have been adopted by countries that have succeeded in changing the structure of exports and production. The experiences of these countries are then compared to that of Chile, the only country in the sample with a long record of trade liberalization.[13]

The most successful long-term experiences with trade policy do not appear to lend support to the contention that import liberalization is a condition for export success. Sachs (1987) argues that Japan, Republic of Korea and Taiwan promoted exports successfully without any significant degree of import liberalization. Import liberalization came after export-oriented industrialization had become well established.

During the 1980s, especially rapid gains as exporters of manufactures were made by a diverse group of countries which includes Indonesia, Turkey, Mauritius, Mexico, Thailand, Sri Lanka and Morocco. With the exception of Mexico, none of these countries can be described as having embraced liberal trade policies, and Mexico only began to do so in 1985. In most of them a comprehensive set of export promotion measures was superimposed on an existing import substitution regime. At the same time, the structure of protection was rationalized and the dispersion of ERPs was significantly reduced.

Generally, there are two factors related to trade exchange rate, and foreign investment policies that largely explain the export and growth success of the established exporters of manufactures of Asia and of the more recent newcomers to international markets for manufactures from that region. In the first place, they succeeded in establishing a domestic economic environment that enabled firms to compete in international markets. This involved the avoidance of currency overvaluation, unrestricted access to imported inputs used in exporting activities at world market prices, access to imported capital goods and investment finance, and the provision to exporters of adequate investment and short-term trade finance at low interest rates. Secondly, these countries found ways of overcoming their lack of technical, managerial and marketing know-how by combining local productive capacity with foreign expertise (Noland, 1990, p. 9; for the experience of Republic of Korea, see Chapter 8, in this volume, Amsden, 1989, and Amsden and Euh, 1990). In some countries, this was achieved by recourse to fairly liberal foreign investment policies. In others (e.g. Republic of Korea), policies favoured either joint ventures or sub-contracting and technology licensing.

The experience of Turkey was similar. Beginning in 1980, Turkish economic policy shifted towards encouraging exports through real exchange rate devaluation and strong export incentives. This policy shift succeeded in reorienting production of manufactures towards export markets, and exports rose rapidly (see Table 4.1). However, import liberalization was cautious and phased in gradually. While most NTBs have been eliminated, tariffs remain relatively high; when account is taken of the import surcharges imposed in recent years, the trend towards lower tariffs has, in effect, been reversed (Aricanli and Rodrik, 1990). The strong increase in exports appears to be associated mainly with exchange rate depreciation and secondarily with the variety of export incentives to which the authorities resorted (see Chapter 9 in this volume). Import liberalization, other than that involved in tariff drawback schemes for exporters, played no role.

Countries experiencing rapid economic growth and sustained export expansion have met other conditions that are unrelated to trade policy. A fundamental factor accounting for the long-term success of the Republic of Korea and Taiwan has been large investments in basic and technical education combined with the maintenance of an incentive system that did not discriminate against exports. The development of human skills facilitated the transfer of labour from agriculture to export-oriented manufacturing (Pack, 1988). There is also evidence that wage repression facilitated the export drive directly and indirectly: the competitiveness of firms was not continuously threatened by a restive labour force, and price and exchange rate stability were easier to maintain.

The Chilean experience is of great interest because of the thoroughness with which trade liberalization was pursued and because sufficient time has elapsed so that its effects should have already been evident in the country's trade and growth record (see Chapter 7 in this volume). As part of a broader set of policy changes designed to leave all microeconomic decision-making to the private sector, between 1976 and 1979 Chile eliminated all NTBs and reduced tariffs to a common rate of 10 per cent.[14]

Since the correction of severe currency overvaluation in 1982, there has been significant export growth and diversification, especially in non-copper natural resource-based products. However, it has not been proven that the greater dynamism of exports has been the result of the dismantling of protection. In fact, the large investments in mining, agriculture, fisheries and forestry that underlie the growth of exports were probably more responsive to the perception that the policy framework would remain favourable to investment (especially, foreign investment) in natural resource industries than to import liberalization affecting the manufacturing sector. As regards entrepreneurs in the manufacturing sector, rather than trying to place production on foreign markets, their response to import liberalization was primarily to become importers of some of the goods they formerly produced.

Moreover, per capita GDP is still not significantly higher than in the early 1970s and, until 1988, the investment rate remained depressed, indicating that the strong export expansion did not carry with it the rest of the economy. At present, the modern export sectors coexist with others in manufacturing, agriculture and services that have remained backward and where factor productivity is still at levels prevailing in the late 1960s.

IV   CONCLUSIONS

Debates about trade policy are among the oldest in the development literature. Undoubtedly, this chapter will not settle them. However, the evidence that has been examined does shed some light on them. There is some support for the proposition that outward orientation, under current conditions, is more conducive to growth than inward-looking policies. Technological change has become the motor of development, and the continuous absorption and adaptation of foreign technology is likely to be fostered more by outward orientation than by a regime that is essentially oriented to domestic markets. The recent reforms announced in India to the effect that a greater outward orientation of policies will be pursued confirm this proposition. The rapid internationalization of the huge and formerly closed Chinese economy is another case in point.

There are important exceptions. In the absence of accompanying import growth, increasing exports can lead to falling output and living standards. For structural adjustment to be successful, more than domestic policy changes is needed. The causes of extreme foreign exchange stringency must be tackled, with the assistance of the international community when they are beyond a country's control.

The potential for export-oriented growth will also depend on the evolution of the international trading system. Small exporters can thrive only in an open multilateral system governed by impartial rules. The entrenched protectionism that has characterized trade policies in developed countries, the growing resort to unilateralism by the major trading powers (and especially by the United States), and the emergence of large and (perhaps) closed trade blocs do not bode well for export-oriented growth strategies. The relationships between the nature of global trading arrangements and the optimal trade strategies of developing countries are an under-researched subject which requires further attention.

The role of import substitution in development in the 1990s and beyond may also require reappraisal. Practically all countries, and particularly the largest, have unexploited possibilities in their domestic markets. For most low-income, commodity-dependent economies, import substitution is inescapable. The trick is to bring it about with moderate and essentially temporary protection, while at the same time compensating the resulting anti-export bias with appropriate export incentives. The suggestion by Bruton (1989, p. 1639) that a moderate degree of real exchange rate undervaluation can serve as a non-distorting means to foster the domestic production of tradeables is worth investigating.

The evidence examined in this chapter is considerably less sanguine as regards the relationship between trade liberalization and export growth. Neither the quantitative information nor the more qualitative evidence lends support to the hypothesis that trade liberalization will induce export growth. This does not mean that high and differentiated protection is the best policy. All of the countries that have succeeded in penetrating international markets for manufactures have pursued pragmatic policies that built on what had already been achieved. Access by exporters to foreign inputs at international prices has been a common feature of policy. So has been the avoidance of extreme protection of the domestic market. But, with the exception of Hong Kong, no successful country has resorted to laissez-faire trade policies.

An adequate level for the exchange rate, as well as its stability, are positively associated with export growth (and also with efficient import substitution). There is considerably less certainty as to the policies that are needed to target the real exchange rate on long-term development objectives and how to improve supply responses to exchange-rate stimuli.

Notes

1. The author wishes to thank Andrew Cornford, Gustavo Franco, Ian Kinniburgh and José Antonio Ocampo for valuable comments and suggestions on earlier drafts of this chapter.
2. Several of these issues have been discussed incisively in a recent article by Helleiner (1990).
3. In most formulations of this issue, it is assumed that the matter consists of calculating one effective exchange rate for a country's exports and another one for its imports (for example, see Bhagwati, 1987, p. 259).
4. In the current international economic environment, however, trade barriers are hampering the expansion of exports even in countries that are very small exporters. In recent years, countries which have only very recently entered international markets for clothing (i.e. Bangladesh, Chile and Fiji) have reported the imposition of quotas by major developed trading partners.
5. This was generally the case for the three developing countries but not for Japan. Bruton (1989, p. 1635) interprets the absence in Japan of a positive relationship between inter-sectoral differences in TFPG and in the contribution of exports to demand growth as evidence that the main causal factor of Japan's phenomenal growth in factor productivity has been the country's autonomous capability to innovate, derived from past policies to foster industrialization. In turn, this capability would also explain Japan's export success.
6. However, as a deliberate policy, import substitution has undoubtedly been taken much farther by the Latin American than by the export-oriented Asian countries. The larger Latin American countries have attempted to extend import substitution to intermediate and capital goods. This has been much less the case in the Asian countries, which switched to a policy of promoting labour-intensive exports after an initial phase of import substitution in consumer goods industries. Production of intermediate and capital goods for the domestic market came much later and was the outcome of an expanding domestic market for such goods and growing domestic capabilities to produce them (see Chen, 1989).
7. For an argument in favour of this sequence and further bibliography, see Thomas, Matin and Nash (1990).
8. For an analysis of the trade effects of external financial openness via the exchange rate and interest rates, see Chapter 6 in this volume.
9. Tobin (1978) pioneered this idea in quite a different context: that of excessive fluctuations of exchange rates for major currencies caused by short-term speculative international capital movements. His proposal was to levy an international tax on such movements.
10. Four countries were excluded from Table 4.3: Taiwan Province of China, because of incomplete data; and Hong Kong, Jordan and Singapore, because they have a significant amount of *entrepôt* trade, which lends an upward bias to their import and export data.
11. Taiwan Province of China is not included in the averages owing to the lack of complete information.

12. The behavioural assumption behind the use of this particular variable is that fairly constant annual changes in the real exchange rate can be anticipated by producers, and that sharp fluctuations in such annual changes are largely unanticipated.
13. In recent years, several countries in the sample have introduced trade liberalization packages, perhaps the most thorough-going of which has been Mexico's. However, these policy shifts have all been recent and have not had sufficient time to be reflected in economic outcomes.
14. The actual rate has varied since then, but the single-rate policy has been retained. Since June 1991, the tariff has been set at 11 per cent.

References

Amsden, A. H. (1989), *Asia's Next Giant: South Korea and Late Industrialization* (New York and Oxford: Oxford University Press).

Amsden, A. H., and Y.-D. Euh (1990), 'Republic of Korea's Financial Reforms: What Are the Lessons?', UNCTAD Discussion Paper No. 30, Geneva, April, processed.

Aricanli, T., and D. Rodrik (1990), 'An Overview of Turkey's Experience with Economic Liberalization and Structural Adjustment', *World Development*, Vol. 18, No. 10, pp. 1343–1350.

Bhagwati, J. (1987), 'Outward Orientation: Trade Issues', in V. Corbo, M. Godstein, and M. Khan, eds, *Growth-Oriented Adjustment Programs* (Washington, DC: International Monetary Fund and World Bank).

Bruton, H. (1989), 'Import Substitution', in H. Chenery and T. N. Srinivasan, eds, *Handbook of Development Economics*, Vol. II (Amsterdam: North Holland).

Chen (1989), E. K. Y., 'Trade Policy in Asia', in S. Naya, M. Urrutia, S. Mark, and A. Fuentes, eds, *Lessons in Development – A Comparative Study of Asia and Latin America* (San Francisco: International Center for Economic Growth).

de Melo, J., and R. Faini (1990), 'Adjustment, Investment and the Real Exchange Rate in Developing Countries', *Economic Policy*, Vol. 11, October, pp. 492–512.

Edwards, S. (1988), *Exchange Rate Misalignment in Developing Countries*, World Bank Occasional Paper No. 2 (Baltimore and London: Johns Hopkins University Press).

Edwards, S. (1989), *Real Exchange Rates, Devaluation, and Adjustment* (Cambridge, Mass. and London: MIT Press).

Helleiner, G. K. (1990), 'Trade Strategy in Medium-Term Adjustment', *World Development*, Vol. 18, No. 6, June, pp. 879–97.

Michalopoulos, C. (1987), 'World Bank Programs for Adjustment and Growth', in Corbo *et al.* (see Bhagwati, 1987).

Nishimizu, M., and S. Robinson (1984), 'Trade Policies and Productivity Change in Semi-Industrialized Countries', *Journal of Development Economics*, Vol. 16, pp. 177–206.

Noland, M. (1990), *Pacific Basin Developing Economies: Prospects for the Future* (Washington, DC: Institute for International Economics).

Ospina Sardi, J. (1989), 'Trade Policy in Latin America', in Naya *et al.* (see Chen, 1989).

Pack, H. (1988), 'Industrialization and Trade', in Chenery and Srinivasan (see Bruton, 1989), Vol I.

Pritchett, L. (1991), 'Measuring Outward Orientation in Developing Countries – Can it Be Done?', PRE Working Paper 566, World Bank, Washington, DC, January.

Rodrik, D. (1990), 'Trade Policies and Development: Some New Issues', Discussion Paper Series No. 447, Centre for Economic Policy Research, London, August.

Rodrik, D. (1992), 'Closing the Productivity Gap: Does Trade Liberalization Really Help?', in Gerald K. Helleiner, ed., *Trade Policy, Industrialization and Development: New Perspectives* (Oxford: Clarendon Press).

Sachs, J. D. (1987), 'Trade and Exchange Rate Policies in Growth-Oriented Adjustment', in Corbo *et al.* (see Bhagwati, 1987).

Solimano, A. (1987), 'Aspectos Conceptuales Sobre Política Cambiaria para América Latina', in R. Cortázar, ed., *Políticas Macroéconomicas – Una Perspectiva Latinoamericana* (Santiago: CIEPLAN).

Thomas, V., K. Matin and J. Nash (1990), 'Lessons in Trade Policy Reform', Policy and Research Series No. 10, World Bank, Washington, DC.

Tobin, J. (1978), 'A Proposal for International Monetary Reform', *The Eastern Economic Journal*, Vol. 4, Nos 3–4, July–October, pp. 153–9; reprinted in J. Tobin, *Essays in Economics – Theory and Policy* (Cambridge, Mass. and London: MIT Press, 1982).

UNCTAD (1989), *Trade and Development Report, 1989*, Part I, Chapter V: 'Trade Policy Reform and Export Performance in Developing Countries in the 1980s', Geneva.

World Bank (1987), *World Development Report, 1987*, Washington, DC.

5 New Theories of International Trade and Trade Policy in Developing Countries

José Antonio Ocampo[1]

This chapter analyses the relevance for developing countries of the new theories concerning imperfect competition and international trade, with emphasis on two main subject areas: economies of scale and the trade matrix, and the implications of imperfect competition for trade liberalization and trade strategies. Although the new theories certainly do not justify the protectionism that has been characteristic of Latin America throughout its industrial history, neither do they support the orthodox proposals now being embraced in the region. On the contrary, they indicate that trade liberalization should be coupled with an active industrial policy, particularly in sectors subject to significant economies of scale, whether they be static or dynamic.

I INTRODUCTION

The theoretical literature on international trade has grown enormously over the past 15 years. The old models based on assumptions of perfect competition and constant returns to scale have given way to a burst of new writings which analyse the implications of imperfect competition and economies of scale for international trade (see, in particular, Helpman and Krugman, 1985 and 1989). A body of knowledge has also been developed in close affinity with these new theories of trade. Examples include the literature on the adaptation and creation of technology in semi-industrialized countries and the development of 'endogenous economic growth' models in which the accumulation of knowledge (human capital) plays the leading role in the expansion of economic activity in the aggregate.

121

Although much of this new literature has been developed to explain phenomena typical of transactions among developed countries and the international market strategies of large corporations in such countries, the recent application of these theories to the analysis of the trade and trade policy of developing countries has been equally noteworthy (see, for example, the reviews of Stewart, 1984; Ocampo, 1986; Krugman, 1988; and Helpman, 1989). Some of these contributions have resurrected old ideas that had long been at the forefront of controversies regarding the development process.

Surprisingly, these contributions have had little impact on prevailing orthodoxies regarding trade liberalization and industrial restructuring in developing countries. In view of the influence that this type of analysis has had on the structural adjustment programmes of the World Bank, this aloofness is both surprising and problematic. The usual recommendations to create neutral trade incentives and to adopt a laissez-faire industrial policy, in particular, clearly conflict with the conclusions derived from these new theories.

In an era when the proponents of a rapid process of internationalization prevail as ideological victors in almost all of Latin America, and at a time when these countries are intent upon an all-out race to open up their economies to external trade (see cases in Part III of this volume), it is imperative that a bridge be built between the implementation of such policies and the new theories. This chapter is a contribution in this direction. It assesses the implications of the new theories and, on that basis, sets forth recommendations regarding the implementation of outward-oriented trade reforms. For reasons of brevity the analysis concentrates on two major issues: economies of scale and the pattern of trade (section II) and the implications of imperfect competition for trade liberalization and trade strategies (section III). The chief policy implications are summarized in section IV.

II ECONOMIES OF SCALE AND THE TRADE MATRIX

The economies of scale discussed in the recent literature can be classified in various ways. For our purposes here, we will use the classification applied by Helpman and Krugman (1985, chapter 2). This differentiates: (a) static intra-firm technological economies of scale (another type of economy of scale, which accounts for the concentration of different plants within a single firm and the formation of conglomerates, will not be dealt with in this chapter); (b) static external economies; and (c) dynamic economies of scale, whether at the company, sectoral or macroeconomic level. Although these various types of economies have a great deal in common, the implications of each in terms of international trade are quite different.

Static Intra-Firm Economies of Scale

Static intra-firm economies of scale can, in their turn, be subdivided into two main categories. The first refers to the existence of a downward curve in the average production costs of relatively homogenous goods which is associated with significant fixed costs (chiefly in the case of highly mechanized production processes), indivisibility and certain other features of production processes. We will refer to this first type as 'traditional' economies of scale. The second category relates less to the scale of production in the firm as a whole than to the degree of specialization in the production of differentiated products. It will therefore be more accurate to refer to this second type as 'economies of specialization'. In this case, a large plant is not needed to produce a design or model of a particular product, but each is none the less subject to decreasing costs. Under these conditions, productivity will depend less on the size of the firm than on its degree of specialization. Although both phenomena may be observed within the same firm, for the purpose of analysis it is convenient to separate them.

The first of these categories has been one of the main focuses of attention in the literature on import substitution in developing countries. Indeed, the fact that the import substitution model seems to be nearing the end of its usefulness is related to the growing weight of branches of industry in which traditional economies of scale prevail as the substitution process advances. This trend accounts for the close correlation between the size of a country and the relative importance within the industrial structure of sectors associated with the inter-mediate and advanced stages of import substitution – paper, chemicals and petrochemicals, iron and steel, motor vehicles and metals and metal manufactures (see, for example, ECLAC, 1981).[2] They are also the basis for the monopolistic or oligopolistic structures typical of these sectors and, in the case of smaller economies, of even more traditional manufacturing sectors. Given the influence of these structures, the gains to be derived from trade liberalization processes will depend to a great extent on how sectors that exhibit economies of scale are affected and on how established companies in those sectors react in strategic terms to such outward-oriented trade reforms (see section III).

Like factor endowments and technological disparity, traditional economies of scale give rise to active *inter*-industry trade between developed and developing countries and, to an increasing extent, between developing countries of different sizes. According to traditional ECLAC thinking (1969, chapter 5), their presence served as one of the basic justifications for integration, since import substitution could only be carried out efficiently in an economy large enough to permit the full utilization of economies of scale. This view was the basis for some of the mechanisms used in a number of integration initiatives in Latin America starting in the 1960s, especially the sectoral industrial development programmes of the Andean Group. Flaws in design and political rigidities prevented these programmes from thriving. Ironically, the aggressive efforts now being made to liberalize trade among Latin American countries may enable the larger countries to augment the benefits of earlier investments in mature import-substitution sectors and may even allow them or some of the mid-sized countries in the region (such as Colombia or Venezuela) to intensify this process.

The centre of attention in the recent literature on international trade has, however, been economies of specialization (see, in particular, Dixit and Norman, 1980, chapter 9; Ethier, 1979 and 1982; Helpman, 1981; Krugman, 1990; Lancaster, 1980). The reason for this is the importance of these economies in accounting for *intra*-industry trade flows, which now account for the bulk of the transactions that take place between developed countries. As had been noted by Linder (1961), these models predict that this type of trade will occur primarily between countries at a similar level of development, whereas the flows between unequal trading partners will continue to be of a chiefly inter-industrial nature. From the vantage point of the developing countries, this suggests that this type of transaction would be most profitable when carried out in the form of reciprocal trade.

The recent literature indicates that the gains from intra-industry trade are related to the possibility of taking full advantage of economies of scale in the production of each particular design and with the greater variety of products that become available to consumers (or to producers if the products in question are intermediate or capital goods). It follows from this that protected markets will be faced with a trade-off between efficiency and diversity. Depending upon the characteristics of the specific sectors concerned, there may be very little variety in the designs of the different products, but each is manufactured at a relatively low cost; or there may be many designs, each of which is produced at a relatively high cost. This type of situation may also stem from a greater concentration of production in the hands of a few firms, in the first case, or the existence of many inefficient firms, in the second. The analysis formulated by Pack (1988) indicates that the main source of inefficiency in many companies in protected economies is, precisely, the abundance of different designs, each of which is the result of excessively short production runs. The effects of outward-oriented trade reforms will differ depending on which of the above situations exists in a given sector.

If the design of new models carries a cost, productive efficiency or an equilibrium exchange rate may not be enough to make a successful transition to export activity. The specifications of local products are – to use Linder's term – geared to 'representative demand' in the domestic market, but there may be no demand for those specifications abroad. Under these circumstances, companies need information on the specifications of products for which there is a demand abroad and have to incur the costs of adapting their designs to the new markets (Keesing and Lall, 1992). The financial and organizational ability of individual companies to make these adjustments may differ, and this may have major implications for the industrial structure of export sectors. Indeed, this may be the reason why export activities tend to be concentrated in the largest firms within a given industry (Rodrik, 1988; Berry, 1992).

External Economies

Unlike economies of specialization, whose importance was, for the most part, ignored in the traditional literature on economic development, external economies sparked a classic controversy. This was the debate between the proponents of 'balanced' development and the proponents of 'unbalanced' development (see, in particular, Rosenstein-Rodan, 1943; Nurkse, 1967; and Hirschman, 1958).

These economies are associated with the cross-sectoral complementarities of the forward and backward linkages that are generated by input–output relationships, the transfer of technology or information between firms or sectors and broader market advantages. According to the more traditional interpretations, these economies are associated with production; however, these types of phenomena may just as easily show up in the area of international marketing (see Keesing and Lall,

1992).[3] Finally, external economies of production and marketing may exist not only for manufactures but for primary commodities as well (Krugman, 1988).

Some of these economies may be of a macroeconomic nature, but others may be specific to certain industries. Their effects will hinge on the degree of mobility or the transport costs of the different factors (including knowledge), inputs or services involved. If their mobility is restricted, a particular process occurs which has been described by different schools of thought alternatively as processes of clustering or 'agglomeration', to use the term of classic location theory (see, for example, Richardson, 1969), 'growth poles' (Perroux, 1961) or, in the terminology of the new literature on trade, 'industrial complexes" (Helpman and Krugman, 1985, chapters 2 and 11). These processes may encompass one or more industries, depending on the relative magnitude of the sectoral or macro economies.

From a dynamic standpoint, these types of economic phenomena are associated with the 'cumulative causation' referred to by Myrdal (1957) in a classic study, or 'uneven development', as it has come to be called in the more recent literature (see, for example, Krugman, 1990, chapter 6, and Dutt, 1986). According to this concept, because of the influence of external economies, an initial difference in levels of development will tend to grow as time passes, thereby generating virtuous or vicious circles, as the case may be. As we will see in the following section, dynamic economies of scale tend to have a similar effect. If the predominant economies are macroeconomic in nature, this cumulative process will tend to be reflected in the overall level of development; if they are specific to one or several sectors, however, they will tend to reinforce the specialization of a region or country in given production activities.

The policy implications of these types of phenomena are not straightforward. Nurkse attributed a great deal of importance to macroeconomic external economies; he defended the need for a 'balanced development' of the various economic sectors. Hirschman criticized this view because such a 'big push' is not feasible in developing countries as it would demand too large a volume of productive resources. He therefore suggested that the most important implication of external economies was the tendency of the development process to generate sectoral imbalances of different types at different stages. Under these circumstances, economic policy should be directed towards selecting the investment strategy that held out the best hope of being self-propelling, i.e. of giving rise to new investment decisions which would tend to correct imbalances generated during earlier phases of the development process.

The implications of the new models of uneven development have a tinge of Nurkse and of the related 'big push' idea, rather than of the fascinating implications of Hirschman's model, which do not jibe very well with the passive approaches now in vogue. The implications of external economies, as well as those relating to dynamic economies of scale, help to account for some critical aspects of world development, particularly the absence of a general trend towards the narrowing of income gaps at the international level and, perhaps, the more recent tendency for export development in the Third World to become concentrated in a few countries. When taken literally, however, they can be used as the underpinnings for strategies that have, in the end, not always proved helpful (e.g. the conscious effort made by some governments to create economic 'miracles'). Some of their less spectacular implications in relation to sectoral external economies are certainly preferable. The most important implication is that the neutrality of incentives and the laissez-faire industrial policy that dominate recent orthodox literature are not necessarily optimum policies. The same conclusion may be drawn, as noted earlier, from the analyses of dynamic economies of scale which are discussed in the next section. Moreover, the absence of external economies could help to explain why macroeconomic stabilization and liberalized trade regimes *per se* have not proved sufficient to bring about a return to economic growth.

Some degree of selectivity and activism is thus necessary, and this includes protection for some sectors and export subsidies for others, direct subsidies for the activities that generate the greatest externalities, and the state's active involvement in the promotion of new activities as well as in the coordination of private investment decisions in sectors where private agents impose major externalities on one another. This policy, which has come to be known as 'picking winners', has been criticized by those who feel that the state lacks the necessary information to design sectoral strategies. Yet there are schemes in which the public sector can act as a partner and coordinator rather than as a planner. This is perhaps the lesson to be learned from the experiences of South-east Asia (see Chapter 8 in this volume). The idea of 'picking winners' is, in any event, somewhat inaccurate, since in a sense it is more a matter of 'creating winners' with the help of the ongoing implementation of a selective policy (Stewart and Ghani, 1992).

Another equally important lesson refers to sectors that may be hurt by trade liberalization. Indeed, in the presence of significant external economies, the initial adverse effects of trade liberalization may become cumulative and lead to the irreversible decline of entire sectors of production, even if the country enjoys a long-term comparative advantage in them. As has been pointed out by a number of authors (see, in particular, van Wijnbergen, 1984, and Krugman, 1990, chapter 7), similar effects can be generated by an appreciation of the real exchange rate as a result of a commodity export boom (Dutch disease) or an extremely tight monetary policy. Special restructuring policies are required in such cases, including the maintenance of tariff protection for the sectors in question while they make the transition (see the case of Chile in Chapter 7 of this volume for the costs that are incurred when such policies are lacking).

Dynamic Economies of Scale

While external economies have been a central focus of attention in the economic development literature and in location theory, the discussion of dynamic economies of scale has invaded the literature more recently from different quarters, including the literature on international trade, the adaptation and creation of technologies in semi-industrialized countries (Katz, 1984; Katz *et al.*, 1986; Pack and Westphal, 1986) and 'endogenous economic growth' models (Romer, 1986; and Lucas, 1988). The endogeneity of the rate of increase of productivity during the growth process has, of course, a long tradition in economic theory which dates back to Young (1928), but also includes Arrow (1962) and, in the Keynesian literature, Kaldor (1978).

According to the new writings on growth, these economies are basically associated with the accumulation of knowledge and, hence, of 'human capital'. This process may be associated with learning by doing, but it also involves a conscious effort to educate and to gain knowledge. For this, however, it is necessary that the use of knowledge should not have diminishing returns at the microeconomic level or that it should not be possible to appropriate entirely its benefits, thereby giving rise to sectoral or macroeconomic externalities associated with its accumulation. Under these conditions, productivity is largely a result of the production process. The recent literature has explored how this human capital formation *per se* generates growth. Alternatively, this notion can be used to show that the growth rate of productivity tends to rise when the growth rate of production speeds up, thereby reversing the causal relationship between the two variables postulated by neo-classical growth theory. This relationship is commonly known as 'Verdoorn's Law' or, in the Keynesian literature, 'Kaldor's Law'.

It should be noted that similar effects to those hypothesized in the new literature can be produced by physical capital formation as well. The development of infrastructure can produce these results via the increased communication among economic agents that it makes possible. They can also be brought about by direct investment in production, if knowledge is incorporated in the equipment concerned. As we will see later on, in the presence of severe inter-sectoral disequilibria during an initial phase, they can also be engendered by the structural change associated with the growth process.

As in the case of the external economies analysed in the preceding section, dynamic economies of scale only have an effect on international trade if knowledge is not perfectly mobile. This is exactly what the new models of technology creation in developing countries posit. According to this body of literature, the development of new products and processes is not a hallmark of technical change in these countries; quite to the contrary, products and processes are to a great extent transferred from more advanced countries. An active process of technological development is none the less taking place in the form of the accrual of knowledge regarding the application of foreign technologies and their adaptation to local conditions. This is not merely learning by doing; it is also a conscious effort on the part of firms and a response to the incentives created by the economic context. In any event, technology transfer cannot be dissociated from a parallel local accumulation of knowledge arising out of the use of that technology and, hence, out of the production process itself. The technological development of developing countries is therefore a process of 'human capital' formation when considered from the vantage point of the new growth theories, even if the technology is first created abroad.

Dynamic economies may be associated with marketing as well as production or, in other words, with the development of marketing and market information networks. Both marketing and production economies can arise in the development of either the domestic or external market. According to Chenery and Keesing (1981), the presence of an active process of learning by doing in connection with exports of manufactures may be the reason why such exports are concentrated in just a few Third World countries. Dynamic marketing economies may play a very important role in the exports of developing countries to developed countries (Keesing and Lall, 1992); yet technological learning tends to be much greater in trade between developing countries as a result of the larger share of more technologically more sophisticated products in this kind of trade (Amsden, 1986).

As discussed in the preceding section, the implications of dynamic economies of scale for trade policy do not differ greatly from those associated with traditional external economies. Depending upon their type, they may serve as a source of support for infant-industry protection, subsidies for the external marketing of new products or the promotion of trade between developing countries. Rather than delving further into these implications, however, we will focus our attention on analysing how close a relationship exists between productivity and the external trade regime. A great deal has been written about this subject during the past two decades along two different but closely related lines of thought: the links between *growth* and the trade regime and the links between the trade regime and *productivity* as such.[4]

The first of these relationships has been exhaustively explored (see, *inter alia*, Michaely, 1977; Heller and Porter, 1978; Tyler, 1981; Balassa, 1985; Jung and Marshall, 1985; Feder, 1986; Chow, 1987; Chenery and Syrquin, 1989; Edwards, 1991). These studies have found a positive correlation between economic growth and export orientation. None the less, this relationship has not necessarily been present at all times or in all the groups of countries studied (Feder, 1986). In the case of Latin America, the simple correlation between these two variables has been unstable throughout the post-war years and, during some periods, it has been negligible (Ocampo, 1988). De Gregorio (1991) discovered that when other variables explaining growth are included, external variables do not play an important role in the relative performance of the various Latin American countries.

For developing countries over all, the correlation is largely a result of a relatively limited number of highly successful cases of export promotion. The list of these cases does not fit in with the 'neutral trade regimes' of orthodox analyses, but it does match up with countries that have combined export promotion policies with aggressive economy-wide or sectoral import-substitution policies or with other types of active industrial policy (Spain, Portugal, Greece, Yugoslavia, South Korea, Taiwan, and others). The *causal* relationship between export growth and overall GDP growth is not, for that matter, clearly demonstrated (Jung and Marshall, 1985; Chow, 1987); its explanation may not be associated so much with the higher

productivity levels of export sectors or with the externalities supposedly generated by their development as with other factors discussed in
the traditional literature on the foreign exchange gap, according to
which expanding export sectors allow countries to relax the foreign
exchange constraint on growth (Feder, 1986).

Additional evidence in this regard is provided by the most recent
writings on *productivity* and export promotion (Pack, 1988; Havrylyshyn, 1990; Tybout, 1990). This literature indicates that in many cases
trade liberalization prompts shifts in firms' efficiency curves, but not a
persistent acceleration of the growth rate of productivity at the sectoral
or microeconomic level. This is not surprising, since, as is shown in
Rodrik's (1992) thorough analysis of the issue, there are no theoretical
reasons to expect such a result.

At the macroeconomic level, however, Verdoorn's Law – i.e. the
existence of a link between increasing productivity and growth – is
backed up by solid evidence (Chenery *et al.*, 1986, chapter 1 and, for
Latin America, de Gregorio, 1991). If, in addition, economic growth is
associated with export promotion, as is asserted by the first group of
theorists discussed here, then there should be a *macroeconomic*
connection between productivity and export growth. Pack (1988)
suggests that this connection can be explained with a simple growth
model under conditions of cross-sectoral disequilibrium, such as that
developed by Chenery (Chenery *et al.*, 1986) and Kaldor (1978, chapters
4 and 5), according to which export promotion permits a dynamic
transfer of production resources from the lowest-productivity sectors to
the highest-productivity ones without causing decreasing returns in the
latter sectors; according to the same author, this process is particularly
favourable when it is the manufacturing sector that is expanding.

This being the case, the exports-growth relationship is not associated
with dynamic economies of scale at the microeconomic level, but rather
with a particular form of 'endogeneity' characterizing productivity in
open economies. This, of course, has profound implications. It
indicates that the success of export-oriented trade policy reform
should not be measured by its contribution to increased productivity
in microeconomic terms, but rather by how much it helps to spur
structural change and, by that means, to increase overall economic
growth. In other words, the programme's direct objective should not be
productivity but rather *production*. Since the first of these variables is
the result of a macroeconomic process, a reform programme will have
the expected results in terms of productivity only if it is implemented
within an expansionary context.

III ECONOMIES OF SCALE, IMPERFECT COMPETITION AND TRADE STRATEGY

The Gains from Trade Liberalization

According to the hypotheses contained in the traditional literature on international trade, the gains from trade liberalization are related to the reallocation of resources from sectors in which a country has no comparative advantage to sectors in which it does; in the case of large countries, these gains may be offset by the deterioration in the terms of trade which a liberalization drive tends to cause. All the traditional types of estimates indicate that the costs of protection associated with a poor inter-sectoral allocation of resources – and, hence, the gains to be realized from liberalization – are not very great (perhaps on the order of 1 or 2 per cent of GDP). Consequently, it comes as no surprise that the traditional orthodox literature has ended up highlighting two entirely different factors: the macroeconomic distortions that interventionist governments tend to bring upon themselves (fiscal deficits, monetization of deficits, disequilibrium and multiple exchange rates, etc.); and the poor resource allocation associated with 'rent seeking', especially the rents to be derived from protection (see, for example, Krueger, 1978; Balassa *et al.*, 1986; World Bank, 1987; Papageorgiou *et al.*, 1990; Thomas *et al.*, 1990).

One of the most interesting implications of this type of analysis and of the traditional estimates of the costs of protection is that the gains from trade liberalization will tend to be fairly small in countries blessed with sound macroeconomic management (e.g. Colombia, within the Latin American arena). In countries with macroeconomic disequilibria, the greatest gains from liberalization will be associated with the re-establishment of a macroeconomic balance rather than with the trade reforms (see Chapters 11 and 7 on Argentina and Chile in Part III of this volume). The tendency to confuse the benefits of stabilization with those of trade reform as such is one of the basic flaws in this body of writing (Rodrik, 1990).

The new literature on international trade has much more complex implications for trade policy (Helpman and Krugman, 1989). Generally speaking, this school of thought contends that free trade is not an optimum policy. The effects of trade policies will be determined by the relative significance of economies of scale in the corresponding sectors and by the corporate strategies used in imperfect markets. The variety of possible situations is quite extensive, and could not be properly summarized in such a short chapter. Therefore, the following paragraphs will focus, first, on the implications of trade policy for the domestic market and, in this connection, on the implications of trade liberalization in imperfectly competitive markets. The next section will take a closer look at 'strategic trade policies', whose relevance is largely associated with competition in external markets.

According to the new literature, the gains in welfare from trade liberalization in a context of imperfect competition are derived from six basic factors: (a) greater access for consumers to products on the domestic market whose international prices are lower than their domestic prices; (b) access to a greater variety of designs for the various products available; (c) the expansion of production in sectors where prices exceed marginal costs; (d) the expansion of production in sectors subject to economies of scale; (e) the effects on the terms of trade; and (f) the effects on productivity (Lancaster, 1984; Krugman, 1988; Helpman and Krugman, 1989; Helpman, 1989; Krugman, 1990, chapter 3; Rodrik, 1990; Sáez, 1990). These latter effects are indeterminate, as we saw in the preceding section, and will therefore not be touched upon in the following discussion.

The first type of gain listed above is simply the traditional gain from trade which, in a context of product differentiation, is augmented by access to a wider variety of designs. The third and fourth factors listed above open up a broad range of alternatives that may either magnify or curtail the gains from liberalization, depending on the circumstances. Gains will be increased if liberalization prompts the growth of industries subject to economies of scale and the reduction of profit margins in those sectors. In that event, and contrary to what is suggested by traditional general equilibrium models, import-substituting sectors will be the ones to benefit the most from liberalization (see, for example, Devarajan and Rodrik, 1989).

If, on the other hand, liberalization leads to a contraction of the sectors subject to economies of scale, then the predictions traditionally made by those models will be borne out, except that the benefits of trade reforms will be substantially reduced. In a more limited market for domestic firms, the existence of intra-firm economies of scale (whether static or dynamic) will be determined by the number of firms remaining in the market; therefore, the process will be less costly if firms are not faced with exit barriers or, in other words, if sector adjustment is more radical. If the predominant economies are external, then the losses will be irreversible and may be independent of the extent of the adjustment effort in industries exposed to greater external competition.

Imperfect competition may result in additional adverse effects. On the one hand, as a rule, a liberalization drive can be expected to discourage collusion among companies, thereby reducing their profit margins and adding to the gains of liberalization. Yet the opposite may occur in oligopolistic sectors if collusive schemes develop to avoid destructive competition. Furthermore, in a situation of monopolistic competition, the reduction of profit margins may push out firms whose product designs are geared specifically to the domestic market. Consumers' access to a greater variety of products is therefore counterbalanced by the increased cost of domestically designed products. This carries significant distributive effects, which may be regressive if the consumers of domestic designs are low-income sectors.

On the other hand, in imperfect markets even small countries can influence their terms of trade. This will necessarily be the case when foreign producers have market power in the importing country or engage in a strategic interaction with importers and/or domestic producers. Under these circumstances, the elimination of quantitative restrictions will usually improve the country's terms of trade, but just the opposite will occur if tariffs are lowered. In the first case, the domestic market power of companies that export to the country will be curtailed by liberalization, while in the second case it will increase. Moreover, if liberalization leads to greater competition among importers in the country, their market power will be reduced, which will have an adverse effect on the country's terms of trade.

Thus, the results of liberalization in imperfect markets subject to economies of scale are both complex and uncertain. Gains may be enhanced if the sectors subject to economies of scale experience growth, if collusion among firms is curbed, if the market power of exporters to the country is reduced and if some of the potential benefits in terms of productivity materialize; quite the opposite will occur, however, if these conditions are not met. Consequently there is no generally applicable presumption in favour of liberalization or in favour of the retention of certain types of protection or regulatory systems. It all depends on the particular circumstances both in the country and sector.

Although the existing literature has mainly concentrated on analysing the domestic effects of protective barriers to imports within a context of imperfect competition, the theoretical constructs that have been developed can just as easily be applied to an analysis of the effects of export incentives on domestic competition. A pioneering work in this connection authored by Valdés (1990) looks into the effects of a drawback system on indirect exporters who are producers of basic inputs and wield market power over direct exporters. I conclude that this system can either reinforce the market power of the former or promote vertical integration, depending on how it is designed.

Strategic Trade Policy

The existing literature has dealt with export sectors mainly in terms of 'strategic trade policy'. This literature explores the conditions under which certain governmental decisions that benefit national companies also increase their ability to obtain monopolistic or oligopolistic rents in foreign markets, thereby adding to national income. This typically occurs in situations where both national and foreign firms have market power. Two basic types of strategic policies are discussed in the literature: (1) policies designed to displace gains towards national firms in imperfectly competitive international markets; and (2) policies that use import substitution as a tool for export promotion (Krugman, 1988; Helpman and Krugman, 1989, chapter 5; Baldwin, 1992).

The first type of policy is seen in cases where there is a limited international market and significant economies of scale which permit only a few firms to enter the sector on a profitable basis. Under such circumstances, the first firm to enter the market has a decisive advantage. In terms of projects, the same thing happens when one company announces that it will make a given investment, thereby leading other companies to abandon similar initiatives that would have competed with that investment. Governments can play an important role by providing various forms of support (subsidies, guaranteed minimum incomes, public co-investment schemes, etc.) in order to reduce the private risk in this type of market. The second type of policy comes into play when domestic protection to a particular sector permits the accumulation of significant economies of scale which enable it to compete more aggressively in the international market.

The existing literature assumes that both types of situations are characteristic of markets in which large economies of scale prevail. Although there are cases in which relatively large developing countries (Brazil in the case of mid-size aircraft and South Korea in the case of some electronics) participate in such markets, they are the exception rather than the rule (Krugman, 1988; Baldwin, 1992). This would seem to suggest that policies of this nature are not very relevant for such countries.

Nevertheless, there are situations other than those focused on in the new literature in which such considerations are indeed relevant for developing countries. The first line of reasoning may be valid over a much wider spectrum as a result of the differentiation of goods and services and to market segmentation as a result of transport costs. Entry into the corresponding market niches thus entails an element of strategic policy if significant economies of scale are to be found in production (owing to the plants' degree of specialization) or, more probably, in marketing. In these cases, export promotion policies are not irrelevant. Even in sectors where competitive activities predominate, state investment in infrastructure or state support for complementary activities subject to economies of scale can also entail a strategic element (Krugman, 1988). Strategic options of this sort may arise quite often in regional markets in the near future as a consequence of the intensive intra-regional trade liberalization process now under way in Latin America. A case in point is that of Colombian versus Venezuelan petrochemicals. Although they started out in more or less even positions, the Venezuelan government took the lead when it announced an aggressive investment programme with state participation and which will no doubt affect investments in Colombia.

In the presence of dynamic economies of scale, the 'import substitution as an export promotion tool' line of reasoning may have other applications as well. Latin America's experience indicates that, over time, a dynamic transition is made from import substitution to export activity in many manufacturing sectors. A similar process may take place in agricultural sectors (cotton and sugar in Colombia, for example). This does give new meaning to the 'infant industry' concept, yet it surely does not justify a permanent form of protection for many manufacturing sectors, as was typical in Latin America, or an overly inward-oriented focus on the part of new industries. In effect, if the arguments summarized above are valid, then the sooner the transition to export markets is made, the greater the advantages offered by dynamic economies of scale will be. Therefore, the 'early' establishment of export targets for these industries and the evaluation of their performance in terms of their penetration into the international market may be pivotal elements in an industrial strategy (Pack and Westphal, 1986).

Furthermore, even in static terms, national markets can often serve as springboards for the conquest of external markets in many industries. In fact, the frequency with which the larger companies charge different prices in domestic and external markets – engaging in dumping on the international market – indicates that the applicability of the arguments made in connection with the new theory of international trade is far from limited. In addition, national markets may be of great strategic value to the firms concerned if they are less unstable in terms of physical sales and prices. Under these conditions, the loss of the domestic market owing to a liberalization programme or a contractive domestic policy has an impact that has frequently been observed in Latin America in recent years: in the short run, firms adopt aggressive sales policies and engage in dumping on the international market; these exports may be a case of 'here today and gone tomorrow', however, if the loss of the domestic market means that earnings will be insufficient to sustain an aggressive sales policy of this type over the long term.

IV CONCLUSIONS

The new trade theories certainly do not provide a justification for across-the-board protectionism but neither do they provide support for 'neutral incentives' and laissez-faire industrial policy. Instead, the new theories corroborate the wisdom of maintaining some selectivity in terms of sectors and markets and firm state support for certain activities that are complementary to the development of the production sectors. Nor have recent theoretical and empirical investigations substantiated the existence of the automatic connection between liberalization and productivity that has figured so conspicuously in traditional orthodox analyses. None the less, they do indicate that macroeconomic relationships may exist that tend to raise productivity in the aggregate in countries where trade policy is effective in promoting economic growth thanks to a dynamic transfer of productive resources from low-productivity to high-productivity sectors.

Sectoral selectivity – in the forms identified in section II of this chapter – is justified in sectors subject to very significant economies of scale. Depending on the sector, this may provide grounds for a defensive protectionist policy (in sectors undergoing restructuring) or an offensive one (infant industries), in combination with active export promotion policies. In terms of markets, the new theories specifically support the liberalization of trade between developing countries. This type of trade appears to offer, in particular, the opportunity to make use of traditional static economies of scale and economies of specialization, as well as dynamic economies, owing to the relatively larger proportion of technologically more sophisticated products involved.

As is typically asserted in the traditional literature, state intervention in international trade does not, in many cases, prove to be the best policy choice. Direct intervention to support sectors with significant economies of scale or to correct distortions to competition is preferable in these cases. Direct subsidies for technological development, for activities that generate externalities in other sectors (including, of course, infrastructure) and for external marketing are, therefore, preferable in many instances.

Obviously, as has often been pointed out, the possibility of adopting the optimum policies proposed by the new literature will depend on the authorities' access to information. This is only possible if close links are established between the public and private sectors. For some this may lead to over-investment in 'rent-seeking' or it might even pervert the very essence of state action. Both sides of the divide over the issue have been based primarily on ideological considerations. It may be that ideology, far from fading into the background, is actually gaining in importance and that, in the final analysis, it continues to outweigh all other factors in determining the basic direction of trade policy.

Notes

1. Translation by Diane Frischman is gratefully acknowledged.
2. In some of these industries, however, and especially metals and metal manufactures, economies of specialization can be much greater.
3. We do not include certain external economies associated with consumption *per se* which play an important role in classic location analyses: the fact that a production centre may lead to an agglomeration of consumers who, in turn, tend to attract consumer goods-producing industries for which transport costs are a major expense.
4. The following discussion does not cover all the issues addressed in this body of literature. For a more comprehensive analysis, see the study by Manuel Agosin in this volume (Chapter 4).

Bibliography

Amsden, A. (1986), 'The Direction of Trade – Past and Present – and the "Learning Effects" of Exports to Different Directions', *Journal of Development Economics*, October.

Arrow, K. J. (1962), 'The Economic Implications of Learning by Doing', *Review of Economic Studies*, June.

Balassa, B. (1985), 'Exports, Policy Choices, and Economic Growth in Developing Countries after the 1973 Oil Shock', *Journal of Development Economics*.

Balassa, G., M. Bueno, Pedro Pablo Kuczynski and Mario Henrique Simonson (1986), *Hacia una Renovación del Crecimiento Económico en América Latina* (Mexico City: Colegio de México).

Baldwin, R. (1992), 'High-technology Exports and Strategic Trade Policy in Developing Countries: The Case of Brazilian Aircraft', in Helleiner (1992).

Berry, A. (1992), 'Firm (or Plant) Size in the Analysis of Trade and Development', in Helleiner (1992).

Chenery, H., and D. Keesing (1981), 'The Changing Composition of Developing Country Exports', in Sven Grassman and Erik Lundberg, eds, *The World Economic Order: Past and Prospects* (London: Macmillan).

Chenery, H., S. Robinson and M. Syrquin (1986), *Industrialization and Growth: A Comparative Study* (New York: Oxford University Press).

Chenery, H. and M. Syrquin (1989), 'Three Decades of Industrialization', *The World Bank Economic Review*, May.

Chow, P. C. Y. (1987), 'Causality between Export Growth and Industrial Development: Empirical Evidence from the NICs', *Journal of Development Economics*.

De Gregorio, J. (1991), 'Economic Growth in Latin America', paper presented at the Fourth Inter-American Seminar on Economics, Santiago, March.

Devarajan, S., and D. Rodrik (1989), 'Trade Liberalization in Developing Countries: Do Imperfect Competition and Scale Economies Matter?', *American Economic Review*, May.

Dixit, A., and V. Norman (1980), *Theory of International Trade* (Cambridge: Cambridge University Press).

Dutt, A. K. (1986), 'Vertical Trading and Uneven Development', *Journal of Development Economics*, March.

ECLAC (Economic Commission for Latin America and the Caribbean) (1969), *América Latina: El Pensamiento de la CEPAL* (Santiago: Editorial Universitaria).

ECLAC (1981), *La Industrialización de América Latina y la Cooperación internacional* (Santiago: ECLAC).

Edwards, S. (1991), 'Trade Orientation, Distortions and Growth in Developing Countries', paper presented at the Fourth Inter-American Seminar on Economics, Santiago, March.

Ethier, W. (1979), 'International Decreasing Costs and World Trade', *Journal of International Economics*.

Ethier, W. (1982), 'National and International Returns to Scale in the Modern Theory of International Trade', *American Economic Review*.

Feder, G. (1986), 'Growth in Semi-industrial Countries: A Statistical Analysis', in Chenery *et al.* (1986).

Havrylyshyn, O. (1990), 'Trade Policy and Productivity Gains in Developing Countries', *The World Bank Research Observer*, January.

Helleiner, G. K., ed. (1992), *Trade Policy, Industrialization and Development: New Perspectives* (Oxford: Clarendon Press).

Heller, P. S., and R. Porter (1978), 'Exports and Growth: An Empirical Reinvestigation', *Journal of Development Economics*.

Helpman, E. (1981), 'International Trade in the Presence of Product Differentiation, Economies of Scale and Monopolistic Competition: A Chamberlin–Heckscher–Ohlin Approach', *Journal of International Economics*.

Helpman, E. (1989), 'The Noncompetitive Theory of International Trade and Trade Policy', in World Bank, *Annual Conference on Development Economics*.

Helpman, E. and P. Krugman (1985), *Market Structure and International Trade* (Cambridge, Mass: MIT Press).

Helpman, E. and P. Krugman (1989), *Trade Policy and Market Structure* (Cambridge, Mass: MIT Press).

Hirschman, A. O. (1958), *The Strategy of Economic Development* (New Haven: Yale University Press).

Jung, W. S., and P. J. Marshall (1985), 'Exports, Growth and Causality in Developing Countries', *Journal of Development Economics*.

Kaldor, N. (1978), *Further Essays on Economic Theory* (London: Duckworth).

Katz, J. M. (1984), 'Domestic Technological Innovations and Dynamic Comparative Advantage: Further Reflections on a Comparative Case-study Program', *Journal of Development Economics*.

Katz, J. M. *et al.* (1986), *Desarrollo y Crisis de la Capacidad Tecnológica Latinoamericana: El Caso de la Industria Metalmecánica* (Buenos Aires: ECLAC).

Keesing, D. B., and S. Lall (1992), 'Marketing Manufactured Exports from Developing Countries: Learning Sequences and Public Support', in Helleiner (1992).

Krueger, A. O. (1978), *Liberalization Attempts and Consequences* (New York: National Bureau of Economic Research).

Krugman, P. (1988), 'La Nueva Teoría del Comercio Internacional y los Países en Desarrollo', *El Trimestre Económico*, January–March.

Krugman, P. (1990), *Rethinking International Trade* (Cambridge: MIT Press).

Lancaster, K. (1980), 'Intraindustry Trade and Perfect Monopolistic Competition', *Journal of International Economics*.

Lancaster, K. (1984), 'Protection and Product Differentiation', in Henryk Kierzkowski, ed., *Monopolistic Competition and International Trade* (Oxford: Oxford University Press).

Linder, S. B. (1961), *An Essay on Trade and Transformation* (Uppsala: Almqvist & Wicksell).

Lucas, R. E. (1988), 'On the Mechanisms of Economic Development', *Journal of Monetary Economics*, July.

Michaely, M. (1977), 'Exports and Growth: An Empirical Investigation', *Journal of Development Economics*.

Myrdal, G. (1957), *Economic Theory of Under-Developed Regions* (London: Duckworth).

Nurkse, R. (1967), *Problems of Capital Formation in Underdeveloped Countries* (Oxford: Oxford University Press).

Ocampo, J. A. (1986), 'New Developments in Trade Theory and LDCs', *Journal of Development Economics*, June.

Ocampo, J. A. (1988), 'Dilemas de la Política Comercial en América Latina', *Coyuntura Económica*, December.

Pack, H. (1988), 'Industrialization and Trade', in Hollis Chenery and T. N. Srinivasan, eds, *Handbook of Development Economics*, Vol. I (Amsterdam: North-Holland).

Pack, H. (1992), 'Learning and Productivity Change in Developing Countries', in Helleiner (1992).

Pack, H. and L. Westphal (1986), 'Industrial Strategy and Technological Change: Theory Versus Reality', *Journal of Development Economics*, June.

Papageorgiou, D., A. M. Choksi and M. Michaely (1990), *Liberalizing Foreign Trade Régimes in Developing Countries: The Lessons of Experience* (Washington: World Bank).

Perroux, F. (1961), *L'economie du XXe siècle* (Paris: Presses Universitaires de France).

Richardson, H. W. (1969), *Elements of Regional Economics* (Baltimore: Penguin Books).

Rodrik, D. (1988), 'Industrial Organization and Product Quality: Evidence from South Korean and Taiwanese Exports', NBER Working Paper No. 2722.

Rodrik, D. (1990), 'Trade Policies and Development: Some New Issues', Discussion Paper 181D, Kennedy School of Government, Harvard University, March.

Rodrik, D. (1992), 'Closing the Productivity Gap: Does Trade Liberalization Really Help?', in Helleiner (1992).

Romer, P. M. (1986), 'Increasing Returns and Long-run Growth", *Journal of Political Economy*, October.

Rosenstein-Rodan, P. N. (1943), 'Problems of Industrialization of Eastern and South-Eastern Europe', reprinted in A. N. Agarwala and S.P. Singh, eds, *The Economics of Underdevelopment* (New York: Oxford University Press).

Sáez, R. (1990), 'La Política de Comercio Exterior en Competencia Imperfecta: Un Ejercicio de Simulación para Chile', *El Trimestre Económico*, July–September.

Stewart, F. (1984), 'Recent Theories of International Trade: Some Implications for the South", in Henryk Kierzkowski, ed., *Monopolistic Competition and International Trade* (Oxford: Oxford University Press).

Stewart, F. and E. Ghani (1992), 'Externalities, Development and Trade', in Helleiner (1992).

Thomas, V., K. Matin and J. Nash (1990), *Lessons in Trade Policy Reform* (Washington: World Bank).

Tybout, J. R. (1990), 'Researching the Trade/Productivity Link: New Directions' (mimeograph), World Bank, August.

Tyler, W. G. (1981), 'Growth and Export Expansion in Developing Countries', *Journal of Development Economics*.

Valdés, S. (1990), 'Drawbacks for Indirect Exporters and Monopoly Power', *Journal of Development Economics*, April.

Van Wijnbergen, S. (1984), 'The Dutch Disease: A Disease After All?', *Economic Journal*, March.

World Bank (1987), *World Development Report* (Washington: World Bank).

Young, A. A. (1928), 'Increasing Returns and Economic Progress', *Economic Journal*, December.

6 Does Financial Liberalization Improve Trade Performance?

Yilmaz Akyüz[1]

I INTRODUCTION

The 1980s witnessed widespread policy reforms in developing countries. This was partly a response to their deep and prolonged crisis, and partly a reflection of a major shift in views regarding the appropriate roles of market mechanisms and government intervention. The sum total of these reforms has come to be expressed as structural adjustment. They are often undertaken in the context of adjustment programmes supported by World Bank lending (World Bank, 1988).

Structural reform has three dimensions: trade, finance, and the public sector. Trade reforms concentrate on exchange rate policy, import liberalization and export promotion; financial reforms on internal and external liberalization; and public sector reforms on the budget (deficit reduction, tax reform and rationalization of expenditures) and state economic enterprises (pricing, rationalization and privatization). All the reforms are expected to provide incentives and mechanisms to promote industrial and agricultural development, and to reduce poverty.

There has been considerable controversy over whether the reforms prescribed can indeed attain their objectives and whether better options are available. The internal consistency of the programmes has also been questioned, for the effects of different reforms may run counter to each other: for instance, financial policies may undermine trade and fiscal objectives, or trade policies may impede the realization of fiscal objectives. This raises the issue of the optimal policy mix, i.e. choosing among a wide range of policy alternatives after considering their effects

142

over the whole range of policy objectives. This is a formidable undertaking, and certainly cannot be expected to yield the same answer for all countries and under all circumstances.

The literature on the sequencing of economic reforms tries to address this issue but does so in a very special way. Its starting point is that liberalization is desirable on efficiency grounds. According to this view, liberalization of a particular market may produce adverse results only if there are distortions and imbalances elsewhere in the economy. On the other hand, since these imbalances and disturbances cannot be corrected at once, liberalization should be undertaken in a particular sequence. The majority view is that domestic financial markets and the current account should be liberalized before the capital account in order to avoid the adverse effects of capital flows on trade and macroeconomic stability, and that fiscal balance and price stability should be attained before any liberalization (Dornbusch, 1983; Edwards, 1984, 1987, 1989; Frenkel, 1983; McKinnon, 1982; Fischer and Reisen, 1992). This literature emerged in large part as an *ex post* theorizing of why the Southern Cone liberalization experiment failed (Corbo, de Melo and Tybout 1986; Corbo and de Melo, 1987; Díaz-Alejandro, 1985) rather than as an inquiry into the optimum policy in developing countries under different circumstances. While this approach has provided some insights, its analysis and prescriptions are limited by its main working assumptions regarding the market mechanism, and by a perception and interpretation of a particular type of experience.

This chapter examines the implications of financial liberalization for trade. Finance is perhaps the most important non-trade policy area influencing trade performance. This is also implied by the sequencing literature. However, our approach is based on a different premise regarding the nature of finance and efficiency of financial markets. We reject the assumptions underlying the mainstream analysis that finance is primarily geared to investment and production and financial markets are efficient in allocating resources. Rather, in modern capital markets finance tends to have a life of its own and there are widespread market failures, particularly in developing countries. Consequently, we argue that financial liberalization creates systemic problems that can undermine growth and competitiveness regardless of the order in which various markets are liberalized and distortions removed. We shall first discuss internal financial liberalization, and then move on to external finance and ask if financial openness of a developing country can help its industry to compete internationally.

II   INTERNAL FINANCIAL LIBERALIZATION

Macroeconomics of Financial Liberalization and Trade

By internal financial liberalization we mean pursuing a market-oriented approach to allocating financial resources and determining interest rates. This implies reducing or eliminating directed credit allocation and preferential credits by easing or removing restrictions on bank portfolios such as compulsory holding of government securities and minimum lending requirements to priority sectors. Although financial liberalization also often involves deregulation of deposit rates, sometimes the central bank continues to set deposit rates or impose ceilings on them, but now determines these with reference to market conditions.

This policy approach is based on the hypothesis, initially due to McKinnon (1973) and Shaw (1973), that regulating interest rates and allocating financial resources through administrative means (i.e. financial repression) depresses savings and creates considerable inefficiencies in their allocation and use. Thus, it is argued that financial liberalization and higher real interest rates will, by increasing the willingness to save and to hold savings in financial assets, increase the availability of investment finance and improve the allocation of resources. However, the evidence suggests that financial liberalization in many developing countries has not succeeded in lifting the level of savings and investment: financial activity has increased, but industry and trade have not been the main beneficiaries (Akyüz and Kotte, 1991; UNCTAD, 1991, part two, chapter 3).

As noted above, it is suggested that financial liberalization should be undertaken under conditions of low and stable inflation in order to avoid sharp increases in interest rates. However, it is also argued that to have an impact on savings, increases in real interest rates should be large and permanent: 'savers may ignore a possible increase from, say, 4 to 6 per cent in rates of return, but they are less likely to maintain consumption-savings patterns when rates of return change, in the context of economic reform, from negative levels to positive 10 or 15 per cent and more' (Shaw, 1973, p. 73). Certainly such large jumps in real interest rates usually occur at relatively high rates of inflation. In any case, in practice in a large majority of developing countries financial liberalization in the 1980s caused sharp increases in nominal and real interest rates because it was undertaken under serious macroeconomic disorder; i.e. as a way out of economic stagnation and instability. Moreover, liberalizations were typically accompanied by monetary restriction, pushing interest rates further. For instance in Turkey the deregulation of deposit rates in the early 1980s raised the real interest rates by more than 40 percentage points with the real lending rate reaching 30 per cent. This was also the experience of some other countries (Akyüz and Kotte, 1991).

In a world of fully competitive markets financial liberalization should help traded-goods sectors and external payments: higher interest rates would reduce the aggregate demand and the prices of non-traded goods relative to traded goods, prices of the latter being determined by world prices, the exchange rate and the degree of protection. In short, it would act like a devaluation as in the orthodox stabilization theory, not only reducing imports but also promoting exports. If, moreover, the resource shift in response to the change in relative prices and the real exchange rate takes place without friction, aggregate domestic output would not shrink – the change will be in the composition of output in favour of traded goods.

However, the immediate macroeconomic effects of financial liberalization may not be favourable to external balance for two reasons, both of which are overlooked or assumed away in the conventional approach. First, the higher interest rates by raising costs have adverse effects on the supply side, causing orthodox policies to be stagflationary (Taylor, 1991). Second, and more important for our purposes, there are widespread imperfections in domestic goods markets which can produce perverse results for trade and external payments.

The effect on supply can be very serious. In developing countries, usually the equity base of corporations is very weak, leverage high, debt maturities short, and corporate debt carries variable rates. The corporate sector borrows heavily not only for investment but also for working capital needs, making the ratio of corporate debt to operating surplus very high. A sharp and sustained increase in real interest rates can therefore impose a very heavy burden on firms, in much the same way as they did on debtor developing countries in the early 1980s. The impact is instantaneous since it operates on the stock of debt. Thus, the share of interest payments in operating surplus can increase considerably even without substantial new borrowing. The evidence from Turkey, for instance, shows that the share of interest in corporate value added doubled after liberalization, equalling and even exceeding the share of wages in total costs (Akyüz, 1990).

While financial liberalization can raise considerably the cost of debt for all firms, those operating in non-traded-goods sectors are much more capable of protecting their profits than those producing traded goods. Typically they operate under oligopolistic competition and can pass the increase of the cost of finance on to consumers by raising prices. By contrast, firms in export sectors, because they work under stiff competition in world markets, have to absorb an increase in the nominal interest rate by reducing their profit margin, all the more so if they use non-traded goods as inputs. The same is also true for import-competing sectors.

Financial liberalization, therefore, can alter relative prices and profitability at the expense of export and import-competing sectors. Production will fall both in the traded and non-traded goods sectors, but when export and import-competing firms have small margins, the impact on them can be very serious and can put them out of business, particularly if the shift in interest rates is large and long-lasting. In any case, the decline in profitability in these industries relative to non-traded goods sectors will discourage investment there.

It may not be possible to offset the adverse effects of financial liberalization and increased cost of finance on exports by currency depreciations. Strong doses of financial liberalization and devaluation taken together can trigger considerable instability, particularly when, as in debt-distressed countries, devaluations have already been taken to limits of tolerance in order to bring about a massive balance-of-payments adjustment and to compensate for trade liberalization (UNCTAD, 1989, part one, chapter IV).

One channel of instability is the reaction of interest rates to price increases. Adjustment of nominal interest rates to increased inflation can exert further cost-push pressure on firms in the non-traded-goods sectors, requiring further devaluations to ensure that production of exports and import-competing goods remains more profitable. Such feedbacks between prices and the rate of interest can increase instability considerably, even though they may not always trigger an inflationary spiral.

More important, devaluation can give rise to destabilizing feedbacks between traded and non-traded goods prices by raising import costs and reducing profit margins in the non-traded sector. Again, the oligopolistic firms can raise prices, thereby preventing the currency from depreciating in terms of non-traded goods. Inflation need not escalate if there is no wage resistance. But then the entire burden of financial liberalization must be shifted on to wages, i.e. increases in the cost of debt in both traded and non-traded goods sectors must be matched by real wage cuts. This can in fact occur under certain circumstances. For instance, a World Bank report on Turkey noted that 'the cost of credits to non-agricultural private enterprises has risen in real terms that cannot be sustained indefinitely. . . . Until now the increase in real interest rates has to a large extent been offset by the decline in real wages, but this is a solution that cannot be maintained in the long run' (World Bank, 1983, p. 18). Indeed, financial liberalization can entail a considerable redistribution of income and wealth (Akyüz, 1991; Díaz-Alejandro, 1985); in Turkey the increase in interest income was about 10 per cent of GDP. This, in combination with the real depreciation of the currency needed to support exports, can exert considerable pressure on real wages.

However, typically strong wage resistance is likely, driving the economy into an inflationary spiral. The consequent distributional struggle between wages, rentier incomes and profits in traded and non-traded-goods sectors can be extremely intense and disruptive. Such a struggle appears to have intensified in Turkey in the second half of the decade when wage claims picked up as a result of changed political circumstances, raising inflation persistently above the levels of the previous years.

It is perhaps for these reasons that many governments have decided to maintain preferential lending to export sectors when deregulating interest rates. In Turkey, for example, interest rates on export credits were kept at around 20–25 per cent during the first half of the 1980s when non-preferential lending rates had almost reached three digit figures. Subsidized credits amounted to more than one-third of the total value of exports, and without them the currency would have had to depreciate by at least another 10 per cent in real terms in order to sustain exports. These subsidies played a crucial role in export expansion during the first half of the 1980s (Ersel and Temel, 1984), and when in 1985 the government eliminated preferential export credits partly as a result of a strong export performance and payments position, and partly as a result of external pressures for further liberalization, exports fell; preferential export credits had to be reintroduced at the end of 1986. The effect of abolishing credit subsidies for exports was much stronger than that of abolishing export tax rebates in 1990; in the latter instance exports did not fall even though there had been widespread over-invoicing.

Even in Korea the preferential treatment of certain export industries was maintained after financial markets were liberalized in the 1980s, although liberalization was undertaken under much more favourable conditions with respect to external payments, growth and price stability than are typical of recent episodes of liberalization in developing countries; consequently a significant increase in real interest rates was avoided. All preferential lending rates were ostensibly abolished in 1982 and the loan rates were unified, and there was a further move to liberalization in 1988 when interest rates were officially deregulated. However,

> in practice . . . the MOF [Ministry of Finance] has tried to prevent a decline in export activity by arranging for certain exporters to receive preferential credit in a form other than subsidized export financing. This form of credit is the same form reserved for targeted industries. Targeted industries receive preferential credit in the form of access to bank loans which . . . carry below-market interest rates, even if not the super "preferential" ones they once carried (Amsden and Euh, 1990, p. 16).

Credit Allocation, Trade and Industrialization

Directed credit allocation at low interest rates indeed played a major role in the industrialization of the successful Asian NICs during the 1960s and 1970s. Contrary to widespread perception, interest rates were generally 'suppressed' under tight ceilings, often resulting in negative real rates, and the preferential rates were much lower. For instance, in Thailand with traditionally liberal economic policies, a World Bank study has found that taken as a group, the ex-post year-end figures for the real ceiling rates on various deposits and loans were positive in only 24 out of 52 instances between 1970 and 1982 (Hanson and Neal, 1985, p. 137). Again, 'bank loan and deposit rates in Korea . . . were consistently negative in real terms throughout the 1974–80 period' (Cho and Khatkhate 1989, p. 33). Targeted industries received loans at lower rates. Thus, 'throughout most of the twenty-five years of Korean industrial expansion, long-term credit has been allocated by the government to selected firms at negative real interest rates in order to stimulate specific industries' (Amsden, 1989, p. 144). Directed allocation of credits at preferential rates has also been applied to foreign capital tapped through official channels. Interest rate subsidies constituted the single most important incentive for sectors with export targets, particularly to highly capital-intensive industries, which also had priority in credit rationing. Such subsidies amounted to 10 per cent of GDP in the 1970s (Bradford, 1986, p. 119). Early in 1991, the government in Korea introduced a plan to increase specialization among the country's large conglomerates by providing credit incentives to concentrate on a smaller number of activities, and to tighten existing credit controls on the others, on the grounds that more focused investment in technology was needed to increase competitiveness in international markets.

In fact, almost all modern examples of industrialization have been accompanied by government intervention in the determination of the cost and availability of finance in the pursuit of selective industrial policies. Governments intervened to ensure that firms facing what is typically a prolonged learning process are not deterred by a lack of funds. 'Learning . . . means that . . . one cannot use current comparative advantage for judgements of how to allocate resources. Moreover, it may be optimal to initially incur a loss; the imperfections of capital markets thus may impose a more serious impediment on LDCs taking advantage of potentials for learning' (Stiglitz, 1989, p. 199). Success in overcoming productivity handicaps in international markets has often stemmed not so much from a lowering of wages as from provision of selective incentives and subsidies. In Korea

government intervention was necessary not just to steer credit in the right direction but to underwrite production during the learning process that was far more involved than what is commonly meant by 'infant industry protection.' Subsidized credit meant the difference between establishing new industries or not, rather than the difference between high or low profits (Amsden and Euh, 1990, p. 31).

Evidence from developed countries also points to the importance of the cost of finance for competitiveness in international trade. A recent study in the Federal Reserve Bank of New York 'estimates cost of capital for corporations in the United States, Japan, Germany and Britain in the period 1977–88 and finds that the United States and Britain labor under a decided disadvantage in relation to the other two economies" (McCauley and Zimmer, 1989, p. 7). In both Japan and Germany where corporations are more leveraged than in the United States and the UK this advantage derives primarily from lower cost of debt. There has been increased concern in the United States in recent years that capital costs may have contributed to the declining competitiveness of that country not only in industry but also in international banking (Zimmer and McCauley, 1991). It has been argued that this enables the firms in Japan to undertake longer-horizon projects than the American firms where high rates of return required to meet the cost of finance impede investments in research and develop-ment projects with delayed payoffs (McCauley and Zimmer, 1989; Poterba, 1991).

There can be no doubt that many countries have directed credit with much less success. The differences between successful and unsuccessful intervention have been partly a result of the selection of priorities, i.e. skill in 'picking winners'. While in this respect governments are not necessarily better equipped than markets, the experience strongly suggests that what is a winner depends on how it is managed. A major factor in the greater success of the Asian countries is that governments have made the provision of support and protection conditional upon good performance, and seen to it that their support and protection were really needed and actually used for the purposes intended, and not simply as a handout. Moreover, such intervention has relied on market-based performance, namely competitiveness in world markets, which provided reliable indicators for assessing the nature and extent of the support needed and whether such support was effectively used (Amsden, 1989; Westphal, 1990).

III   EXTERNAL FINANCIAL LIBERALIZATION

Financial Openness in Developing Countries

External financial liberalization consists of policy actions that increase the degree of financial openness, i.e. the ease with which residents can acquire assets and liabilities denominated in foreign currencies and non-residents can operate in national financial markets. Financial openness depends on the degree of liberalization of three broad types of transaction. First, inward transactions; namely, allowing residents to borrow freely in international financial markets, and non-residents to invest freely in domestic financial markets. Second, outward transac-tions; namely, allowing residents to transfer capital and to hold assets abroad, and non-residents to issue liabilities and to borrow in domestic financial markets. Third, domestic transactions in foreign currencies; namely, allowing debtor–creditor relations among residents in foreign currencies such as bank deposits and lending in foreign currencies. This definition of financial openness is thus wider than capital account liberalization because it includes financial transactions among residents denominated in foreign currencies. These are an important part of banking and finance, and have international characteristics that affect the national economy in ways similar to cross-border financial transactions (Bryant, 1987, chapter 3).

The first wave of external liberalization in developing countries generally took the form of liberalizing inward transactions, particularly allowing the private sector to borrow abroad in order to attract foreign exchange and capital. The Southern Cone experience is the best-known, and was set in a broad programme of liberalization. However, external borrowing by residents was liberalized also in a number of countries where domestic financial markets continued to be highly regulated (e.g. Turkey in the 1970s, former Yugoslavia, and the Philippines). Resident banks were often involved as intermediaries between international capital markets and domestic borrowers. In countries with a sizeable flow of workers' remittances, a particular form of such borrowing took place on a large scale, namely foreign currency deposits offering attractive terms and carrying government guarantees. In almost all these episodes there was a massive build-up of foreign exchange liabilities by private financial and non-financial corporations (Díaz-Alejandro, 1985; Rodrik, 1986; Akyüz and Kotte, 1991). The subsequent debt crisis also served to open the financial markets of developing countries by generating new prospects for arbitrage and windfall profits (through the so-called market-based menu), which significantly raised the amount of equities and domestic-currency debt assets held by non-residents in highly indebted countries (UNCTAD, 1989, pp. 105–7). More recently, access of non-residents to national equity markets has been encouraged in the context of privatization programmes. Today inward transactions are virtually free in a large number of countries, particularly in Latin America where external borrowing by the private sector is not subject to approval except for capital market issues. Similarly, there are few restrictions on the access of non-residents to domestic capital markets.

In recent years an increasing number of developing countries have liberalized outward transactions and adopted capital account convertibility – some to an extent not found in most industrialized countries – although many countries still maintain restrictions on transferring capital and holding assets abroad. Liberalization of transactions among residents in foreign currency, however, has gone much further. Indeed, there has been a tendency to encourage residents to hold foreign exchange deposits with banks at home, increasing the importance of foreign currency in the economy (dollarization). The share of foreign currency in total deposits in recent years reached 50 per cent in a number of developing countries in Latin America as well as in Asia (e.g. Philippines), the Middle East and Europe (e.g. Turkey and former Yugoslavia), a figure well above the levels found in some international financial centres such as London, where the share of total bank claims (including inter-bank claims) on residents in foreign currencies barely exceeds 20 per cent (Bryant, 1987, chapter 3; Akyüz, 1992). Interest offered on such deposits is usually above world levels. These deposits are highly liquid (even sight deposits earn considerable interest) and much more easily accessible than their counterparts in most industrial countries where minimum limits and/ or charges and commissions are applied.

As a result of progressive liberalization of inward and outward operations and domestic transactions in foreign currencies, the degree of internationalization of finance has gone much further than trade. Indeed in many countries in Latin America and elsewhere the share of foreign exchange assets and transactions in the financial system is far greater than the share of foreign trade in GDP.

Capital Flows, Exchange Rates and Trade

Financial openness increases the substitutability between domestic and external funds for resident borrowers, and between domestic and foreign currency assets for lenders, thereby making it very difficult to delink the rates of return on domestic financial assets from those prevailing abroad and to decouple interest and exchange rates. Capital flows exert a considerable influence on exchange rates and financial asset prices, and are themselves influenced by expectations regarding rates of return on financial assets denominated in different currencies. This means not only that domestic policies have a new channel of influence on exchange rates, trade, balance of payments and, hence, the level of economic activity (namely, through their effects on capital flows), but also that these will all be influenced by financial policy abroad and by events at home and abroad that alter expectations. This effect of openness is known as loss of policy autonomy, i.e. reduced ability of governments to achieve national objectives by using the policy instruments at their disposal (Bryant, 1980, chapter 12). The conventional view assumes that the benefits of financial openness more than compensate for the possible costs of the loss of policy autonomy. The benefits claimed for financial openness are generally based on the assumption that the internationalization of finance allows savings to be pooled and allocated globally through the movement of capital across countries in response to opportunities for real investment, thereby improving the allocation of resources internationally and equalizing rates of return on investment everywhere. Accordingly, external financial liberalization in developing countries is expected to give rise to capital inflows provided that it comes after the deregulation of interest rates. This is seen as a one-off phenomenon of adjustment of domestic interest rates to world levels as capital scarcity is reduced through an increase in the underlying capital flows.

However, evidence strongly suggests that capital flows do not improve the international allocation of savings. There has been no narrowing of differences in rates of return on capital investment in the major industrial countries, or in real long-term interest rates; nor has the link between the levels of savings and investment in individual countries been considerably weakened (see OECD, 1989, table 53; 1991, table 58; UNCTAD, 1987; Akyüz, 1992; Kasman and Pigott, 1988; McCauley and Zimmer, 1989). The main reason is that most international financial transactions are portfolio decisions, largely by rentiers, rather than business decisions by entrepreneurs. Capital movements are motivated primarily by the prospect of short-term capital gains, rather than by real investment opportunities and considerations of long-term risk and return. The speculative element is not only dominant but also highly variable, capable of generating gyrations in exchange rates and financial asset prices by causing sudden reversals in capital flows for reasons unrelated to policies and/or the underlying fundamentals.

Thus, financial openness tends to create systemic problems regardless of the order of external liberalization. The exposure to short-term, speculative capital flows is much greater for developing than for developed countries because their instability provides greater opportunities for quick, windfall profits on short-term capital movements while their ability to influence capital flows through monetary policy is much more limited.

While internal financial liberalization strengthens the link between inflation and interest rates, external financial liberalization (unlike trade liberalization) weakens the link between inflation and the exchange rate, causing the latter to be dominated by capital flows instead of trade balances and the relative purchasing power of currencies; i.e. inflation differentials are more readily reflected in nominal interest rate differentials than in the movement of the nominal exchange rate. Thus, although short-term capital inflows motivated by the lure of quick windfall profits are often associated with positive real interest rate differentials in favour of the recipient, such a differential is not always necessary or sufficient. Capital inflows usually occur when there are nominal interest rate differentials that markets do not expect to be matched by a nominal exchange rate depreciation.

Such differentials often emerge when domestic inflation is much higher than abroad and domestic financial markets have been liberalized. Since in many developing countries inflation rates close to those prevailing in the major OECD countries are very difficult to attain, the scope for big arbitrage opportunities to emerge is much greater. Similarly, an expectation that equity prices will rise faster than domestic currency depreciation can prompt an inflow of capital. Both types of expectation can be self-fulfilling since the inflow of funds, if large enough, can itself maintain the value of the currency and boost equity prices.

Such inflows are typically initially a response to a favourable shift in market sentiment regarding the recipient country. This shift may result from external causes such as a sudden rise in export prices, or from internal ones such as reduced inflation, better growth prospects and greater political stability and confidence in the government's policies. After the initial shift in market sentiment, bandwagon-type behaviour often develops and creates a speculative bubble where people are lending or investing simply because everybody else is doing the same. Such booms do not always end with a soft landing; a recently liberalized, well-performing economy can suddenly find favour with foreign capital of all sorts, but if things go wrong for some reason, the capital disappears just as rapidly. When the bubble bursts and the currency comes under pressure, even a very large positive real interest rate differential may be unable to check the capital outflow.

These conditions were broadly fulfilled during the liberalization episodes in the Southern Cone in Latin America in the 1970s, when high domestic interest rates, overvalued exchange rates, freedom to borrow abroad and plentiful international liquidity combined to induce capital inflows. There are strong signs that a similar process has recently been under way in a number of Latin American countries. It is estimated that the region as a whole received about US$40 billion in 1991, three times the level of 1990, the main recipients being Mexico, Brazil, Argentina, Venezuela and Chile. While not all capital inflows have been for short-term uses, much of it does appear to have been so, particularly in Argentina and Brazil (UNCTAD, 1992, part two, annex II). In the majority of these countries capital inflows continued at an accelerated pace in the early months of 1992. In Chile, where 'the monetary authorities adopted a cautious approach based on the assumption that the oversupply of foreign exchange was only temporary and was due to the unusually high price of copper and the low international interest rates' (ECLAC, 1991, p. 41), short-term capital inflows slowed down considerably in 1992 thanks to various measures designed to reduce the arbitrage margin.

This experience shows that destabilizing capital inflows do not always arise from inappropriate policies. Indeed, the recipient countries not only are in quite different positions compared to the 1970s, but they also differ among themselves with respect to inflation, fiscal posture, and exchange rate and trade policies.

While Brazil has had a large fiscal deficit and a very high inflation, others, particularly Chile and Mexico, have had balanced budgets or fiscal surpluses, and moderate inflation. Currency appreciation has played an important role in attracting capital in Chile, Mexico and particularly Argentina, but not in Brazil where the underlying factor has been very high real interest rates. Currency appreciation is the result of exchange rate policy in Argentina (namely, to using the exchange rate as a nominal anchor to reduce inflation), but not in Chile and Mexico where it is market-generated. It has led to a considerable deterioration of the trade balance, especially in Argentina and Mexico.

That such capital flows can easily be reversed is evident from the experience of Turkey following the liberalization of its capital account and lifting of restrictions on private borrowing in August 1989. Turkey received $3 billion of short-term capital in 1990 compared to a net outflow of $2.3 billion in the year before, and its currency appreciated considerably. Capital flows were reversed in early 1991 with the outbreak of the Gulf War and political uncertainty at home. Net short-term outflows reached $3 billion in 1991, the currency depreciated sharply against the dollar and foreign exchange reserves dropped. What is remarkable about this experience is that real domestic interest rates were barely different between the two phases: the major difference was in the state of expectations and the direction of capital and exchange rate movements.

The ideal response to such capital inflows is a corresponding increase in domestic investment in traded-goods sectors. This not only prevents a sharp appreciation of the currency by raising imports of capital goods, but can also enhance export capacity that may be needed when capital flows dry up or are reversed. But higher investment is not always possible when domestic interest rates are prohibitive and long-term investment with funds borrowed abroad at lower rates carries considerable exchange rate risk. The dilemma is that the high interest rates and/or currency appreciation that attract short-term capital also deter investment. In Latin America recent capital inflows resulted in a sharp swing in the transfer of resources abroad by about 4 per cent of the region's GDP, but investment has remained depressed; in Brazil and Argentina the investment ratio in fact fell below the levels of the 1980s when these countries were making large transfers abroad.

The problems of macroeconomic management in the face of a massive capital inflow are familiar. Sterilization of these inflows by issuing domestic debt could impose a serious burden on the public sector, particularly when the arbitrage margin is large. In Brazil, for instance, the cost of carrying an extra US$5 billion of reserves purchased in this way amounted to about US$2 billion per annum, and added considerably to domestic public debt during 1992 (UNCTAD, 1992, part two, annex II; Junior, 1992). Furthermore, sterilization itself tends to raise domestic interest rates and, hence, the arbitrage margin by increasing the stock of government debt. If, on the other hand, the currency is allowed to continue to appreciate, it can lead to a payments crisis as the competitiveness of the domestic industry is undermined, possibly triggering a sharp reversal in short-term capital flows.

Instability in short-term capital flows combined with the inherent volatility of capital held in stocks exposes the economy to even greater risks when a close link develops between capital and currency markets. Since opening up domestic capital markets requires some form of currency convertibility for non-resident equity investors, such a link can develop even in countries where the capital account is not fully open. This may be potentially a serious problem in Latin America because of the increased presence of non-residents in capital markets. In Mexico, for instance, equity holding by non-residents in the second quarter of 1992 is estimated to have amounted to more than $25 billion, or about a quarter of the market's capitalization (*Latin American Economy and Business*, May 1992, p. 4), compared to about 5 per cent in the major capital markets such as New York and Tokyo. Moreover, the link between these two potentially unstable markets is also strengthened by the dollarization of the economy.

This link increases the potential for the emergence of foreign exchange and/or stock market crises. Since the return on investment to the foreign investor depends largely on the movement of the exchange rate, a serious shock (e.g. a terms of trade deterioration) that makes a devaluation appear inevitable can trigger both a sharp decline in equity prices and an outflow of capital.

Similarly, the mood in equity markets can exert a strong influence on the exchange rate – e.g. bullish expectations can trigger capital inflow, leading to appreciation. By contrast, a bearish mood in the capital market and/or massive profit-taking in dollars by non-residents can prick not only the speculative bubble in the stock market, but also lead to a currency crisis. Recent evidence suggests that strong destabilizing influences between financial and currency markets can easily develop: for instance, when the bubble burst in the Tokyo stock exchange at the beginning of 1990, there was a massive shift out of yen-denominated assets, causing also considerable drops in the government bond index and the currency (Akyüz, 1992).

Financial openness creates adverse systemic effects on trade and industrialization because sharp swings in the direction of capital flows and instability of exchange rates tend to reduce investment, particularly in the traded-goods sectors. This effect operates through the borrower's risk. The 'entrepreneur's or borrower's risk . . . arises out of doubts in his own mind as to the probability of his actually earning the prospective yield for which he hopes. . . . [I]t is a real social cost, though susceptible to diminution by . . . an increased accuracy of foresight' (Keynes, 1936, p. 144). Thus, while the borrower's risk is inherent in all investment decisions, its level depends, among other things, on the stability of economic conditions. The expected rate of return on investment must be high enough to cover both the borrower's risk and the cost of finance.

For investors in traded-goods sectors the real exchange rate is the single most important relative price affecting profits. Firms in non-traded goods sectors are also affected, depending on the imported inputs they use. In both sectors large swings in exchange rates result in considerable uncertainty regarding prospective yields of investment. This will raise the borrower's risk and, hence, the average rate of return required to undertake investment, particularly in the traded-goods sectors, and depress the level of investment to be undertaken at any given rate of interest.

The importance of the exchange rate as a variable influencing investment decisions increases with the share of foreign trade in the economy. It is thus of growing importance in the developing world because of widespread import liberalization and greater dependence on exports for growth. But simultaneously the exchange rate is becoming a variable pertaining to the sphere of finance, determined largely by capital flows delinked from trade and investment. Instability in exchange rates can thus undermine the success of the new 'outward oriented' strategy by depressing investment in traded goods sectors. The evidence suggests that such adverse effects have occurred even in industrial countries where firms are better equipped to hedge against unexpected swings in exchange rates, and that exchange rate stability has been an essential feature of countries with sustained export growth (UNCTAD, 1987; UNCTAD, 1989, part one, chapter 5).

Openness and Cost of Finance

Another systemic effect of volatile capital flows on trade and industrialization is through the cost of capital. Contrary to the orthodox view, financial openness in developing countries tends to raise interest rates. This effect operates through the lender's risk as the most important determinant of the rate of interest (Keynes, 1936, pp. 144–5). The lender's risk arises from a number of sources. First, the risk due to the possibility of involuntary default by the borrower: in other words, in a system of borrowing and lending, the borrower's risk is at least partly duplicated in the interest rate. Second, voluntary default, or what Keynes calls the moral risk: the lender must make allowance for the dishonesty of the borrower and non-enforcement of contracts. Third, the lender also runs a risk regarding the capital value of his assets, as a result of uncertainties over future interest rates, asset prices and the price level.

Increased borrower's risk discussed above raises the lender's risk and the interest rate since it increases the probability of involuntary default. Increased volatility of interest rates and prices of financial assets, including equities, lead to greater capital-value uncertainty which, in turn, raises liquidity preference and lowers the demand for capital-uncertain assets. The result is to shorten the maturities of financial assets and push up interest rates, especially the long-term ones.

Increased competition between assets denominated in the domestic currency and in foreign currency tends to raise the cost of finance also because there is greater risk and uncertainty in developing countries. The fact that most developing countries are economically and politically more unstable than developed countries, together with the weaknesses in their financial and legal systems in ensuring enforcement of contracts, makes financial investment in these countries more hazardous. That is why spreads over LIBOR in international lending are much higher for developing than for developed country borrowers, and why foreign exchange deposits in developing countries have to offer higher rates than those in world markets. In a financially closed economy there are considerable transaction costs in shifting into foreign exchange assets, at least for a large number of small savers, which tend to offset the safety premium on such assets. Financial openness reduces these costs considerably. Consequently, domestic assets need to carry much higher rates of return than external assets to make up for their additional risk.

When enterprises in developing countries have to pay higher real interest rates than their counterparts in developed countries, even greater reliance has to be placed on lowering wages in order to compete in world markets. This may cause serious problems. Competitiveness cannot always be restored through adjustments in exchange rates because they are governed by capital flows rather than trade. Furthermore, there may not exist a level of wages compatible simultaneously with competitiveness, macroeconomic stability and social peace.

Controlling Capital Flows

Complete isolation of the financial system in a developing country from the rest of the world is neither feasible nor desirable, if only because successful export performance requires close interaction of banks at home with world financial markets in order to provide trade-related credits and facilitate international payments. However, particular care needs to be given to the design of external financial policies, since mistakes in this area tend to be very costly and difficult to reverse. Allowing residents uncontrolled access to international capital markets has proved damaging in many developing countries, and short-term speculative capital flows have proved extremely troublesome even for industrial countries. Most developing countries need to exercise considerable control over external capital flows in order to minimize their disruptive effects and gain greater policy autonomy to attain growth and stability.

Given the drawbacks of external financial liberalization, tapping foreign capital primarily through official channels may be the most effective way of alleviating the capital shortage in many developing countries. For instance, for many years a principal feature of the external financial strategy of Korea was to control external borrowing through official approval and guarantees, and allocate foreign capital via the government-owned Development Bank. Even in the late 1980s the government prohibited firms outright from borrowing abroad and put tight controls on short-run speculative capital inflows (Amsden and Euh, 1990, p. 23).

There are a number of techniques to control private capital flows with different degrees of restrictions and effects which were widely used in industrial countries in the 1960s and 1970s (OECD, 1972, pp. 239–44; Swidrowski, 1975; Swoboda, 1976). Quantitative restrictions over short-term capital inflows through banks include reserve requirements on foreign liabilities, limits on their external or foreign-currency positions or liabilities, and minimum holding periods and blocking of foreign deposits for such periods. Similarly, a number of measures may be applied to restrict the external borrowing by non-banks, including reserve requirements on their foreign liabilities, and exchange controls such as prohibition of borrowing other than commercial or supplier credits for importers, control on domestic foreign currency credits to importers and exporters, and regulations regarding the timing of export and import settlements. Limits on banks' net external or foreign currency positions and exchange controls regarding non-banks can also be applied to restrict outflows. Restrictions on interest payments on non-resident deposits and negative interest rates were also used to deter capital inflows.

Taxes may also be used to reduce the arbitrage margin and discourage speculative capital flows. The interest equalization tax used in the United States in the past can be especially effective in checking capital inflows in developing countries where inflation and interest rate differentials with developed countries tend to be large. The tax rate can be used flexibly according to the behaviour of capital flows and the objective pursued. Another is a tax on financial transactions, long advocated by Keynes (1936, pp. 155–6) for domestic capital markets, and recently elaborated by Tobin (1978) to apply to international financial transactions in order to 'throw some sand in the wheels' and 'deter short-term financial round-trip excursions'.

Various restrictions may also be introduced on the access of non-residents to capital markets. One common measure is to limit foreign ownership to approved country funds and allow transactions on such funds only among non-residents in order to control the flow of foreign funds in and out of the country via capital markets. This can be combined with the requirement that such funds be managed by local managers who are generally more amenable to 'moral suasion' by the authorities. It should be kept in mind that in several industrialized countries capital markets have been opened up to non-residents only very recently. In Japan, for instance, they were largely closed until the 1984 agreement with the United States, and in Europe there were considerable restrictions on entry into capital markets in a number of countries until the completion of a single market. Again, Korea only recently opened up its capital market to non-residents, but restricted foreign acquisition to 10 per cent of total equity capital, and to 2 per cent in some strategic industries.

Some of these techniques have recently been used in Latin America in order to slow down short-term capital inflows, including reserve requirements for foreign currency liabilities (Chile and Mexico), compulsory liquidity requirements on the short-term foreign exchange liabilities of commercial banks (Mexico), minimum holding periods (Chile), extension of the fiscal stamp tax to foreign credits (Chile), restrictions on company borrowing abroad through stock and bond issues (Brazil), and limits on the dollar amounts that banks can raise in deposits abroad as a proportion of their total deposits (Mexico). However, such measures have not always been successful. Governments are often very shy in applying effective controls for fear of fending off genuine, long-term capital and investment. This is certainly a legitimate concern, particularly in Latin America, after a decade-long foreign exchange strangulation. However, experience shows that capital controls might have to be introduced anyway if the process develops into a payments crisis and capital flight. It may be easier to restrict short-term inflows and prevent debt accumulation early on than to check capital flight in a crisis.

Controls on capital flows are not always effective if there are large arbitrage opportunities. It is thus important to bear in mind that price stability is vital for a financially open economy, since high inflation and wide interest rate differentials with reserve-currency areas often lead to large arbitrage opportunities and encourage unsustainable capital flows. Furthermore, exchange rate management plays an important role. Explicit or implicit exchange rate guarantees tend to reduce the risk involved in arbitrage and encourage capital flows. As noted above, this has been an important factor in attracting short-term capital to Argentina. By contrast in Chile, 'the monetary authorities moved to resist revaluation of the peso by introducing changes to create uncertainty concerning yields on short-term capital flows' (ECLAC, 1992, p. 40). These measures included the ending of the practice of advance announcement of devaluation of the peso, widening of the currency band, and linking the peso to a basket of currencies instead of the US dollar. They appear to have played an important role in slowing down short-term capital inflows and securing greater real exchange rate stability by introducing uncertainty regarding the movement of the exchange rate. In Mexico too the authorities widened the differential points for the peso–US dollar exchange rate to allow larger fluctuations, although its effects on capital flows seem to have been limited (Banco de Mexico, 1992, p. 144).

Finally, measures to control capital inflows are not equally effective in stemming capital flight, especially under economic and political instability. It is important to bear in mind that capital controls are needed not in order to pursue inappropriate policies and exchange rates, but to minimize the disruptive effects of short-term capital flows, and gain greater policy autonomy to attain growth and stability. Indeed, historical experience clearly shows that capital controls are no panacea when the underlying policies are not sustainable.

Note

1. The views expressed in this chapter are those of the author and do not necessarily reflect the views of the UNCTAD secretariat. The author is grateful to Shahen Abrahamian, Manuel Agosin and Cem Somel for valuable comments and suggestions.

References

Akyüz, Y. (1990), 'Financial System and Policies in Turkey in the 1980s', in T. Aricanli and D. Rodrik, eds, *The Political Economy of Turkey. Debt, Adjustment and Sustainability* (London: Macmillan).
Akyüz, Y. (1991), 'Financial Liberalization in Developing Countries: A Neo-Keynesian Approach', UNCTAD Discussion Paper, No. 36, March.
Akyüz, Y. (1992), 'Financial Globalization and Instability', in Uner Kirdar, ed., *Change: Threat or Opportunity?* Vol. 3, Market Change, UNDP, New York.
Akyüz, Y., and D. Kotte (1991), 'Financial Policies in Developing Countries: Issues and Experience', UNCTAD Discussion Paper, No. 40, August.
Amsden, A. (1989), *Asia's Next Giant. South Korea and Late Industrialization* (New York: Oxford University Press).
Amsden, A., and Yoon-Dae Euh (1990), 'Republic of Korea's Financial Reform: What Are The Lessons?', UNCTAD Discussion Paper, No. 30, April.
Banco de Mexico (1992), *The Mexican Economy 1992*, Mexico.
Bradford, C.I. (1986), 'East Asian "Models": Myths and Lessons', in J.P. Lewis and V. Kallab, eds, *Development Strategies Reconsidered* (Washington, DC: Overseas Development Council).

Bryant, R. (1980), *Money and Monetary Policy in Interdependent Nations* (Washington, DC: The Brookings Institution).

Bryant, R. (1987), *International Financial Intermediation* (Washington, DC: The Brookings Institution).

Cho, Yoon-Je, and D. Khatkhate (1989) 'Lessons of Financial Liberalization in Asia. A Comparative Study', World Bank Discussion Paper, No. 50.

Corbo, V. and J. de Melo, (1987), 'Lessons from the Southern Cone Policy Reforms', *The World Bank Research Observer*, Vol. 2, No. 2.

Corbo, V., de Melo, J. and J. Tybout (1986), 'What Went Wrong with the Recent Reforms in the Southern Cone', *Economic Development and Cultural Change*, Vol. 34, No. 3.

Díaz-Alejandro, C. (1985), 'Good-Bye Financial Repression, Hello Financial Crash', *Journal of Development Economics*, Vol. 19 (1-2).

Dornbusch, R. (1983), 'Panel Discussion on the Southern Cone', *IMF Staff Papers*, Vol. 30, No. 1.

ECLAC (1991–92), *Economic Panorama of Latin America* (Santiago: United Nations).

Edwards, S. (1984), 'The Order of Liberalization of the Balance of Payments', World Bank Staff Working Paper, No. 710.

Edwards, S. (1987), 'Sequencing Economic Liberalization in Developing Countries', *Finance and Development*, March.

Edwards, S. (1989), 'On the Sequencing of Structural Reforms', Working Paper, No. 70, OECD, September.

Ersel, H. and A. Temel (1984), 'Turkiye nin 1980 Sonrasi Dissatim Basariminin Degerlendirmesi Uzerine Bir Deneme (A Test for the Assessment of the Post-1980 Export Success of Turkey)', Toplum ve Bilim, Autumn.

Fischer, B., and H. Reisen, (1992), *Towards Capital Account Convertibility*, Policy Brief No. 4, OECD Development Centre.

Frenkel, J. (1983), 'Panel Discussion on the Southern Cone', *IMF Staff Papers*, Vol. 30, No. 1.

Hanson, J.A. and C.R. Neal, (1985), 'Interest Rate Policies in Selected Developing Countries, 1970-1982', World Bank Staff Working Papers, No. 753.

Junior, P.A. (1992), 'Política Monetaria e Ingresso de Divisas: O Caso Brasileiro Recente', paper presented to the meeting of the technicians of Central Banks of the American Continent, Barbados, November 16-20.

Kasman, B., and C. Pigott (1988), 'Interest Rate Divergence among the Major Industrial Nations', *Federal Reserve Bank of New York Quarterly Bulletin*, Autumn.

Keynes, J.M. (1936), *The General Theory of Employment, Interest and Money* (London: Macmillan).

McCauley, R.N., and S.A. Zimmer (1989), 'Explaining International Differences in the Cost of Capital', *Federal Reserve Bank of New York Quarterly Bulletin*, Summer.

McKinnon, R.I. (1973), *Money and Capital in Economic Development* (Washington, D.C.: The Brookings Institution).

McKinnon, R.I. (1982), 'The Order of Economic Liberalization: Lessons from Chile and Argentina', in K. Brunner and A. Meltzer, eds, *Economic Policy in a World of Change* (Amsterdam: North Holland).

OECD (1972), *Economic Outlook*, No. 12, December.

OECD (1989), *Economic Outlook*, No. 45, June.

OECD (1991), *Economic Outlook*, No. 50, December.

Poterba, J. M. (1991), 'Comparing the Cost of Capital in the United States and Japan: A Survey of Methods', *Federal Reserve Bank of New York Quarterly Review*, Winter.

Rodrik, D. (1986), 'Macroeconomic Policy and Debt in Turkey During the 1970s: A Tale of Two Policy Phases', Discussion Paper, Harvard University John Fitzgerald School of Government, November.

Shaw, E. S. (1973), *Financial Deepening in Economic Development* (New York: Oxford University Press).

Stiglitz, J. E. (1989), 'Markets, Market Failure and Development', *American Economic Review*. Papers and Proceedings, May.

Swidrowski, J. (1975), *Exchange and Trade Controls* (Aldershot: Gower Press).

Swoboda, A. K. (1976), in *Capital Movements and their Control* (Geneva: Institut Universitaire de Hautes Etudes Internationales).

Taylor, L. (1991), 'Economic Openness: Problems to the Century's End', in T. Banuri, ed., *Economic Liberalization: No Panacea* (Oxford: Clarendon Press).

Tobin, J. (1978) 'A Proposal for International Monetary Reform', *The Eastern Economic Journal*, July/October.

UNCTAD (1987), 'The Exchange Rate System', in *International Monetary and Financial Issues for the Developing Countries* (Geneva: United Nations).

UNCTAD (1989–92), *Trade and Development Report*s (Geneva: United Nations).

Westphal, L. E. (1990), 'Industrial Policy in an Export-Propelled Economy: Lessons from South Korea's Experience', *Journal of Economic Perspectives*, Summer.

World Bank (1983), *Turkey. Special Economic Report. Policies for the Financial Sector*, Washington, DC.

World Bank (1988), *Adjustment Lending. An Evaluation of Ten Years of Experience*, Washington, DC.

Zimmer, S. A. and R. N., McCauley (1991), 'Bank Cost of Capital and International Competitiveness', *Federal Reserve Bank of New York Quarterly Bulletin*, Winter.

Part III

Country Studies in Trade Policy Reform

Part III

Country Studies in Trade Policy Reform

7 Trade Liberalization and Growth: The Chilean Experience, 1973–89[1]

Ricardo Ffrench-Davis, Patricio Leiva and Roberto Madrid

I INTRODUCTION

Many countries in Latin America have undertaken thorough-going efforts to restructure their economies and open them up to external trade because they see that this is the only way out of a crisis whose end is otherwise nowhere in sight. Against this backdrop, the Chilean experience can be regarded as an example of a long-term effort from which a number of lessons can be derived. In particular, the sacrifices made along the way and the costs paid over so many years – many of which could have been avoided, as we shall see in the following pages – should be borne very much in mind. The sweeping changes made in the Chilean economy have been implemented in a series of stages which span the period from 1973 to the present. The complexity and variety of the wealth of experience that has thus been gained in the micro- and macroeconomic spheres will be invaluable both in helping Chile to meet the many economic challenges it still faces and as an example for other countries that are now just beginning to undertake trade liberalization.

Chile is certainly not in chaos, but it is also far from being a miracle. The main conclusions presented in this chapter therefore aim to provide policy lessons and point to scenarios that can be expected during the implementation of liberalization. It is important to keep in mind that this experience was carried out within a particular historical, economic and political context, and that therefore policies that were applicable then cannot simply be extracted and applied without further thought to processes now under way in other countries in a democratic context.

II   THE MACROECONOMIC CONTEXT OF TRADE LIBERALIZATION

After the military coup of September 1973, economic policies underwent a radical transformation in Chile with the adoption of an orthodox experiment. As a result, exports expanded rapidly and became more diversified, the fiscal budget began to show either balance or a surplus, and inflation ended up being very low in comparison with the levels that were usual in the period towards the end of the 1980s. However, in the period 1974–89 internal reforms and the transmission of huge external shocks combined to produce what was, by the standards of the 1960s, a low average rate of economic growth, a fall in the investment rate, and a deterioration in the distribution of income and wealth.

An examination of the Chilean economy at the macroeconomic level leads to the identification of two sub-periods with significant differences, 1973–81 and 1982–9. The first corresponds to the putting in place of the 'pure' model, and during which the greater part of the process of deregulation and liberalization was accomplished. This included a strong dose of privatization of economic activities and the weakening of public economic policies. After the debt crisis of 1982, certain regulations were reintroduced, while at the same time the process of privatization was continued and large subsidies were given to private firms in financial distress. Throughout both periods, economic liberalization advanced hand in hand with the application of severe restrictions on political and social organizations. On the international front, Chile, as well as other developing countries, experienced the sharp external shocks of the mid-1970s and early 1980s. As a consequence of these external shocks and the nature of domestic economic policies, Chile experienced two great cycles, with deep recessions and vigorous recoveries (see Table 7.1).

The Main Reforms since 1973[2]

In 1973 the Chilean economy was experiencing sharp macroeconomic imbalances. The economy was also overregulated, and private and public firms alike were subject to excessive 'microeconomic' controls. The sheer magnitude of these imbalances and the inconsistency of previous interventionist measures prompted the application of an extreme orthodox approach after September 1973. The principal reforms related to fiscal matters, finance, external trade and the public

Table 7.1   Output, unemployment, wages and investment in Chile: peaks and troughs in the 1975 and 1982–3 recessions

	GDP	Per capita Manufacturing	Unemployment (%)	Real wages	Per capita public social spending	Investment rate[a] (%)
	(1)	(2)	(3)	(4)	(5)	(6)
1970	100.0	100.0	5.9	100.0	100.0	20.4
1974	101.6	101.2	9.1	65.0	75.9	17.4
1975	83.4	73.3	21.9[b]	62.9	61.9[b]	12.7
1981	109.6	84.6	15.1	97.6[c]	104.4[c]	19.4
1983	90.4	65.7[a]	31.3	83.2	84.0[d]	12.9
1989	117.4	91.1	9.1	92.0	91.2[e]	18.6

Notes: [a] Gross fixed capital formation as a percentage of GDP, expressed in pesos at 1977 prices.
[b] 1976.
[c] 1982.
[d] 1985.
[e] 1987.

Sources: Authors' calculations, based on Ffrench-Davis and Raczynski (1990) and CIEPLAN (1990).

ownership of the means of production. Measures adopted in the field of international trade included the elimination of virtually all non-tariff barriers and a rapid reduction of tariffs using a phased approach that brought tariff rates down from the very high simple average of 94 per cent in 1973 to a uniform 10 per cent tariff on all goods in 1979 (see Table 7.2). Along similar lines, trade liberalization measures resulted in the elimination of the existing mechanisms for partially blocking the transmission of external instability to the local economy. In the case of exports, the main policy tools used were the exchange rate and an across-the-board liberalization of imports. Between 1973 and 1979, exchange rate policy provided for a system of mini-devaluations; however, the monthly rate of devaluation began to lag behind the rate of inflation in 1976, and in mid-1979 the nominal rate was frozen as the authorities switched to a monetarist approach to the balance of payments which was expected to lower domestic inflation to international levels.

Far-reaching financial reforms were undertaken in 1975. Banks that had been nationalized under the preceding government were returned

Table 7.2   Real exchange rates, tariffs and real interest rates: Chile, 1970–89 (indexes [1977 = 100] and percentages)

| | Real exchange rate, deflated by | | Average tariff[c] | Real interest rate[d] |
	CPI^a	Wage index[b]		
1970	82.8	59.2	94.0[e]	6.7
1974	108.1	117.7	75.6	n.a.
1975	148.2	168.0	49.3	15.4
1976	119.8	130.4	35.6	51.2
1977	100.0	100.0	24.3	39.2
1978	111.0	104.3	14.8	35.1
1979	108.5	94.2	12.1	16.6
1980	94.7	75.6	10.1	12.2
1981	80.5	59.0	10.1	38.8
1982	93.5	68.7	10.1	35.1
1983	112.1	92.3	17.9	15.9
1984	115.5	95.0	24.4	11.3
1985	144.1	123.8	25.8	11.1
1986	162.7	136.9	20.1	7.7
1987	167.1	140.8	20.0	9.4
1988	174.0	138.5	15.1	7.4
1989	163.4	126.8	15.1	11.9

Notes: [a] Nominal exchange rate (pesos per US dollar), multiplied by external price index (EPI) and deflated by the consumer price index (CPI).
      [b] Nominal exchange rate, multiplied by the EPI and deflated by the wage index.
      [c] *Ad valorem* tariff rate in percentage.
      [d] Nominal short-term interest rate on loans, deflated by the CPI.
      [e] December 1973.

Sources: Central Bank of Chile and CIEPLAN (1990).

to private ownership. Interest rates were deregulated; all regulations concerning maturities and credit allocation were eliminated, new financial institutions were authorized to set up operations with few restrictions, and foreign banks were given easy access to the economy. Finally, the restrictions applying to capital movements were gradually eased as well.

The process of transferring the means of production – in both the manufacturing and agricultural sectors – to private ownership was equally intense. In the manufacturing sector, a huge increase in the flow of credit from international commercial banks supplied a substantial part of the financing which a few large Chilean economic groups needed to purchase the companies that were put up for sale. In the agricultural sector, about 30 per cent of the land that had been expropriated was returned to its former owners and 20 per cent was auctioned off to urban buyers. A scant 30 per cent of this land was parcelled out to peasants, many of whom later had to sell off all or part of their holdings. Indeed, a bustling land market grew up that later contributed to the modernization of an expanding segment of the sector and to the agricultural export drive. The prevailing inequality of opportunity led to the impoverishment of many small-scale farmers, the bankruptcy of a number of cooperatives and the displacement of many peasant farmers, who were pushed off the land that was covered by the reforms.

Results: 1973–81

Even official figures show that overall economic growth in 1973–81 was slow, and its pattern reflected the resulting vulnerability of the economy. First, in 1975 Chile slipped into a severe domestic recession which had the effect of trebling the recessionary effects of the deterioration in the country's terms of trade. The result was a 13 per cent decline in GDP. For the period 1974–81 as a whole, the average annual growth rate was only 2.6 per cent, which was just 1 per cent more than the population growth rate (see Table 7.1).

Secondly, the rate of gross fixed capital formation (as a percentage of GDP) for 1974–81 was below that which the historical figures indicate as 'normal' levels and, since the share accounted for by foreign capital rose, the performance of national saving was even worse than it would otherwise appear to be. Investment was low for a number of reasons. High interest rates were an important factor, but the drop in public investment also played a significant role, as did the swift liberalization of imports (which pushed up the relative cost of imported capital goods, discouraged the domestic production of importables[3] and sharply boosted imports of consumer goods) and the low rate of capacity utilization. Thus, employment prospects and the outlook for wage hikes were dimmed by the low level of investment and capacity utilization.

Thirdly, the external debt burgeoned after 1976 as the domestic economy accommodated itself to a mounting deficit on current account. In 1981, the deficit was equivalent to 18 per cent of GDP,[4] which was more than double the figure for Latin America as a whole. With a frozen exchange rate, an absence of non-tariff barriers, a uniform 10 per cent tariff and easy access to foreign credit, the economy fell victim to rapidly mounting disequilibria. Unlike other countries that channelled external financing to investment, Chile did not embark upon a 'debt-led economic growth process';[5] instead, it ran up a 'debt-led deficit on current account' which adversely affected domestic production and investment, as imports crowded out nationally produced goods from the domestic market. On the one hand, inflation was held in check, the public-sector budget was balanced, exports soared and a modern sector of firms and entrepreneurs was beginning to account for a larger and larger share of production; on the other hand, severe trade imbalances were building up, as was a considerable external debt, unemployment was high and the investment rate was below the average coefficient recorded for the 1960s. As for the social situation, income and wealth were heavily concentrated in the upper strata of the population at the expense (in absolute terms) of the great majority of the people. Unemployment climbed to an average of 18 per cent in 1975–81, the percentage of 'informal' workers increased, and average wages were below their 1970 level in each and every year of the period in question.

The 1982–3 Recession and Subsequent Recovery

When the international crisis broke out in the early 1980s, the trade and current-account deficits were extremely large and debt, measured as a percentage of GDP, was one of the highest of all developing countries. Thus Chile had to cope with the downturn in international trade and financial flows at precisely the same time that it found itself obliged to find a way of sharply reducing its external deficit.

The limitation of developing countries' access to external financing in the early 1980s was accompanied, in Chile's case, by a steep drop in copper prices, an urgent need for fresh funds, a government that trusted so much in the automatic adjustment effect of the 'dollar standard' that it had abandoned all other mechanisms of economic regulation, and a weakened production system that was overloaded with debt. Consequently, the external shock – which was strong in and of itself – was magnified within the domestic economy, and GDP (even after allowing for the deterioration of the terms of trade) plunged by 14 per cent in 1982.[6] Manufacturing again suffered a severe blow, as value added fell by 22 per cent. In fact, the drop in output was the largest in all of Latin America.

Economic performance in 1982 and the following years was very similar to what it had been during and after the 1975 recession (see Table 7.1). Production slumped sharply in 1982, as did employment and investment. Later on, all three variables began to make a gradual recovery. As late as 1989, however, real wages (and the real minimum wage as well) were still below their 1970 levels.The thrust of economic policies remained basically the same with some minor changes in recognition of some of the glaring errors committed during the most dogmatic phase of laissez-faire.

Production capacity did not experience rapid growth during this period, except in the export sector; yet the substantial expansion and diversification of exports was not sufficient *per se* to galvanize the rest of the economy. This trend is consistent with the overall stagnation of per capita GDP since the early 1970s. In 1982–7, for example, the increase in installed capacity is estimated to have been only slightly greater than the 1.7 per cent annual rate of population growth (Marfán and Artiagoitía, 1989). The investment rate rose only in 1988–9, and it allowed an estimated expansion of installed capacity to an annual rate of about 3.5 per cent for the biennium.

III THE EFFECTS OF LIBERALIZATION ON GROWTH

The effects of foreign trade policy on economic growth are multi-faceted. Trade policy certainly influences the efficiency of activities producing tradeables. A greater exposure to outside competition clearly tends to boost the productivity of the surviving firms. The overall net impact is less clear cut, however. Are the factors of production that had been used in the activities that were hurt by increased competition speedily reallocated to other activities or do they remain idle for a long time? Does the sum total of new investment opportunities increase or decrease? Is the development of new comparative advantages facilitated or hampered? Does the increased competition involve unfair practices, such as dumping, and hinder an efficient allocation of resources owing to highly unstable prices? What happens to macroeconomic efficiency while an economy adjusts to external shocks? Some of these questions will be addressed in this section on the basis of a review of Chile's experience in these respects.

Traditional approaches generally characterize the liberalization of imports as an essential component of export growth. Exchange rate adjustments are to be used as a means of striking a balance between the growth of imports and exports. This will supposedly ensure that the negative impact that the reversal of the import substitution process may have on domestic production will not outweigh the positive impact of the expansion of exports. In order to determine the relative intensity of these two forces during the 1970s, the lag in the real exchange rate that resulted from the nominal exchange rate freeze of 1979 must be excluded. This is done by considering events only up to 1979.

The Volume and Structure of Imports

In the course of the sweeping changes during this period imports were affected by a number of variables outside the sphere of import policy. Among the most important factors were the sharp contraction of aggregate demand in 1975–6, the low level of investment throughout this period, and the rise in oil prices.[7] Thus the pattern of imports was influenced by a series of rapidly changing variables, of which the reduction of tariffs was only one.

The choice of a base year for purposes of comparison is difficult and, inevitably, somewhat arbitrary. Therefore, Table 7.3 gives data for all the years during which the policy associated with this period was applied, as well as for the immediately preceding year. As is well known, however, 1973 was quite abnormal in many respects, and

Table 7.3   Imports: Chile, 1970–9 (millions of dollars at 1977 prices)

		1970	1973	1974	1976	1978	1979
I.	Consumer goods, food	107.4	267.7	85.5	51.8	115.7	130.2
II.	Consumer goods, non-food	191.6	199.3	236.8	114.4	410.7	528.7
III.	Capital goods	550.2	360.8	336.3	443.0	566.6	668.7
	Breeding stock	16.3	13.2	3.9	1.0	2.1	2.5
	Machinery and equipment	380.9	225.9	244.7	256.6	321.6	378.4
	Transport equipment	153.0	121.7	87.7	185.4	242.9	287.8
	(ships, boats and aircraft)	(50.2)	(3.9)	(66.6)	(77.6)	(77.2)	. . .
IV.	Intermediate goods	1,005.2	1,322.1	1,769.7	1,253.5	1,575.8	1,925.9
	Wheat	26.7	123.8	308.1	182.3	144.5	105.7
	Maize	6.4	5.1	32.7	10.0	28.5	20.9
	Fuels and lubricants	114.7	199.9	329.3	422.5	419.9	681.5
	Other	907.4	1,073.3	1,099.6	638.7	982.9	1,117.8
V.	TOTAL	1,904.4	2,149.9	2,428.3	1,862.7	2,668.8	3,253.5

Source: Ffrench-Davis (1986), table 3.

figures are therefore shown for 1970, a relatively 'normal' year. Total imports climbed by 71 per cent between 1970 and 1979, while total imports other than fuels and lubricants expanded by 44 per cent (23 per cent in per capita terms). These figures seem quite modest in view of the fact that an entire decade had passed and that the liberalization effort was so comprehensive. Three factors need to be taken into account, however. First, rising oil prices are a permanent fact of life for Chile, and it therefore has no choice but to find some way of financing the larger outlays required, whether by reducing other imports or expanding its exports. Secondly, even in 1979 imports of machinery and equipment were still too low to sustain historical economic growth rates. Thirdly, per capita GDP exhibited nearly zero growth during the period in question. The result of all this was that, measured in points of GDP, imports other than machinery and equipment grew by 52 per cent between 1970 and 1979.

In sum, total imports, measured in terms of constant purchasing power, rose significantly in relation to the level of domestic economic activity. This was to be expected, given the scope of the import liberalization effort. Since per capita output was virtually unchanged, the increase in imports was not the result of an income effect but rather primarily of the liberalization and of exogenous changes in the supply and demand of importables (e.g. oil prices and changes in the distribution of income and wealth).

The performance of the various import items differed a great deal. The influence of liberalization, in the aggregate, is apparent mainly in the category of non-food consumer goods, which included most of the country's 'non-traditional' imports. Compared to the above-mentioned 44 per cent increase in imports other than fuel and lubricants between 1970 and 1979, imports of non-food consumer goods jumped by 176 per cent, accounting for 43 per cent of the real increase in imports.[8] As a consequence of this rapid growth, consumer goods came to represent 20 per cent of all imports, which was more than total imports of machinery and equipment.

Imports of machinery and equipment showed no growth between 1970 and 1979, while their share of the total slipped from 20 per cent to 12 per cent. Similarly, their share of GDP (aggregate demand at constant terms of trade) shrank by one-fifth. This decline is a reflection of the low level of investment associated with the economic policy pursued during this period. It is quite probable that this investment trend was not unrelated to the abrupt and extreme manner in which imports were liberalized, as will be discussed later on.

Most of the 'non-traditional' imports were made up of what are usually regarded as non-essential consumer goods. In many cases, the new imported products were not produced locally, although they did take the place of other domestically produced items. Hence, a significant diversification of consumption did in fact take place.

In spite of this marked diversification of imports in terms of product types and models, the consumption of the fastest-growing imports was highly concentrated. This is, of course, related to the concentration of income and wealth; it should be noted, however, that, by income bracket, the consumption of the importables in question is even more concentrated than is total consumption (see Ffrench-Davis, 1986). Obviously, the low-income sectors of the population did indeed gain access to new varieties and new consumer products, but the extent of that access was limited by their low income levels.

Overall Effects of Liberalization on Manufacturing

Evaluating the effects of the liberalization process is a highly complex undertaking. First of all, each one of its stages seems to have had widely differing impacts. Secondly, many other major changes took place concurrently with the liberalization effort. On the one hand, aggregate demand and wages slumped, unemployment was high and fixed capital investment was low, all of which plays a crucial role in determining the nature of the adjustment process. On the other hand, the expansion of exports, which began before the liberalization had gained momentum, helped to bring about some increase in economic activity and to open up investment opportunities in the sector. Finally, in 1979 the adjustment process was still under way.

Manufacturing was severely affected by recession in 1975. In 1979, after the reforms had been in place for six years, value added in the manufacturing sector was 8 per cent lower than it had been in 1974 and was 15 per cent lower in per capita terms. Its share of GDP fell sharply from 26 to 20 per cent. The decline was also reflected in employment within the sector, which remained far below its 1970 level between 1976 and 1979. This was partly attributable to the decline in the market position of labour-intensive manufacturing activities, such as those of the textiles and clothing industries, but employment also slipped in branches of industry whose gross output rose. Obviously, the liberalization of imports did not 'destroy' industry, but it did play a role in the poor overall performance turned in by the sector, and by the economy as a whole, between 1973 and 1979.

The manufacturing sector adapted to external competition in three ways. One was simply to declare bankruptcy or to close down industrial plants. In other cases, a greater degree of intra-industry specialization was attained either through business mergers or, less ambitiously, via the suspension of product lines within a firm. Finally, many surviving firms not only cut down on their number of product lines but also began to import the products they used to produce.

Dynamism and Efficiency

It has already been noted that the speed of the adjustment seems to have been different in those sectors that were hurt by the change in trade policy and those that benefited from it. Presumably, its reallocative signals came through more clearly for the former, and the message was reinforced by the widespread downturn in aggregate demand and high interest rates, which reached annual levels of nearly 40 per cent in real terms (see Table 7.2). This further jeopardized the continued survival of the firms in these sectors, regardless of how efficient they might have been under 'normal' or socially optimal conditions.

A very low rate of gross domestic investment added to the asymmetry of the adjustment. Obviously, adjustment is easier with high growth rates. Stagnation made it necessary for many of the adversely affected sectors to undergo a contraction in absolute terms in order for a relative adjustment to be accomplished. Furthermore, the relative lack of sectoral and regional mobility of resources and the low rate of investment hindered an effective reallocation of the resources that became available as a result of that contraction.

The only counterbalancing factor was the expansion of the export sector, which began to absorb an increasing share of what little domestic investment there was. This investment had previously been concentrated in natural-resource intensive activities, while activities with greater value added were of less significance. Indeed, it has proved easier to identify comparative advantages with a clearly defined natural resource base than to ascertain what other types of comparative advantages might be developed. This was one of the reasons why the rate of domestic investment was so low during the period.

Competition and Efficiency

Increased competition within the domestic market was one of the expected results of the liberalization of imports. This was to be achieved by means of the potential or actual presence of importables, which would in effect put a 'cap' on domestic prices – and, to a significant extent, this is exactly what did occur. Clearly, the sectors that survived tended to be more efficient than the average firm was prior to the reform. In fact, taken as a group, the surviving businesses are more modern, flexible and innovative than the average pre-reform firm. However, they are also smaller and account for less value added.

Moreover, there were major departures from the types of relationships associated with a 'competitive' economy. First, a considerable percentage of the 'non-traditional' imports were items in which product differentiation plays a decisive role. In those cases, competition among suppliers therefore focused on product differentiation rather than on sales price; the segmentation of the capital market (i.e. gaps between domestic and external interest rates) also added an element of 'competition' in the credit terms for such sales. Secondly, marketing channels were not completely open to potential entrants and, as a result, in a number of cases import-substituting enterprises began to import products that competed with the goods they produced. Thirdly, trade liberalization fostered a greater concentration of the management and ownership of domestic production activities; this process was furthered by the contraction of aggregate demand and by the way in which the capital market operated, in that it gave a significant advantage to economic groups with ties to financial activities and access to external credit. Finally, in the case of commodities such as wheat and sugar, domestic prices were put in line with external prices, but instability increased. The elimination of 'water' in the tariffs and the absence of non-tariff stabilizing mechanisms meant that fluctuations in world markets were rapidly transmitted to the Chilean economy. Thus, production was exposed to international price swings and to dumping, which can prompt an inefficient reallocation of resources, as well as creating a situation in which economic agents fail to take advantage of investment opportunities that could help to promote development.

In the final analysis, the lessons to be learned from Chile's experiences in the 1970s point in a heterodox direction. Before the reforms, a large number of importable products were over-protected; in consequence, a major trade liberalization drive was called for, as was an effort to seek a more dynamic form of complementarity between import substitution and export promotion. However, the liberalization programme went overboard and was poorly timed. What was lacking, as in other areas of economic policy, was an adaptation of theoretical postulates to the specific features of the Chilean economy. Finally, the conventional hypothesis that indiscriminate liberalization will promote the expansion of labour-intensive activities and the contraction of capital-intensive ones appears to have been at least partially refuted by the types of changes that occurred in the production structure and the rate of utilization of available resources. This may have been linked to the timing of the trade liberalization initiative, its excessive intensity and indiscriminate implementation, and the passive role imposed upon the public sector.

IV   MACROECONOMIC ADJUSTMENT: 1981–9

In the early 1980s, the country suffered three major external shocks. The strongest had to do with external capital flows, which, after having climbed to 18 per cent of GDP, plunged to half that figure in 1982 and to one-fourth their former level in 1983. Clearly, the 18 per cent figure registered in 1981 was the result of a blatant error on the part of economic policy-makers, who allowed the economy to overborrow. Indeed, ever since 1977 the Chilean economy had been adapting both its production structure and spending patterns to a level of capital inflows that was simply unsustainable over the medium term. Thus, even without the international debt crisis, an adjustment would still have been necessary in the immediate future (Ffrench-Davis, 1983). The second shock was delivered in the form of an increase in interest payments which arose out of both greater indebtedness and higher interest rates. The third was the deterioration of the terms of trade, which was led by the drop in copper prices.

In conjunction with these external shocks, a severe domestic recession hit the economy in 1982. Aggregate demand had far outstripped domestic production when a drop was registered in international reserves owing to the effects of the above-mentioned external shocks. Then, the 'automatic adjustment' in the money supply triggered by the decrease in reserves sparked a steep drop in domestic liquidity and in aggregate demand.[9] This, in turn, led to a drop in the rate of capital formation, as well as causing per capita GDP to plummet by 15.5 per cent in 1982 (the largest decrease in all of Latin America). Economic activity and investment gradually recovered in the years that followed.

In an ideal adjustment process, excess aggregate demand can be eliminated without reducing production (or, more accurately, the growth rate). In a perfectly flexible economy, the decline in production, if any, should be negligible. On the other hand, in an economy that starts out with under-utilization of its production capacity for tradeables, an adjustment that includes a suitable dose of reallocative policies may lead to an increase in the rate of resource use and in production. In an economy with inflexible prices and imperfect factor mobility, however, 'neutral' policies to curb demand – i.e. even-handed policies which lead to a decrease in all components of expenditure alike – may result in a significant slide in production. This is because they dampen demand for tradeables as well as non-tradeables, thereby prompting lower utilization of installed capacity and a slowdown in the rate at which new production capacity is created.

Selective policies that have reallocative effects in terms of the *composition* of both production and expenditure can soften the impact of the decrease in output. The right combination of spending cuts and reallocation policies can allow a result that is closer to a constant rate of utilization of potential GDP (see Ffrench-Davis and Marfán, 1989). Clearly, if there is an excess of expenditure over production capacity, as was the case in 1981, aggregate demand must be curtailed. However, this can be done in conjunction with the implementation of reallocation policies that will bring down the demand for tradeables more sharply than the demand for non-tradeables while also helping to boost the supply of tradeables and investment.

An 'automatic adjustment' mechanism such as that used in 1982 relies heavily on the shock effects of policies to reduce demand. Generally speaking, after an abrupt fall in domestic expenditures some spontaneous reallocation in the composition of supply and demand does eventually take place; and in an 'orderly' economy, that reallocation tends to gain momentum with the passage of time. This endogenous reallocation was furthered by a number of sizeable devaluations which went beyond making up for the deterioration of the real exchange rate up to 1982. This real devaluation was carried out gradually by means of a series of 'jumps' in the crawling peg then in use. These measures made possible, given the scale of the external shocks, a gradual recovery of production and expenditure. None the less, in 1988 per capita GDP was still 1 per cent below its 1981 level, while per capita investment was still 14 per cent lower. Production levels in 1988 were, of course, determined by the average rate of investment during the whole of the adjustment period, which was just 14.9 per cent of GDP for 1982–8.

In the external sector, the effects of the automatic adjustment were initially felt more keenly in the form of a decrease in imports, while exports rose more slowly; as was to be expected, imports were more elastic than exports in response to the sharp fall in domestic expenditure. This was reinforced by the considerable depreciation of the currency entailed by a real increase in the price of the dollar of nearly 100 per cent between 1981 and 1985. The decision to raise the uniform tariff temporarily from 10 to 35 per cent worked in the same direction. In this case, too, the passage of time brought a change in the behaviour of exports and imports. Thanks to the stimulus provided by the significant depreciation of the currency, exports expanded more swiftly during the final portion of the adjustment period. The average per capita volume of merchandise exports for 1982–9 was 23 per cent above the 1981 level and, in 1989, the export index was 56 per cent higher than its 1980 peak,[10] while per capita GDP was only then rising above its 1981 level. As a result, the exports/GDP coefficient climbed by nearly 40 per cent between 1980 and 1989 to one-third of GDP; however, this development was accompanied by a quite modest expansion of per capita output, which did not manage to overtake its previous 1981 peak level until 1989.

Hence, this was not a case of export-led economic growth but rather quite the opposite: an export boom prompted by external constraints and a recessionary adjustment of production. This adjustment also brought about a reallocation of a fairly constant pool of resources.[11] The rapid growth of exports did, of course, contribute to the economic recovery, but it was not great enough to offset the decline in the production of non-exportables. None the less, this strong export performance provided a foundation for future economic growth.

V LESSONS OF THE CHILEAN EXPERIENCE

In examining Chile's experience, a distinction must be drawn between two different phases. The first, during which sweeping reforms were introduced in trade policy (and in many other fields as well), began in 1974 and ended with the crisis of 1981–2. The second phase spans the years from 1982 to 1989. This period began with a severe recession which prompted the formulation of more pragmatic policies and the rectification of the more blatant policy errors committed during the preceding years.

The reforms launched in late 1973 and early 1974 were meant to overcome serious macroeconomic imbalances reflected in high inflation coupled with a deep recession. Trade liberalization boosted exports, but at the same time acted as a strong disincentive for import-substitution activities and did, in fact, bring about a reversal of import substitution that proved to be more powerful than the export drive. This facet of liberalization tended to depress economic activity even more.

In the second phase (1982–9), the factors promoting an expansion of exports proved to be much stronger than those giving rise to a reversal of import substitution. This turnabout is attributable to the fact that the economy had by this time already carried out its trade liberalization programme. Tariffs even rose somewhat, which stimulated import substitution. In addition, the average real exchange rate (pesos per dollar) was considerably higher in the 1980s than it had been in the 1970s.

Another element that sets the two phases of this process apart is the fact that only the most powerful companies survived into the second phase because shaky firms, as well as businesses that under normal circumstances might have been profitable, had gone bankrupt. Hence, most firms in the export sector and the surviving companies in the manufacturing sector are, today, for the most part, quick-reacting, powerful, dynamic enterprises. The high costs of this process in terms of bankruptcies and the disarray of the production structure could perhaps have been avoided if exchange rate policy had been more realistic, trade liberalization had been more gradual, and international capital movements had been controlled more carefully.

It is important to note that during the trade reform implemented in the 1970s, exchange rate policy was at odds with trade policy. As is well known, the adverse effect that reductions in tariffs and other import restrictions have on economic activity can be offset by a real devaluation. Such a devaluation helps to reallocate resources, shifting them away from non-tradeable or highly protected goods and services and towards other tradeables that receive little or no protection. In other words, a compensatory devaluation facilitates the development of exports and of efficient import substitution. In Chile, non-tariff barriers were dismantled and both average tariff rates and tariff dispersion were sharply reduced, but the dampening effects of the liberalization on the relative prices of tradeables as a whole were not counterbalanced by a real devaluation; on the contrary, the local currency rose steeply in real terms.

This was a result in part of the fact that trade liberalization was accompanied by other significant changes in economic policy, particularly external financial liberalization. Large capital inflows beginning in 1977 allowed the authorities to carry out a real revaluation (see Table 7.2). In addition, in 1976 the authorities began to use the nominal exchange rate as a tool in their fight against inflation. Gradually, this led (in 1979) to fixing the nominal exchange rate. Contrary to the government's expectations, however, domestic inflation did not converge fast enough to international levels, which meant that the real exchange rate (pesos per dollar) declined sharply. Heavy borrowing from international banks sustained the reorientation of exchange rate policy.

This mismatch between a liberalization-oriented trade policy and an exchange rate policy that played an increasingly important role as a monetary and anti-inflationary tool was one of the reasons why the disincentives to import substitution outweighed the incentives for export growth or more efficient production for the domestic market. The financial liberalization that accompanied the liberalization of trade was also a decisive factor. The lessons to be drawn from this are quite clear: to a major extent, the success of a liberalization scheme and the costs it entails are determined by how the exchange rate is handled; in addition, the degrees of freedom for determining the real exchange rate are influenced by policies towards international financial flows.

An examination of the overall performance of the Chilean economy reveals that GDP grew at an annual rate of 2.6 per cent during both phases, but this figure is a weighted average of periods of very slow growth and of very rapid growth. This low average annual growth rate is accounted for by the low investment rate that characterized both periods.[12] When investment is low, it becomes much more difficult to restructure supply than it would otherwise be; therefore, under such circumstances, a sudden liberalization of imports tends to engender an adjustment process whereby the economy moves very gradually from inefficient forms of production (the result of protectionism) towards the optimum production frontier, but it will do so by recessionary means and will lose a great deal of production potential along the way. By the end of this process, the economy will have arrived at a point on that frontier where it is more intensive in tradeables and, within that category, in exportables, but it will have sacrificed a great deal of production potential in the course of the adjustment.

As for the behaviour of investment, it is usually the case that, at the time that trade reforms are initiated, imports of consumer goods are severely restricted; in heavily protected economies, imports of capital goods, on the other hand, are normally duty free. Therefore, the logical outcome of a reform that includes a devaluation and the application of a uniform tariff to all imports, even if it is low, is that capital goods will become more expensive as a consequence of the tariff and devaluation whereas consumer goods will become less expensive. In other words, the signals sent out by changes in relative prices encourage consumption and discourage investment. If the possibility that these adverse forces may materialize is borne in mind, however, mechanisms can be found to neutralize them.

With regard to the issue of graduality, it is not a question of reforming everything gradually or doing everything suddenly. There are some measures that should be implemented rapidly. If a country has a fixed exchange rate, it should change over to a crawling peg and should do so in one go. If tariffs are too high and redundant, all the 'water' can be eliminated at a single blow. The substitution of tariffs for quantitative restrictions can be done abruptly as well. In the remaining areas, however, a gradual programme, pursued in a way that will lend it credibility, is the best means of ensuring that adjustments will be made along the production frontier and of promoting its more rapid expansion. Even in cases where it appears that the entire reform programme can only be implemented suddenly, because otherwise it will lose political credibility, it is necessary to be aware of the costs of doing so and to have an idea of how long the population will have to bear those costs. The decision to embark upon liberalization should not be arrived at in a vacuum, but rather in the light of its possible effects on resource allocation and economic growth. Reform is not an objective in and of itself, but rather a means of achieving development with social equity.

Notes

1. Translation by Diane Frischman is gratefully acknowledged.
2. This is an overview. A more detailed analysis of the model and a wide range of references are found in Ffrench-Davis (1982), Foxley (1982), Ramos (1986) and Vergara (1985). The distributive aspects are summarized in Ffrench-Davis and Raczynski (1990). A discussion of the situation as it stood in 1973 appears in Bitar (1979). Foxley (1982) and Ramos (1986) undertake a comparative analysis with other 'neo-conservative' experiments in Latin America. See also Balassa (1985), Corbo (1985) and Harberger (1982) for analyses that are more in keeping with the views of the authorities of that period. Official reports and addresses are to be found in the Central Bank's *Estudios Monetarios* series and in publications of the Ministry of Finance.

3. Despite the growth and diversification of exports, their response to these trade and financial reforms was much weaker than that of imports.
4. Figures are at 1977 prices.
5. See Bacha (1983) for a comparison of the strategies used by Argentina, Brazil, Chile, Colombia and Mexico.
6. According to official national accounts, the deterioration in the terms of trade was equivalent to 4.7 per cent of GDP between 1980 and 1982. Capital movements in 1982 were US$ 2.3 billion lower than in 1981, but were somewhat higher than in 1980.
7. The figures given in the following discussion, unless otherwise indicated, do not include imports brought into the country through its customs-free areas owing to the difficulty of obtaining information on these transactions. The figures, expressed in dollars at current prices, have been deflated by the external price index (Ffrench-Davis, 1984).
8. The figures for the period during which the bulk of the liberalization measures were implemented, i.e. 1973–9, are 164 per cent and 61 per cent respectively.
9. It should be remembered that, at the time, policy-maters were following the monetary approach to the balance of payments. The nominal exchange rate was fixed and monetary policy was passive.
10. It should be noted that in 1981 the volume of exports was on the decline due to exchange rate appreciation. The rate of utilization of export production capacity made a rapid comeback in 1982–3, however, following the devaluations that were carried out during those two years.
11. Between 1981 and 1989, per capita exports of goods climbed by 10.4 points (25.3–14.9). Since per capita GDP grew by 7.1 points (107.1–99.0), it is calculated that the remaining (non-export) per capita GDP declined by 3.3 points. See Ffrench-Davis, Leiva and Madrid (1991), table V.4.
12. Without a doubt, the productivity of capital is much greater today than it was in the 1970s. This is a reflection of the increased competition to which the economy was exposed when it was opened up to foreign trade, since this motivated economic agents to become more innovative and to make greater use of economies of scale.

Bibliography

Bacha, E. (1983), 'Apertura Financiera y Su Efecto en el Desarrollo Nacional', in R. Ffrench-Davis, ed., *Relaciones Financieras Externas: Su Efecto en La Economía Latinoamericana* (Mexico City: Fondo de Cultura Económica).

Balassa, B. (1985), 'Policy Experiments in Chile, 1973–83', in G. Walton, ed., *The National Economic Policies of Chile* (Connecticut: J.A.I. Press).

Bitar, S. (1979), 'Transición, socialismo y Democracia: La Experiencia Chilena', Siglo XXI, Mexico City.

Cieplan (1990), 'Set de Estadísticas Económicas', Santiago, May–June.

Corbo, V. (1985), 'Reforms and Macroeconomic Adjustment in Chile during 1974–84', *World Development*, August.

Ffrench-Davis, R. (1982), 'El Experimento Monetarista en Chile: Una Síntesis Crítica', *Colección Estudios CIEPLAN*, No. 9, Santiago, December; also published in English in *World Development*, November 1983.

Ffrench-Davis, R. (1983), 'El Problema de la Deuda Externa y la Apertura Financiera en Chile', in ICI, ed., *América Latina: Deuda, Crisis y Perspectivas*, Madrid, 1984; in M. Wionczek, ed., *Politics and Economics of the External Debt Crisis* (Boulder: Westview Press, 1985); and in *Colección Estudios CIEPLAN*, No. 11, Santiago, December.

Ffrench-Davis, R. (1984), 'Indice de Precios Externos: Un Indicador para Chile de la Inflación Internacional, 1952–83', *Colección Estudios CIEPLAN*, No. 13, Santiago, June.

Ffrench-Davis, R. (1986), 'Import Liberalization: The Chilean Experience, 1973–82', in J. S. and A. Valenzuela, eds, *Military Rule in Chile*, (Baltimore and London: The Johns Hopkins University Press) (an earlier version was published in *Colección Estudios CIEPLAN*, No. 4, Santiago, December 1980).

Ffrench-Davis, R., P. Leiva and R. Madrid (1991), 'La Apertura Comercial en Chile: Experiencias y Perspectivas', *Estudios de Política Comercial*, No. 1, UNCTAD, Geneva.

Ffrench-Davis, R., and M. Marfán (1989), 'Selective Policies under a Structural Foreign Exchange Shortage', *Journal of Development Economics*, Vol. 29.

Ffrench-Davis, R., and D. Raczynski (1990), 'The Impact of Global Recession on Living Standards: Chile 1973–1989', *Notas Técnicas*, No. 97, CIEPLAN, Santiago, February.

Foxley, A. (1982), 'Experimentos Neoliberales en América Latina', *Colección Estudios CIEPLAN*, No. 7, Santiago, March, special issue.

Harberger, A. (1982), 'Crisis, Stabilization, Reform', in K. Brunner and A. Meltzer, eds, *Economic Policy in a World of Change*, Carnegie Rochester Conference Series on Public Policy, Vol. 17.

Marfán, M., and P. Artiagoitía (1989), 'Estimación del PGB Potencial: Chile 1960–1988', *Colección Estudios CIEPLAN*, No. 27, Santiago, December.

Ramos, J. (1986), *Neoconservative Economics in The Southern Cone of Latin America, 1973–83* (Baltimore: The Johns Hopkins University Press).

Vergara, P. (1985), 'Auge y Caída del Neoliberalismo en Chile', FLACSO, Santiago.

8 Trade Policy and Economic Performance in South Korea

Alice H. Amsden[1]

F13, 019

I THE IMPORTANCE OF HARD-TO-QUANTIFY SUBSIDIES

Beginning in the early 1980s, both Korea and Taiwan set the goal of liberalizing their capital markets and foreign trade. But according to Yung Chul Park, a former Korean government economic adviser, 'In spite of this, the two economies have hardly followed classical liberal principles of laissez-faire' (Park, 1991, p. 152). Park goes on to argue:

> Policymakers have been by and large passive and conservative in liberalizing the Korean and Taiwan economies, in that they have implemented reforms mostly when they were forced to do so by internal and external developments. Even when they were compelled to liberalize, they were reluctant to make policy changes unless disruptions to the economy could be minimized.

Park concludes: 'Ever since the outward-looking strategy was launched, liberalization has been carried out on most occasions to attain certain policy objectives, *such as improved growth or stability,* and seldom for the sake of improving the allocative efficiency of the economy [emphasis added]' (p. 153).

All this creates something of a conundrum. If, according to Park, the Korean and Taiwan governments liberalized for reasons of improving 'growth or stability', then for what reasons did they intervene and depart from the free market paradigm in the first place? Were their interventions superfluous, or were they also related to growth and stability?

The conventional wisdom is that if a developing country 'gets the prices right' and follows its comparative advantage in exporting, then there is no need for government intervention, certainly not on the scale found in Korea and Taiwan. Governments may have to create the institutional framework necessary for a market economy to work, and to invest in infrastructure, the environment, and a 'social safety net.' But not much more, as the World Bank's chief economist, Lawrence Summers, warned (Summers, 1992).

Korea is generally regarded, justifiably, as having got its exchange rate 'right' in its 1964–5 reforms. Professor Kwang-Suk Kim, an expert on Korean trade policy, observes that the reforms established a 'more realistic official exchange rate'. He further notes that, thereafter, 'Although Korea had experienced substantial price inflation, particularly until 1982, the PPP-adjusted official exchange rate did not show any wide fluctuation over more than two decades, indicating that the nominal exchange rate was often adjusted to prevent any significant overvaluation of the "won" currency' (Kim, 1991b, pp. 15–16).

Nevertheless, despite a more realistic exchange rate, the Korean government still intervened extensively to support import substitutes, exports and, *a fortiori*, exports of import-substitution products. The relationship between the nominal market exchange rate and domestic inflation was such that from 1966 through to 1980, the real private cost in Korea of borrowing abroad was negative (Park, 1985). This is one example of a handsome subsidy to those targeted firms lucky enough to be allocated foreign loans (domestic commercial bank credit was also negatively priced in the 1970s and was also allocated at the government's discretion).

Did Korea and Taiwan deviate from liberal policies for non-economic reasons, or because markets did not generate the industrial development that conventional theory predicts?

In addition to reviewing Korea's trade 'liberalization' policies, the purpose of this chapter is to try to answer the question of why the Korean government had to intervene in trade matters at all.

As discussed next with respect to Korea's 1964–5 trade reforms and export promotion generally, the degree to which the government did, in fact, subsidize exports is still open to question despite extensive empirical work. The degree of subsidization is contentious because its measurement is sensitive to how net *indirect* subsidies are handled. Westphal (1978), Krueger (1979), and Kim (1991a and 1991b) all found that *net* export subsidies (which exclude subsidies that simply offset barriers to importing at world prices) accounted for only a very small proportion of the effective exchange rate and were eliminated entirely after 1982 (see Table 8.1). Their measures, however, generally excluded net *indirect* subsidies. If one includes not just direct subsidies to exports

Table 8.1 Purchasing-power-parity adjusted effective exchange rates for exports and imports: Korea 1965–90 (direct subsidies only)

Year	Official rate	Effective rate for		Anti-export bias	Export subsidy size
		Exports	Imports		
	(1)	(2)	(3)	(4)	(5)
1965	265.4	275.3	293.1	0.94	.036
1970	240.2	256.2	260.0	0.99	.062
1973	320.6	327.6	336.2	0.97	.021
1975	274.4	281.7	288.5	0.98	.026
1978	272.0	278.2	296.1	0.94	.022
1980	250.1	260.0	265.7	0.98	.038
1983	264.5	264.5	283.6	0.93	.000
1985	290.6	290.6	307.4	0.95	.000
1988	319.3	319.3	341.0	0.94	.000
1990	289.1	289.1	305.2	0.95	.000

(1) Official rate × purchasing power parity (PPP) index.
(2) PPP index × effective rate for exports which is measured as official exchange rate plus net export subsidies per US dollar of exports. *Net* export subsidies are net of subsidies to imports to arrive at a free trade price for imports. They include direct cash subsidies (in effect in 1958–64), export dollar premia (1958–61 and 1963–4), direct tax reduction on export income (1962–73) and export (working capital only) credits (1958–82) (Kim, 1991a, p. 33).
(3) PPP × official exchange rate plus actual tariffs and tariff equivalents per US dollar of imports.
(4) (2)/(3).
(5) [(2)−(1)]/(2).
Source: Calculated from Kim (1991b, p. 17).

(say, preferential export credit and export income tax exemptions), but also indirect subsidies (such as negatively priced credit for long-term investment), then the extensiveness of subsidies is far greater than they report.

The uncertainties inherent in attributing indirect subsidies to either export or import substitution activity also complicate the measurement of trade bias. Kim (1991b) has argued that between 1965 and 1990, Korea's trade policies demonstrated a slight but persistent *anti-export* bias (see Table 8.1). If indirect net subsidies are included, this anti-export bias would increase, if only because most indirect subsidies (say, government support of targeted industries by means of inexpensive land sites or preferential long-term credit) are oriented towards lowering investment costs, and investments in the early stages of growth are for import substitution (or to satisfy domestic demand generally). Exports, if they occur, usually follow import substitution with a time lag (only the most labour-intensive goods may be able to begin exporting at once). Therefore, it is plausible to attribute investment subsidies to import substitution activity rather than to export activity. If, however, Korea did *not* follow an 'export promoting' trade regime (see the definition of Bhagwati, 1988), then one must explain how it managed to squeeze exports out of import substitution projects and why exports grew so fast (see Table 8.2).

The second part of the chapter examines import liberalization. During Korea's Sixth Five-Year Plan (1987–91), import liberalization increasingly took a *two track* approach, reminiscent of the 'negative' and 'automatic approval' trade regime of the 1950s. One track, which might be called a 'fast-track', included an increasingly large number of imports that were no longer given any sort of protection because they obviously no longer needed it; they could be produced in Korea and compete abroad at market-determined costs and existing quality levels. Another track, which might be called a 'tech-track', included a small but critical number of high technology products that Korean industry was still in the process of learning how to produce competitively. The

Table 8.2   Changes in key economic indicators in Korea (average percentage change)

	1962–9	*1970–9*	*1980–9*
Real GNP	12.7	8.9	8.3
Real exports	41.7	38.1	15.7
Real imports	27.5	29.6	11.8
Wholesale prices[b]	12.8	16.6	6.1
Consumer prices[b]	13.7[c]	15.2	7.8

Notes: [a] Preliminary.
            [b] Rates of increase compared with the last month of the previous year.
            [c] 1966–9.
Sources: Bank of Korea, various years; imports and exports – *International Trade Statistics Yearbook, 1991,* New York, United Nations, 1991.

success of Korea's trade policy depended on art rather than science with respect to the sequencing of a product's graduation from the 'tech-track' to the 'fast-track'. The switch-over, one of the least-discussed aspects of Korean trade policy, appears to have depended on a mix of considerations, such as short-term efficiency, pressures from US trade representatives, domestic politics and, perhaps most important of all, shrewd judgements about whether domestic firms were ready to compete openly against foreign rivals.[2]

II MAKING MANUFACTURING MORE REMUNERATIVE: THE 1960s

Import liberalization in Korea in the mid-1960s mainly took the form of tariff drawbacks for exporters. The aim of liberalization was to lower tariffs and non-tariff barriers on imported inputs (mostly raw materials and intermediates) used in export-oriented industries in order to raise these industries' profitability. Liberalization of imports for its own sake was not pursued. Indeed, 'the policy reforms of 1964–65 brought about some *increase* in the level of protection for domestic industry' (Kim, 1991b, p. 15, emphasis added).

Two industries that trade policy almost entirely insulated from foreign competition at that time were textiles and clothing (Park, 1991). But, one may ask, why the need for the heavy-duty protection against labour-intensive imports in a country with low wages, high educational levels, and modern infrastructure by the standards of most developing countries? The answer seems to lie in the fact that all but Korea's most labour-intensive industries (say, wigs and plywood) could not compete at market-determined prices, and at the exchange rates prevailing at the time, against the higher quality and productivity of Japan. Korean cotton spinning and weaving companies began receiving modest subsidization as early as the 1920s (Eckert, 1991). Then in the 1950s they were a major recipient of subsidized American loans to help them finance imports of textile machinery. Cotton textiles were regarded as one of the most modern industries in Korea in the 1950s and early 1960s in terms of equipment, technology, management and firm size. Yet at market-determined production costs and at prevailing exchange rates, the textile industry could still not compete against the Japanese textile industry, which benefited from greater efficiency, higher quality, superior marketing, as well as the below-national-average wage rates that Japan's highly segmented labour markets afforded textile firms (Amsden, 1989).

One objective of Korean trade policy in the 1960s, therefore, was to protect a wide array of domestic industries against competition from Japan, both in the form of keeping out Japanese exports and limiting Japanese foreign investment.

Another objective was to stimulate exports, and one of the strongest political lobbies that inspired the introduction of export subsidies was the large integrated cotton textile companies, which had organized themselves into a powerful industry association (Kim, 1991b). The subsidized investments its members had undertaken in the 1950s had resulted in excess capacity, which was exacerbated by the recession in the early 1960s that accompanied an American-inspired price stabilization. The motives behind the government's export-promotion measures in the mid-1960s were varied (the dwindling of postwar reconstruction demand, the winding-down of American foreign aid and its short-term foreign exchange shortages, and the realization, evident from Japan's then recent experience, that a resource-scarce country needed an on-going mechanism to generate hard currency). Not least, the government subsidized exports as a way to support those industries that were suffering as a result of recession and over-supply. The textile industry lobbied hard for additional government support, and textiles accounted for 29 per cent of manufactured exports in 1963 and 41 per cent in 1965 (Hong, 1979).

The military government of Park Chung Hee first responded to business pressures by offering *industry-specific* export subsidies. The discriminatory character of this policy was strongly opposed by American aid officials. By way of compromise, the government agreed (wisely) to offer subsidized working capital to *all* exporters regardless of industry (Cole and Lyman, 1971). The very fact that Korea had to compromise its policies to appease American aid advisers provided another reason to expand exports, which was viewed by Park Chung Hee as a way to reduce dependence on American aid for foreign exchange and, therefore, American influence over Korean policies (Amsden, 1989, p. 72).

The overall reforms of 1964–5 ultimately amounted to a comprehensive package. The exchange rate was unified, then devalued, and finally pegged (after floating experimentally at the behest of some of Korea's American advisers). Export incentive measures included: (a) preferential export credit, which was significant especially for the seven years (1965–72) when Korean interest rates on ordinary bank loans were liberalized (raised) as a result of financial reforms; (b) tax breaks on export income (abolished in 1973); (c) wastage allowances for imported raw materials used in exports, along with indirect domestic tax exemptions on intermediate inputs used for export production and on export sales; (d) accelerated depreciation allowances for fixed assets of major export industries; (e) preferential rates on electricity and railroad transportation; and (f) the drawback system, or tariff exemptions on imports of raw materials (mainly cotton and lumber) used in export production (Frank, Kim and Westphal, 1975; Nam, 1981).

Excluded from this list is the preferential long-term investment credit that targeted industries (including cotton textiles) received in the 1960s. In the case of textiles, this list also excludes the government-subsidized investments in the import substitution of synthetic fibre production. The establishment of a domestic synthetic fibre industry reduced the requirements of spinners for hard currency to import raw cotton. Their reduced imports (raw cotton was estimated to account for over 60 per cent of total costs) allowed the nominal exchange rate to be devalued periodically with less of a negative effect on production costs than otherwise.

Finally, it is noteworthy that in the 1964–5 reforms, access to imports was linked to export performance. Because this linkage system is not reflected in the effective exchange rate for imports and exports in Table 8.1, the calculations on trade bias do not capture the extent to which exports were *coerced*. This linkage system is one of the first examples of the performance-related subsidy allocation system that enabled Japan, Korea and Taiwan to grow so fast (see Amsden, 1989). Later, the policy of making the right to import conditional on export performance was changed to making protection from foreign imports conditional on exporting (in the same industry). In effect, exporters received a subsidy in the form of being allowed to sell part of their output above world prices in the protected domestic market. This was possibly the most lucrative subsidy of all, and possibly also the cheapest from the government's viewpoint, as first pointed out by Cole and Lyman (1971). Protection is also another major subsidy to exporters which fails to be incorporated into the typical calculation of export incentives.

III DEEPENING THE INDUSTRIAL BASE: THE 1970s

Korea's trade policy in the 1970s became supportive of its overall objective to deepen its industrial structure, principally by means of

massive investments in heavy industry, including increasingly sophisticated electronic manufactures. In order to deepen its industrial
structure, Korea also deepened its incentives to import substitution
industries. Some heavy and chemical industry products (especially
machinery and transportation equipment) were put back on the
'negative list', meaning they could not be imported without prior
government approval (Luedde-Neurath, 1986). It became almost
impossible for enterprises other than exporters to import products in
'targeted' industries (Kim, 1988). Concerning investment funds, the
government controlled capital allocations not just for particular
industries but also for particular projects, and 'policy loans' received
preferential interest rates. According to estimates of Hong (1990), the
yearly provision of interest rate subsidies increased from 3 per cent of
GNP in 1962–71 to 10 per cent of GNP in 1972–9. Government-
controlled interest rate subsidies on foreign loans to the private sector
averaged about 6 per cent of GNP each year in the 1970s. Given the
magnitude of these subsidies, Korea could be said to have developed
on the basis of getting the prices 'wrong' (see Amsden, 1989).

Thus, instead of liberalizing imports in the 1970s, Korea apparently
moved in the opposite direction. As for exports, net *direct* subsidies
decreased. According to Kwang-Suk Kim:

> The government abolished direct tax reduction on income earned
> from export and other foreign exchange earnings activities with effect
> from 1973. In 1975 the system of outright tariff exemptions on imp-
> orts of raw material for export was changed to a drawback system,
> thereby increasing the financial burden of export firms. By early 1978,
> the preferential export credit was the only scheme that continued to
> provide some net subsidies for export (Kim, 1991a, pp. 67–8).

Despite the alleged reduction in export subsidies, and in spite of the
increase in subsidies to import substitution, exports of import-substitu-
ted items were precisely those that began to grow the fastest. According
to a study undertaken at the Korea Development Institute by Yoo:

> Increases in Korean exports in the 1980s have been most visible in
> such products as various kinds of consumer electronics, semicon-
> ductors, other computer related products, telecommunications
> equipment, and passenger cars. These were mainly the products of
> 'heavy' industries that were greatly favored under the industrial
> policy of the 1970s (Yoo, 1990, p. 110).

By the mid-1980s heavy industry had become Korea's new 'leading sector.'

IV PUSHING OUT EXPORTS

How Korea managed to extract exports from import-substituting industries that operated under a 'pro-IS' incentive system (whereby the effective exchange rate in won per U.S. dollar for imports exceeded that for exports) is an issue of general interest to other developing countries. The magnitude of the problem is evident from the distaste that export targets elicited from many Korean firms. This distaste is suggested by a survey of exporters conducted at the height of the drive into heavy industry. In response to the question, 'What has been the effect of export targets on your firm?', only 37 per cent of respondents in 1976 said that targets contributed to a more rapid increase in production, and only 10 per cent said that they made no difference to them. The remainder of respondents intimated that having to meet export targets was an unwelcome interference, to the extent that it caused them to divert sales from the domestic market, led to unprofitable production, higher costs, and so forth (see Table 8.3).

Several theories have been advanced to explain how, under these conditions and a pro-IS trade regime generally, Korea managed to extract exports from import substitution industries. According to Kim (1991b, p. 19), 'the fact that Korea could maintain a stable level of real effective exchange rate after 1965 was very important for export expansion', presumably because stability enabled exporters to plan for the future. According to Yung Chul Park, exports in Korea followed in the train of import substitution because import substitution was predicated on the principle of economies of scale and the creation of large scale plants. Park (1991, p. 156) states:

> Perhaps the most important reason is that although import-substitution industries have been subsidized as infant industries, they have from the beginning been developed as the export industries of the future and not just for meeting domestic demand. As a result, firms in import-substitution industries have been encouraged to build large plants . . . and to sell abroad as soon as they begin operating.

Nevertheless, although scale economies were critical in Korea's industrial growth (see Kwon, 1986), they constitute an incomplete

Table 8.3   Korean firms' perception of the effect of export targets, 1974, 1975, 1976

Responses of firms to the question: 'What has been the effect of export targets fixed for your firm?

Effect	1974	1975 (% composition)	1976
Contributed to a more rapid increase in production	42	32	37
Made no difference to the growth of production	14	16	10
Caused firm to divert sales from the domestic to export markets	20	15	18
Reduced profitability	7	12	9
Led to price-cutting and other unprofitable competition	5	11	10
Led to some unprofitable exports	4	8	5
Raised unit costs due to employment of inexperienced personnel or other reasons	7	7	10
Led to some deterioration of product quality	1	1	1
Total percentage of firms	100	100	100
(number of responses)	115	152	155

Note: 105 firms in total replied to this question, some more than once, and some only for one or two years.
Source: Adapted from Rhee, Ross-Larson and Pursell, 1984, Table A-10, p. 91.

explanation of export activity. Not all large-scale industries were dependent on export markets or oriented towards exporting from the start of their operations, as the scale argument suggests. Some required long learning periods before they could export.

For instance, the centrepiece of Korea's heavy industrialization, the integrated Pohang Iron and Steel Company (POSCO), like most big companies was constructed in stages, in tandem with rising demand rather than ahead of it. Initially, POSCO was designed to serve the domestic market, and enjoyed a 25 per cent duty on steel sold to non-exporting users. In the early stages of POSCO's development, domestic demand was rising faster than POSCO could supply; POSCO did not have to export. Nevertheless, as a strategic state-owned enterprise, POSCO elected to export 30 per cent of its output. It did so to (a) increase the certainty of a steady flow of orders in order to operate at full capacity for all types of steel; (b) earn foreign exchange to repay its debt; (c) take advantage of government export subsidies; and (d) drive a stake in the international market in anticipation of possible future capacity expansions (Amsden, 1989, p. 301).

Although an operation like the shipbuilding division of Hyundai Heavy Industries was designed with exports immediately in mind, other more technologically complex operations, such as Hyundai Motors, were not, and delayed exporting for a long time until product or production technique could be improved. The Korean automobile industry began assembly operations in the 1960s (or earlier, in the case of one company). Its learning process lasted at least 25 years, during which time no foreign cars were to be seen on Korean roads and no Korean cars were to be seen on foreign roads. In theory, Korea's three motor vehicle producers competed with each other in the domestic market. In practice, such a heavily protected oligopoly was an open invitation to inefficiency and abuse, and proved to be so in many other late-industrializing countries.

Korea succeeded (exports of Korean cars, for example, boomed by the mid-1980s) where other countries failed because of the discipline that the Korean government imposed not just on labour but also on capital (Amsden, 1989 and 1992). Whereas slow-growing late-indus-trializing countries allocated subsidies according to the principle of 'giveaway', fast-growing late-industrializing countries such as Korea and Taiwan allocated subsidies according to the principle of 'recipro-city', in exchange for concrete performance standards, including exports. Park Chung Hee, Korea's former President responsible for its heavy industry drive, indicated the connection between scale and discipline when he stated:

One of the essential characteristics of a modern economy is its strong tendency towards centralization. Where the appalling power of mammoth enterprise is concerned, . . . there is no free competi-tion. . . . Therefore, the key problems facing a free economic policy are *coordination and supervisory guidance, by the state,* of mammoth economic strength (Park Chung Hee, 1962, as cited in Amsden, 1989, p. 50; emphasis added).

Korea was assisted in creating an efficient corps of exporters, while maintaining a highly protected domestic economy, by the initial *underdevelopment* of its manufacturing sector, and the fact that its industrial growth was characterized by a *late spurt* rather than a *gradual evolution* over a relatively long time period, as in India and Latin America. The relative primitiveness of industry at the beginning of Korea's spurt allowed machinery and intermediate imports to be exempted from restrictions (when embodied in exports) without stepping on established producers' toes. As Table 8.4 suggests, by comparison with selected Latin American countries, manufacturing activity in Korea in the mid-1950s was rudimentary, as measured by the ratio of manufacturing to agricultural net product. The ratio for India, which had a relatively long history of industrial development, would be much higher than indicated in Table 8.4 were it not for India's huge agrarian population. A sharp discontinuity in industrial development allowed Korea and other East Asian countries to

Table 8.4   Ratio of manufacturing to agricultural net product and net value of manufacturing per head of population, Latin America and Asia, 1955

	Ratio of manufacturing to agricultural net product	*Net value of manufacturing per head (US$)*
Latin America		
Argentina	1.32	145
Brazil	0.72	50
Mexico	1.00	60
Venezuela	1.43	95
Chile	1.35	75
Colombia	0.42	45
Peru	0.52	25
Asia		
S. Korea	0.20	8
Indonesia	0.20	10
Philippines	0.32	13
Thailand	0.28	10
India	0.30	7

Source: Maizels (1963), as cited by Freeman (1992).

sequence their protection of the home market more efficiently, moving towards protecting capital goods manufacture relatively late, and allowing consumer goods producers to enjoy the free importation of machinery and intermediates at world prices and quality standards. A weak manufacturing base also went hand-in-hand with a weak political lobby of manufacturers, which made the discipline of such manufacturers easier for the government.

V FINANCING SUBSIDIES

The way in which Korea financed its subsidies to business was a further reflection of government discipline over economic agents, including taxpayers and consumers. The three methods of finance were through taxation, savings and foreign loans. Table 8.5 indicates that the gross tax burden to GNP increased steadily over time, reaching approximately 17 per cent by 1979. This burden was less than the average for

Table 8.5 Key economic indicators in Korea

	1962	1970	1979	1990
Per capita GNP (US$)	87	252	1,644	5,570
Current account balance (Bil. US$)	−0.05	−0.62	−4.1	−8.8
Gross domestic investment ratio (%)	11.8	27.9	35.9	37.1
Gross saving ratio (%)	11.0	18.0	28.8	35.3
Gross tax burden to GNP	7.1[b]	14.3	17.4	19.0
Foreign debt as a % of GNP	4.1[c]	31.5[d]	31.7	..

Note: [a] Preliminary
      [b] 1964.
      [c] 1963.
      [d] 1973.
Sources: Bank of Korea; tax burden – Economic Planning Board.

the OECD countries (35 per cent in 1980), but unlike many developing countries, Korea taxed both business and personal incomes (OECD, 1991). Throughout the period 1962–90, corporations accounted for roughly 10 per cent of Korea's total tax revenues. Until 1977, non-incorporated businesses accounted for another 10 per cent. Thereafter, the business tax (but not the corporation tax) was phased out and replaced by a value added tax (in conjunction with a decline in the share of the income tax). By the 1980s, indirect taxes in Korea accounted for over 40 per cent of total tax revenues, compared with only about 30 per cent previously. Nevertheless, Korea's tax system was relatively efficient and served as an integral part of industrial policy. In a developmental way, the government used threats of tax audit to pressure firms to behave socially. (In a negative way, it used them to pressure them to extend political support.)

Table 8.5 also indicates the steady rise in the proportion of income saved. The gross saving ratio rose from 18.0 per cent in 1970 to 28.8 per cent in 1979, although real deposit interest rates were negative: −1.92 per cent from 1972 to 1976 and −1.52 per cent from 1977 to 1981. Previously, in conjunction with financial liberalization in 1967–71, real deposit interest rates became strongly positive (10.7 per cent), but not for long. Thus, investors in heavy industry in the 1970s received 'subsidized' credit in so far as the real interest rate they paid was below that which market forces dictated (the real curb market interest rate in the 1970s was about 22 per cent). But credit was not subsidized from the government's point of view in so far as state banks' deposit rates did not exceed their lending rates (Amsden and Euh, 1993). The savings ratio increased in the 1970s despite (or because of?) negative real interest rates; savings have been found to be fairly inelastic with respect to real interest rates in Korea (Yu, 1988). Savings may rise the *lower* are real interest rates if savers have a target level of savings they wish to achieve (say, to buy a dwelling), and, therefore, must save more as real interest rates decline.

Finally, the government financed overall investments in heavy industry with foreign loans: total foreign debt rose from $4.3 billion in 1973, the beginning of the drive into heavy industry, to $20.5 billion in 1979, the end of the drive. The government accounted for around 40 per cent of these loans (Park, 1985). Nevertheless, despite the large rise in foreign loans, foreign debt as a percent of GNP remained unchanged at the beginning and end of the period (as indicated in Table 8.5), a tribute to the disciplined way in which Korean industry pushed out exports.

VI STRIVING TO REACH THE WORLD TECHNOLOGICAL FRONTIER: THE 1980S AND BEYOND

Despite Korea's high ratio of exports to GNP, its current balance of goods and services was almost always in deficit. Export growth was extremely rapid (31 per cent annual average increase, 1962–89), but import growth was rapid as well (22 per cent annual average increase over the same period from a relatively large base) (see Table 8.2). Import growth was rapid despite extensive controls, and the government was highly sensitive to balance of payments disequilibria in pacing further liberalization. Moreover, given the implicit policy of using protection against imports to subsidize fledgling export industries, the Korean government delayed taking any major initiatives towards import liberalization until 1978.

Korea registered a big current account surplus in 1986–89, due partly to the real depreciation of the won against major currencies, and partly to favourable world trade conditions. Korea's current account surplus and general increase in affluence gave rise to two conditions that pressurized policy-makers to liberalize imports further. First, a growing number of Korean college graduates could afford to study in the United States. As the number of American-trained Korean economists (A-TKEs) mushroomed (from 204 degree recipients in 1970–9, to 466 in 1980–9, to 131 in 1990 alone – compared to a total of only 305 American-trained Japanese economists over the same period), a strong lobby favouring free markets emerged (Amsden, forthcoming). Second, with a sharp rise in both Korea's aggregate trade surplus and bilateral trade surplus with the United States, Washington began breathing down Korea's neck to open its markets and to revalue the won.

Thus far, trade policy has been discussed primarily in terms of export incentives. Direct net subsidies to exporters, in the form of tax exemptions and interest rate preferences on export finance, were phased out by 1983 (Kim, forthcoming). Indirect net export subsidies continued to be given to exporters in targeted industries in the form of investment credits at below-market interest rates, access to low-cost land sites (particularly in industrial parks near Seoul, where most professional people preferred to live and where real estate prices were exceptionally high), aid to R&D, and assistance in technology acquisition and demand stabilization in conjunction with government infrastructure and procurement projects (such as telecommunications and high-speed rail transportation). The issue in trade policy that received the most attention in the 1980s, however, was import controls, and these will now become our focus of attention.

VII TRADE OBJECTIVES: EFFICIENCY CONSIDERATIONS ON THE BACK-BURNER

American-trained Korean economists advocated free trade on the grounds of efficiency. The case for liberalization on efficiency grounds intensified with accelerated wage demands after democratization (beginning in 1987), which undermined Korean exporters' cost-effectiveness. Nevertheless, for those government officials in Korea who operated with a long-term growth perspective, trade policy by the late 1980s revolved around building technological capabilities in high-tech, and two other considerations unrelated directly to efficiency.

First, it became critical for Korea not to antagonize the United States since the latter accounted for such a large share of Korea's exports (around 35 per cent in the late 1980s: Bank of Korea, 1991). Trade policy became oriented towards shifting imports from Japan to the United States (for an analysis of the triangular trade between the United States, Japan and Korea, see Park and Park, 1991). To reduce their dependence on the United States, the big business groups also made intense efforts to develop new export markets (in Eastern and Western Europe, the former Soviet Union, and China – not to mention North Korea).

Second, it became critical for Korea not simply to achieve a balance in its current account but to aim for a *sustained surplus*. It was pointed out by a Presidential Commission on Industrial Restructuring convened in 1988 that the world's most competitive economies at the time – Japan, West Germany, Taiwan, not to mention Korea – were all running trade surpluses. A surplus was an advantage in financing the technology imports necessary for Korea to reach the world frontier. In the 1960s and 1970s, Korea's technology requirements could be satisfied through imports of capital goods, technical assistance, and foreign licences. By the late 1980s and 1990s, it could only be fully satisfied through the acquisition of foreign high-tech firms and the establishment of Korean R&D centres overseas. For example, in order to learn how to design major improvements in its consumer products line, Samsung Electronics Company (SEC) not only beefed up its R&D in Korea (R&D expenditures accounted for as much as 7 per cent of SEC's sales) but also established R&D facilities in Osaka (the home of Matsushita Company, the Japanese electronics giant) and New Jersey (the home of Bell Labs and RCA) (Amsden, forthcoming). Foreign-based R&D and acquisitions of foreign high-tech companies were believed to be time-effective and cost-effective ways to infuse the leading-edge technology that could no longer be purchased easily in the marketplace.

A current account surplus was proving useful in other ways as well: (1) to relocate labour-intensive production stages in low-wage countries (Asia), and thereby reduce production costs; and (2) to establish production facilities overseas in order to create export markets for domestically manufactured parts and components or final products. According to the Bank of Korea, Korea's overseas investments reached almost $1 billion in 1990 (a rise of nearly 70 per cent over 1989) but then levelled off as the trade surplus vanished.

VIII THE JAPANESE CONNECTION

Japan typically accounted for almost 90 per cent of Korea's total trade deficit. Allegedly Japanese counterpart customs duties on 16 major Korean exports to Japan also ranged from 10 per cent to 25 per cent, impeding a rise in Korea's traditional exports to Japanese buyers (Sohn, 1992). To achieve a shift in import origin, the Korean government adopted a set of policies that was anything but liberal. First, it offered special subsidized credit to Korean importers to 'Buy American' (Ministry of Trade and Industry, 1991). In a gentle twist of irony, the Korea Traders' Association went as far as conducting surveys of the Korean market to help American exporters penetrate it, focusing on the quality and other non-price problems from which many American manufacturers suffered (Min, 1989). The highly politicized nature of Korea's import liberalization is suggested in Table 8.6. Between 1986 and 1989, the growth rate of liberalized items from the United States was much higher than the growth rate of liberalized items from either Japan or the European Community.

Second, the Korean government reinforced trade barriers against Japanese goods made in Japan. It also imposed special import restrictions on Japanese goods made in South-east Asia. The second measure protected Korean enterprises in their home market from low-wage/Japanese brand-name competition, while the first gave them a breathing spell to upgrade their own technological capabilities.

Because Korea's major competitor in all the high-tech industries it wished to penetrate was first and foremost Japan, import policy in the

Table 8.6   Yearly growth rate of import-liberalized items in Korea (percentages)

Year	Growth rate of liberalized imports from:				Growth rate of all imports
	All countries	USA	Japan	EC	
1986	26.6	25.5	20.2	30.1	1.4
1987	17.8	29.6	9.2	25.1	29.9
1988	0.9	34.1	−18.8	−12.3	26.3
1989	9.4	166.6	−32.9	−87.7	18.6

Sources: Hong *et al.* (1991) and Bank of Korea (1991).

early 1990s mirrored that in the 1960s: it was targeted defensively against Japan and it was illiberal at the core.

IX   A 'TWO-TRACK' IMPORT REFORM STRATEGY

To meet the contradictory pressures for short-term liberalization and long-term technological development, the Korean government also implemented what could be described as a *two-track* system of trade reform, comparable in selectivity to the one operating in Japan.[3] A *'fast-track'* was geared to the *average* Korean manufacturing industry. By the late 1980s, much of Korean industry had already become globally competitive and could withstand the immediate withdrawal of import controls. By contrast, a *'tech-track'* was geared to shielding advanced-technology industries that were still in need of protection as they strove to reach the world frontier. To move an industry from the tech-track to the fast-track, the government devised an 'advance notice' warning system, whereby strategic industries were to be given adequate time to prepare to face foreign competition at home. Thus, one can differentiate qualitatively two phases of import liberalization in Korea. Towards the end of the 1960s, import liberalization took the form of a one-stage approach in so far as the 'degree of liberalization made a sudden jump by the loosening of QRs in 1967, but made no further progress for a long time'. Beginning in 1978, by contrast, liberalization followed a 'gradual, multi-stage approach' through the system of 'advance notices' (Kim, forthcoming).

By way of illustration of two-track trade reform, Table 8.7 indicates the Korean government's plan to liberalize import tariffs and bring them into conformance with levels prevailing in other countries. Nevertheless, both strategic and politically sensitive industries continued to be shielded and subsidized by non-tariff barriers. These trade impediments were distasteful to many of the American-trained Korean economists who served on the Subcommittee on Internationalization of the Korean Economy of the Presidential Commission on Economic Restructuring. 'Unfortunately', the Commission's Report stated, 'there seems to remain a considerable discrepancy between intention and reality given existing non-tariff import barriers for manufactured products, especially consumer goods' (p. 29). The Report goes on to note:

To begin with, a number of products [including motor vehicles and consumer electronics] are regulated by Korea's so-called *import source diversification* policy which restricts imports of designated products from Japan [and after 1988, from Japanese companies operating overseas in low-wage economies], the justification being Korea's chronic and large bilateral trade deficit with Japan. In addition, a small number of products are regulated by an *import surveillance* policy which prevents import surges in designated products. 'Consumer' laws dealing with pharmaceuticals, agricultural chemical management, fertilizer management, quality of manufactured products, electrical safety, telecommunications, and environmental protection [constitute] another type of non-tariff import barrier.

Table 8.7   Korea's planned tariff reform (*ad valorem* tariff in percentages)

	Before reform (1988)	Planned reform (as of 1988)	Foreign countries, 1988			
			Japan	USA	EC	Taiwan
All products	18.1	7.9	5.9	6.2	7.9	11.7
Manufactures	16.9	6.2	n.a.	n.a.	n.a	n.a.
Agricultural products	25.2	16.6	n.a.	n.a.	n.a.	n.a.

Source: Ministry of Finance, 'The Tariff Reform Plan', as cited by Presidential Commission on Economic Restructuring (1988).

The Report concludes:

> The bureaucratic excesses and procedural complexities represented by these laws as well as the influence of domestic producer organizations in their administration seem to serve as serious import impediments . . . [affecting] about twenty per cent of all industrial product classes (Presidential Commission on Economic Restructuring, 1988, p. 29).[4]

The Presidential Commission was writing in 1988, after which time still more products were transferred from the 'tech-track' to the 'fast-track' in response to the Korean government's desire to qualify for membership in the Paris-based Organization for Economic Co-operation and Development (OECD). Nevertheless, not only did the 'tech-track' still exist, despite the smaller number of products it comprised, it also appeared to include the critical products Korea was cradling for future growth.

X   THE NEGLIGIBLE ECONOMIC EFFECTS OF LIBERALIZATION

Studies of import liberalization in Korea suggest that, contrary to the fears of some government officials, liberalization did not negatively affect key macroeconomic variables, such as GNP, employment, exports, imports, or the balance of payments (at least not up until the late 1980s, the cut-off date for available evidence).[5] On the other hand, neither did liberalization fulfil the optimistic expectations of Korea's American-trained economists and raise efficiency. According to Kim, who made careful estimates of the effects of trade liberalization: 'The system of export incentives established in the 1960s was clearly effective in increasing the country's exports, making rapid industrialization possible thereafter. The actual impact of import liberalization on the domestic economy has not been so visible' (Kim, forthcoming).

Apparently liberalization had no effect whatsoever on productivity: 'There is no clear indication that liberalization had *any significant effect* on domestic industrial productivity, either during the period 1966–70 or 1975–85' (emphasis added).

These are rather striking findings given the importance placed on abolishing import controls by the Bretton Woods institutions and the

A-TKEs. It is Kim's opinion that these results arose 'probably because liberalization has been cautious and gradual'. Another explanation is that a large share of Korea's imports were controlled by big business groups, which tended not to import products that competed directly with those of their own subsidiaries. Therefore, removing barriers to imports did not raise efficiency. Still another hypothesis is that the Korean economy was not nearly as inefficient as the A-TKEs feared. Consequently, the removal of import barriers did not increase efficiency as much as anticipated.

In support of the last hypothesis, it must be remembered that Korea was a very open economy since the late 1960s, and a large share of its imports took the form of producer goods – machinery, transport equipment, chemicals, and other intermediate products (see Table 8.8). In 1970, 1985 and 1990, machinery and transport equipment accounted for 30 per cent or more of total imports. The share of consumer goods amounted at most to 6 per cent or 7 per cent. Since imports already catered for production rather than consumption, their further liberalization made little dent in productivity; indeed, it was consumer goods that figured prominently in the late 1980s' import surge.

That the Korean economy was not as inefficient as feared is suggested by the results of a study which estimated the welfare cost of both labour and capital market distortions for the year 1978, the

Table 8.8   The composition of Korean imports, 1970, 1985 and 1990 (percentage of total imports)

Industry	1970	1985	1990
Commodities and processed foods[a]	37.3	17.5	17.6
Mineral fuels[b]	6.9	23.6	15.8
Chemicals[c]	8.3	9.0	10.6
Manufactures[d]	47.6	49.9	56.0
Machinery and transport equip.[e]	29.7	34.2	34.3

Notes: Standard Industrial Trade Classification (SITC):
   [a] SITC 0-2 and 4.
   [b] SITC 3.
   [c] SITC 5.
   [d] SITC 6-9.
   [e] SITC 7.
Sources: Bank of Korea, *Economic Statistics Yearbook*, various years, Seoul.

height of Korea's heavy industry drive. Using a computable general equilibrium model, the study found that removing labour market distortions increased output by less than 1 per cent of the base year GDP, and removing capital market distortions, which were rife during the 1970s, increased base year GDP by only 3.2 per cent (Kwon and Paik, 1992). While statistical exercises of this type usually generate small welfare losses, these estimates are especially small. The authors conclude:

> These results cast doubt on the importance of the efficiency loss argument associated with factor price distortions. They support, albeit indirectly, the view that dynamic efficiency gains (i.e. from x-efficiency, the spread of new technological knowledge, [scale economies], and so forth), resulting from larger and more concentrated capital stock, especially in an export-oriented environment, may have more than offset allocative inefficiency (p. 24).[6]

That the Korean economy was not as inefficient as the A-TKEs feared, and, therefore, import liberalization did not increase efficiency as much as was expected, is also indicated by data on economic concentration. Market concentration in Korea peaked in the late 1970s but then decreased as markets deepened. From 1970 to 1977, to 1987, the share of oligopolies in shipments went from 35.1 per cent, to 48.6 per cent, to 40.2 per cent, while the share of competitive market structures went from 39.9 per cent, to 26.1 per cent, to 44.3 per cent (Lee, Urata and Choi, 1986; and Lee and Lee, 1990). As both competitive and oligopolistic market structures increased their share of total output, the importance of monopolies declined.

XI CONCLUSION: THE LESSONS

If estimates of government support to business in Korea are calculated to include not just direct but also *indirect* net subsidies (in the form of preferential credit for long-term investment, access to land sites at below-market cost, support for R&D, public procurement externalities, and so forth), then government support for both export and import substitution activity in Korea has been much greater than direct subsidies alone suggest.

In the 1960s, subsidization was required because Korea could not out-compete Japan – on the basis of market-determined production costs – in a wide range of labor-intensive industries, including cotton textiles. In the 1970s, subsidization was necessary in order to enable Korea to compete against Japan in heavy industries. Starting in the 1980s, it was necessary to enable Korea to compete against Japan in increasingly complex technology-based sectors.

Once indirect subsidies are introduced, not only was government support to business in Korea greater than direct subsidies alone suggest, they also involved more *anti-export bias*. Given a pro-IS trade regime, it is of no small interest to other countries to understand how Korea managed to increase exports. In large part, exports flourished for reasons that operated *outside the price mechanism*. Exports were a strategic part of the national misssion to develop. As part of an activist industrial policy that emphasized the need for a resource-poor country like Korea to survive on the basis of manufactured exports, the government disciplined subsidy recipients and imposed performance standards on them, with export targets representing the most important, transparent, and easily monitored performance criterion of all.

The conditions faced by underdeveloped countries in the 1990s are different from those that Korea faced beginning in the 1960s. In two respects, the conditions may make subsidies as extensive as those that were characteristic of Korea *less* necessary. For one, garment manufacture and electronics assembly have replaced cotton spinning and weaving as leading sectors, and are relatively more labour-using than textiles. Therefore, low wages may bestow a more decisive competitive edge to local producers. For another, implicit subsidies to business in the 1980s in the form of real wage *decreases* (in the order of roughly 50 per cent in Mexico, for example) have significantly reduced wage costs themselves. If, as a consequence of these two factors, poor countries today can compete in world markets by getting the prices 'right', so much the better. If they cannot — just as Korea could not – then they will have to consider the trade-off between lowering wages further (if politically or physiologically possible) or deviating from laissez-faire. The latter policy is likely to be both socially preferable and quicker, *but only if* the subsidization process can be made disciplined and performance standards can be imposed on business in exchange for government support, as exemplified in the Korean case.

Concerning import controls, trade policy in Korea gradually became more liberal in the 1980s as a result of pressures from American-trained Korean economists, the US government, and the achievement of competitiveness in the great majority of industries, such that continued import controls were no longer necessary for survival. Imports were slowly liberalized according to an 'advance warning system' (whereas in the 1960s a few import items had been liberalized in one jump, with no follow-up until the late 1970s).

Nevertheless, just as imports were subject to either 'negative' or 'automatic approval' in the 1950s, import reform in the 1980s progressed along two tracks, which could be called a 'fast-track' and a 'tech-track'. The former applied to imports that did not seriously threaten the competitiveness of domestic industry. These products were quickly liberalized. The latter applied to imports that did seriously threaten the competitiveness of advanced-technology industries in the process of catching up. They continued to be restricted by various means, such as an 'import diversification system' supposedly in effect to reduce Korea's huge trade deficit with Japan. Although this system was estimated to cover only about 2.2 per cent of tradeables by 1989, it covered the strategic imports that Korea was planning on developing into leading sectors in the future.

The Korean trade regime would be misrepresented to developing countries if only the 'fast-track' system were emphasized.

Notes

1. I'd like to thank Gerry Helleiner and Jene Kwon for helpful suggestions.
2. The difficulties researchers have encountered in finding a correlation between exports and growth have led them to emphasize the importance of openness in terms of facilitating the absorption of foreign know-how. In this spirit, whichever line of argument is adopted, the key issue is one of sequencing, or deciding (a) when it is time to restrict the open importation of high-tech products in order to allow domestic producers to learn how to produce these products themselves, if, indeed, they are still unable to do so competitively at market-determined production costs and world quality standards, or (b) when it is time to stop protecting high-tech production and let domestic producers compete openly in world markets. These issues are of considerable importance but are not discussed systematically in this chapter.
3. Japan's two-track approach is evident from the following example: although Korea's exports to Japan often incurred duties of 15–25 per cent, as mentioned earlier, Japan's average tariff in 1992 was only about 3 per cent. In this example, Japan was protecting low-end products from Korean competition to protect domestic employment. Some of the products that Korea continued to protect in the 1990s may also have shared this employment-preserving objective.

4. In 1988, formal import restrictions covered only 0.6 per cent of all manufactured products (including processed raw materials), measured at the 8-digit level of the Customs Council Commodity Nomenclature (CCCN). The 0.6 per cent of commodities carried an average tariff rate of 17 per cent, and, if elected as a strategic industry, received additional support such as subsidized investment credit, R&D assistance, and government procurement privileges. All 99.4 per cent of the remainder of manufactured products could be imported freely. Nevertheless, considering tariffs as well as special laws and quantitative restrictions, Kim (forthcoming) estimated that in 1988, the overall degree of import liberalization of the Korean economy was 83.9%.

5. A study conducted by Choi (1988) for KIET (the Korea Institute for Economics and Technology) examines the export behaviour of the same set of commodities whose importation was liberalized in the period 1978–87. Choi finds that while the growth rate of liberalized imports was 32.9 per cent, the export growth rate of the same bundle of commodities was greater, 37.5 per cent. He attributes this to manufacturers' easier access to raw materials and to a technological factor: in the case of products that the Korean economy was capable of imitating, through reverse engineering, liberalization stimulated exports, by providing exporters with better designs to copy. By contrast, the manufacturers who suffered the most were those who were unable to imitate foreign products, because either their production scale was too small or their technological capabilities were too low (as in the case of manufacturers of consumer chemicals).

6. Gunasekera and Tyers (1991) have simulated the effects of liberalization on the Korean economy and find that the reduction of import controls could raise GNP by as much as 7 per cent. Nevertheless, 'the model results are quite sensitive to the values chosen for minimum efficient scale, and in particular, for the elasticity of substitution between imports and domestic goods' (p. 240).

References

Amsden, A. H. (1989), *Asia's Next Giant: South Korea and Late Industrialization* (New York and Oxford: Oxford University Press).

Amsden, A. H. (1990), 'The Rise of Salaried Management', in J. K. Kwon, ed., *Korean Economic Development* (New York: Greenwood Press).

Amsden, A. H. (1991), 'The Diffusion of Development: The Late-Industrializing Model and Greater East Asia', *American Economic Review*, Vol. 81, No. 2, May.

Amsden, A. H. (1992), 'A Theory of Government Intervention in Late Industrialization', in L. Putterman and D. Rueschemeyer, eds, *The State and the Market in Economic Development* (Boulder: Lynne Rienner).

Amsden, A. H (forthcoming), 'The Specter of Anglo-Saxonization Is Haunting South Korea', in L.-J. Cho and Y.-H. Kim, eds, *Korea's Political Economy: Past, Present, and Future,* (Hawaii: East West Center).

Amsden, A. H. and Y.-D. Euh (1993), 'South Korea's 1980s Financial Reforms: Good-bye Financial Repression (Maybe), Hello New Institutional Restraints', *World Development,* March.

Bank of Korea (1991), *Economic Statistics Yearbook,* Seoul.

Bhagwati, J. N. (1988), 'Export-Promoting Trade Strategy: Issues and Evidence', *Research Observer,* Vol. 3, No. 1, January.

Choi, S.-Y. *et al.* (1988), *The Analysis of the Effect of Import Liberalization on Korean Domestic Industry* (in Korean) (Seoul: KIET).

Cole, D. C., and P. N. Lyman (1971), *Korean Development: The Interplay of Politics and Economics* (Cambridge, Mass.: Harvard University Press).

Dornbusch, R., and Y. C. Park (1987), 'Korean Economic Growth', *Brookings Papers on Economic Activity,* 2.

Eckert, C. (1991), *Offspring of Empire: The Koch'ang Kims and the Colonial Origins of Korean Capitalism, 1876–1945* (Seattle: University of Washington).

EPB (Economic Planning Board) (1962), *Economic Survey,* Seoul.

EPB (Economic Planning Board), Various Years. *Major Statistics of Korean Economy,* Seoul.

Frank, C. R. Jr., K.-S. Kim and L. Westphal (1975), *Foreign Trade Regimes and Economic Development: South Korea* (New York: NBER).

Freeman, C. (1992), 'Catching Up in World Growth and World Trade', mimeo, Science Policy Research Unit, University of Sussex.

Gerschenkron, A. (1962), *Economic Backwardness in Historical Perspective,* (Cambridge, Mass.: Harvard University Press).

Gunasekera, D. and R. Tyers (1991), 'Imperfect Competition and Returns to Scale in a Newly Industrialising Economy: A General Equilibrium Analysis of Korean Trade Policy', *Journal of Development Economics,* Vol. 34.

Haggard, S. (1990), *Pathways From the Periphery: The Politics of Growth in Newly Industrializing Countries* (Ithaca: Cornell University Press).

Hikino, T., and A. H. Amsden (forthcoming), 'Staying Behind, Stumbling Back, Sneaking Up, Soaring Ahead: Late Industrialization in Historical Perspective', in W. Baumol, R. Nelson and E. Wolff, eds, *Historical Perspectives on the International Convergence in Productivity.*

Hong, K.-M., *et al.* (1991), *Analysis of the Effect of Import Liberalization on Imports From the United States* (in Korean) (Seoul: KIET).

Hong, W. (1979), *Trade, Distortions, and Employment Growth in Korea,* (Seoul: Korea Development Institute).

Hong, W. (1990), 'Market Distortions and Polarization of Trade Patterns: Korean Experience', in J. Kwon, ed., *Korean Economic Development,* (New York: Greenwood Press).

Kim, K.-S. (1987), 'The Nature of Trade Protection by Special Laws in Korea', Discussion Paper No. 87-0l, Graduate School of Business Administration, Kyung Hee University, Seoul.

Kim, K.-S. (1988), *Economic Impact of Import Liberalization and Industrial Adjustment Policy in Korea* (in Korean) (Seoul: Korea Development Institute Press).

Kim, K.-S. (1990), 'Import Liberalization and Its Impact in Korea', in J. K. Kwon, ed., *Korean Economic Development* (New York: Greenwood Press).

Kim, K.-S. (1991a), 'Korea', in D. Papageorgiou, M. Michaely and A. Choksi, eds, *Liberalizing Foreign Trade* (Cambridge, Mass. and Oxford: Basil Blackwell).

Kim, K.-S. (1991b), 'Trade and Industrialization Policies in Korea: An Overview', Conference on Trade and Industrialization Reconsidered sponsored by the United Nations University World Institute for Development Economics, mimeo (Seoul: Kyung Hee University).

Kim, K.-S. (forthcoming), 'Industrial Policy and Trade Regimes in Korea: Past, Present, and Future', in L.-J. Cho and Y.-H. Kim, eds, *Korea's Political Economy: Past, Present, and Future* (Hawaii: East West Center).

Krueger, A. O. (1979), *The Developmental Role of the Foreign Sector and Aid* (Cambridge, Mass.: Harvard University Press).

Kwon, J. K. (1986), 'Capital Utilization, Economies of Scale, and Technical Change in the Growth of Total Factor Productivity: An Exploration of South Korean Manufacturing Growth', *Journal of Development Economics*, Vol. 24.

Kwon, J. K., and H. Paik (1992), 'Factor Price Distortions, Resource Allocation, and Growth: A Computable General Equilibrium Analysis', mimeo, Northern Illinois University, DeKalb, Il. 60115.

Lee, K.-U., S. Urata and I. Choi (1986), 'Recent Developments in Industrial Organizational Issues in Korea', mimeo, Korea Development Institute and the World Bank, Washington, DC.

Lee, K.-U., and J.-H. Lee (1990), *Business Groups and Economic Power Concentration* (in Korean) (Seoul: Korea Development Institute).

Luedde-Neurath, R. (1986), *Import Controls and Export-Oriented Development: A Reassessment of the South Korean Case* (Boulder and London: Westview Press).

Maizels, A. (1963), *Industrial Growth and World Trade* (Cambridge: Cambridge University Press).

Min, S. (1989), 'Appreciation of the Yen and Japanese Exports to Korea', DBA dissertation, Harvard Business School, Boston.

Ministry of Trade and Industry (1991), *Trade and Industry White Paper* (in Korean), Seoul.

Nam, C. H. (1981), 'Trade and Industrial Policies, and the Structure of Protection in Korea', in W. Hong and L. B. Krause, eds, *Trade and Growth of the Advanced Developing Countries in the Pacific Basin* (Seoul: Korea Development Institute).

OECD (Organization for Economic Co-operation and Development) (1991), 'Revenue Statistics of OECD Member Countries, 1965–1989', Paris.

Park Chung Hee. (1962), *Our Nation's Path: Ideology for Social Reconstruction* (Seoul, Dong-A).

Park, Y.-C. (1985), 'Korea's Experience with External Debt Management', in G. Smith and J. Cuddington, eds, *International Debt and the Developing Countries* (Baltimore: Johns Hopkins University Press).

Park, Y.-C. (1991), 'Liberalization in Korea and Taiwan', in A. Koves and P. Marer, eds, *Foreign Economic Liberalization: Transformations in Socialist and Market Economies* (Boulder and Oxford: Westview Press).

Park, Y.-C., and W. A. Park (1991), 'Changing Japanese Trade Patterns and the East Asian NICs', in P. Krugman, ed., *Trade with Japan: Has the Door Opened Wider?* (Chicago: University of Chicago Press for the National Bureau of Economic Research).

Petri, P. A. (1990), 'Korean Trade as Outlier: An Economic Anatomy', in J. K. Kwon, ed., *Korean Economic Development* (New York: Greenwood Press).

Presidential Commission on Economic Restructuring (1988), *Realigning Korea's National Priorities for Economic Advance: Presidential Commission Report on Economic Restructuring,* Seoul.

Rhee, Y.-W., B. Ross-Larson, and G. Pursell (1984) *Korea's Competitive Edge: Managing the Entry into World Markets* (Baltimore: Johns Hopkins University Press).

Sohn, J.-A. (1992), 'Too Close for Comfort', *Business Korea*, February.

Summers, L. H. (1992), 'Knowledge for Effective Action', *Proceedings of the World Bank Annual Conference on Development Economics, 1991* (Washington, DC: World Bank).

UN (United Nations) (1991), *International Trade Statistics Yearbook, 1989*, (New York: United Nations).

Westphal, L. E. (1978), 'The Republic of Korea's Experience with Export-Led Industrial Development', *World Development*, Vol. 6, No. 3.

Yoo, J.-H. (1990), 'The Industrial Policy of the 1970s and the Evolution of the Manufacturing Sector in Korea'', Korea Development Institute Working Paper No. 9017, October, Seoul.

Yu, B-H. (1988), 'Household Savings in Korea', *Monthly Bulletin* (in Korean), Bank of Korea, September.

9 Trade Policies and Economic Performance in Turkey in the 1980s[1]

Ercan Uygur

F13, 019

The primary purpose of this chapter is to examine critically Turkey's trade policies and economic performance. The emphasis is on the decade of the 1980s, a period during which policies and developments were shaped largely by an adjustment programme that aimed at outward orientation and liberalization. The chapter concentrates more on the analysis of exports than of imports, in line with the priority that the adjustment programme gave to export promotion over import liberalization.

I INTRODUCTION

Over the last two decades, the Turkish economy has gone through various experiences with foreign trade policies and growth. In the 1970s, policy-makers of different governments and with different political colours pursued and staunchly defended inward-looking import-substitution policies. In the 1980s, there was a radical shift towards outward-looking policies. The 1980s started with an adjustment programme, which had elements of both stabilization and liberalization. Implemented with strong outside support from both individual Western countries and multilateral organizations such as the Organization for Economic Co-operation and Development (OECD), the International Monetary Fund (IMF) and the World Bank, the programme was often cited as an example of successful structural reform in the 1980s.

The primary purpose of this chapter is to evaluate critically the trade policies and macroeconomic achievements of the Turkish economy in the 1980s. In the second half of the 1970s, Turkey's import-substitution industrialization had reached its more difficult phase, and at the end of

215

the decade Turkey went through a balance of payments and foreign debt crisis which gave birth to the 1980 adjustment programme. Section II describes the nature of the programme and the way stabilization and liberalization were implemented.

The chapter concentrates more on exports than on imports, since the adjustment programme gave priority to export promotion over import liberalization, primarily for fear of recurrent balance of payments problems. Section III deals first with the export policies of the adjustment programme and makes an assessment of export performance in the 1980s. It is argued that exchange rate and export policies created uncertainties from the mid-1980s onwards. Export promotion schemes, as measures to counteract the large overhead costs of entry to the world markets, are found to have an important role to play in explaining Turkey's export success. However, in the long run, an appropriate exchange-rate policy is found to be more effective than export incentives.

Import and capital account liberalization and an evaluation of macroeconomic developments in the 1980–90 period are the subjects of section IV. This section starts by describing the contents of the import liberalization programmes since 1980. Thus it is argued that the liberalization of imports has not significantly reduced the anti-export bias of the trade regime, because exporters have access to duty-free imports worth up to 80 per cent of the value of their exports.

Section IV finally looks at macroeconomic achievements during the 1980s. In this regard, the emphasis is on the record of inflation and growth, although developments concerning employment and income distribution are also briefly mentioned. Achievements in terms of growth were clearly better than those in terms of inflation, but the sustainability of growth can be called into question, in view of the fact that the industrial growth of the 1980s was not spearheaded by investment.

II THE 1980 ADJUSTMENT PROGRAMME

As already noted, up until 1980, the Turkish economy developed basically on an import substitution model. In response to a severe balance of payments crisis, significant policy changes were introduced in January 1980. January 1980 witnessed the beginning of the reversal of the earlier policies and, from then on, a series of changes was introduced amounting to a stabilization and liberalization programme.

The programme was supported by multilateral organizations including the IMF, the OECD and the World Bank and also by bilateral creditors, especially the major OECD countries. There were two equally important reasons for the sympathy with which the multilateral organizations and the major OECD countries greeted the programme. First, the adjustment programme was of an orthodox type, similar to those proposed by the IMF. Secondly, it was outward-looking and had a market-oriented approach with an expressed desire to liberalize the economy.

The first concern of the programme was to reduce the rate of inflation, while not causing a major slow-down in the growth of output. The second aim was to promote exports, through continuous adjustments of the exchange rate and export incentives, and, subsequently, to liberalize imports. The third aim was financial liberalization, which, it was thought, would increase private savings and investment. The fourth, longer-term, aim was to liberalize foreign capital movements and take measures towards making the lira convertible. A final major aim of the programme was to reduce the role of the public sector in the economy.

The Turkish adjustment programme implemented stabilisation and liberalization policies simultaneously. As far as the sequencing of liberalization is concerned, the programme addressed first the product market, then foreign trade and domestic financial markets and, finally, foreign capital transactions. The sequencing of the liberalization process, therefore, agrees with the pattern prescribed by most economists in the field.[2] As regards the speed of the liberalization policies, gradualism was their characteristic in all spheres, including foreign trade and financial markets.

The first moves aimed to correct price misalignments and to eliminate disequilibria in certain important markets. To this effect, multiple exchange rates were abolished and, after a large devaluation, a uniform rate of TL70 per US dollar was established in January 1980. Government-controlled prices were likewise increased sharply. Wage earners did not have enough time to adjust to these changes, however, since in September 1980 the military ousted the civilian government and banned wage bargaining by the trade unions. The real wage declined continuously and in the mid-1980s it had reached levels that were only half what it had been in the late 1970s. These developments blocked the dialogue with broad sections of society from the start and a broad political participation could not be achieved on this important policy turnaround.

In May 1981 the Central Bank was authorized to make daily adjustments in the exchange rate. The commercial banks were allowed to fix their own rates within a narrow band around the official rate. With continuous adjustments, the lira depreciated in real terms and the Real Effective Exchange Rate (REER)[3] increased considerably and consistently until 1987–8. The margin between the official rate and the market rate for the US dollar was eliminated in the mid-1980s, as can be seen in Table 9.1. Changes in the direction of domestic financial liberalization were made in the period up to mid-1982, but were later reversed. A notable change in December 1983 was that residents were allowed to open foreign exchange deposits with commercial banks.

Table 9.1   Turkey: exchange rates and inflation rate, annual averages

Years	Exchange rates				
	Market[a]	*Official*[a]	*EER*[b]	*REER*[c]	*Inflation rate*
1977–9	32.9	24.6	31.8	83.5	46.5
1980	84.5	76.0	100.0	100.0	103.8
1981	124.6	112.7	141.2	108.2	41.9
1982	182.8	164.1	202.4	125.4	27.5
1983	259.1	230.0	280.7	137.5	28.0
1984	374.2	372.8	446.4	149.3	50.1
1985	536.5	525.2	629.3	146.7	43.9
1986	700.6	685.2	870.1	150.4	31.0
1987	901.2	868.3	1,152.0	145.7	38.4
1988	1,484.0	1,452.0	1,929.0	151.9	65.7
1989	2,135.0	2,140.0	2,807.0	138.4	66.9
1990	2,643.0	2,641.0	3,593.0	120.3	54.4

Notes: [a] Market and official rates are the averages of end of month figures
   [b] EER is the effective exchange rate and is calculated from the official rates for the $ and the DM. Following the practice at the Central Bank of Turkey, computations are made with weights of 0.75 for the $ and 0.25 for the DM. Figures are index numbers with 1980 = 100.
   [c] REER is the real effective exchange rate and is computed by making use of wholesale price indices for the United States and Germany and the GNP deflator for Turkey. Figures are index numbers with 1980 = 100.

Sources: *World Currency Yearbook*, 1986; Central Bank of Turkey, *Quarterly Bulletin*, several issues; IMF, *International Financial Statistics*, several issues; Uygur (1987 and 1991).

However, there were speculative attacks on the exchange rate on several occasions, to which the Central Bank responded by raising, and later freeing, interest rates on deposits.

III EXPORT POLICIES AND EXPORT PERFORMANCE, 1980–90

Export Promotion Polices in the 1980s

Export promotion measures were in operation even in the heyday of the import-substitution strategy. In the 1980–4 period, the adjustment programme used the exchange rate exclusively to promote exports. From 1985 to 1988, the exchange rate was almost neutral regarding export promotion. Helped also by the current account surpluses in 1988 and 1989, the lira appreciated in real terms considerably from mid-1988 onwards, when the exchange rate was used almost exclusively as a tool to fight inflation.

In addition to exchange rate policy, up to 1985 manufacturing exports were encouraged by several incentive schemes. These incentives were significantly weakened thereafter, contributing to the uncertainties to which the changes in exchange rate policy gave rise.

Export incentives were all linked to the issuance of an export incentive certificate by the State Planning Organization (SPO). Important incentive schemes included the following:[4]

(i) An export tax rebate by which exporters were refunded the indirect taxes paid during the process of production. The maximum rebate rate was 15 per cent in January 1980 and was raised to 20 per cent in May 1981. In addition to the basic rebate rates, there were additional rebates for large exporters. These were used to channel exports through foreign trade companies; until April 1984, they varied between 6 per cent and 10 per cent. The tax rebate rates were almost halved in late-1984, mainly because the system was being abused. The scheme was terminated in 1988. In 1980–8, about 90 per cent of the exports eligible for tax rebates were in the manufacturing sector (Uygur, 1993). The industries that benefited most from them were iron and steel, transportation equipment and machinery industries (Milanovic, 1986, pp. 14–15).

(ii) Payment of cash premiums to exporters. At the time when the tax rebate rates were reduced in 1984, plans were made to compensate at least for part of the reduction. Another selective premium system was instituted in December 1986. Owing to budgetary constraints and the prohibition of such subsidies in GATT's Subsidies Code (of which Turkey is a signatory), these subsidies have been used decreasingly since then. Export promotion in recent years has been implemented increasingly through indirect measures such as tax exemptions and subsidized export credits.

(iii) Subsidized export credits, by which exporters receive medium- and short-term credits at interest rates lower than those on general (non-preferential) credits. Although instituted in 1968, the rate of subsidy was the highest in 1980–1 and declined sharply in 1984. Maturities on these credits were also shortened in the same year. The scheme was terminated in January 1985, but it was reintroduced in November 1986.

(iv) Foreign exchange allocations to exporters for imports at the official exchange rate and duty-free importation of raw materials and intermediate goods used by exporters. Until the end of 1983, such allocations could not exceed 60 per cent of the FOB value of pledged exports. This rate was reduced to 40 per cent at the end of 1983, raised to 50 per cent in 1985 and to 80 per cent in 1986. The allocation scheme was valuable especially when there were foreign exchange shortages and when the market exchange rate carried a premium over the official exchange rate. This premium, which constituted a subsidy to exporters, stopped being significant after 1983, as the official exchange rate approached the market rate. The duty-free importation of inputs used in exports started in 1980 and has operated on the same basis as the foreign exchange allocations. The subsidy element of this scheme is equivalent to the tariffs and surcharges not paid by the exporters who qualify.

(v) Partial exemption from corporate taxes (introduced in 1980). According to this scheme, industrial firms that export over $0.25 million are allowed to deduct up to 20 per cent of their export revenues from taxable earnings. If exports are made through a trading company, one-fourth of the tax allowance is forwarded to that company. The allowance was also made applicable to exporters of fruits, vegetables, flowers and seafood in 1981.

Apart from the above mentioned benefits, exporters are also exempt from VAT and some other taxes. Outward orientation has also been stimulated by the establishment of export-processing zones that began in 1989. The firms that operate within these zones are exempt from all taxes. The volume of foreign trade through these zones has not yet reached a significant amount.

Table 9.2 contains subsidy rates to manufacturing exports, as well as percentage changes in the REER. As can be seen from Table 9.2, export promotion in terms of both subsidies and real exchange rate changes was substantial in the early years of the 1980s. The former reached a peak of about 36 per cent of the value of exports in 1983. The increase in REER peaked at 33 per cent right at the beginning, in 1980. Secondly, there was a rather sharp downturn in export promotion in general in 1984–5, after which exchange rate policy was either neutral or had a negative role. Thirdly, after 1985, the sum of all subsidies did not reach the levels of the early 1980s, but was nevertheless still high at about 25 per cent of the value of exports.

Growth and Structure of Exports from 1980 to 1990

In the 1980–7 period, both the growth and the change in the composition of exports were impressive. During this period, exports more than tripled, and the share of manufacturing in total exports increased from about 36 per cent to about 79 per cent (see Table 9.3).

Table 9.2   Turkey: subsidy rates on manufacturing exports (percentages)[a,b]

Years	Direct payments (1)	Export credits (2)	Duty allow. (3)	Tax allow. (4)	Total sub (2+3+4+5) (5)	REER change (6)
1979	11.0	9.9	0.31	0.0	21.21	−6.0
1980	5.6	14.9	4.15	2.0	26.65	33.3
1981	9.1	13.0	3.31	2.0	27.41	8.2
1982	15.1	10.8	3.63	2.0	31.53	15.9
1983	17.4	10.5	5.99	2.0	35.89	9.6
1984	17.3	5.9	2.03	2.0	27.23	8.6
1985	10.0	2.0	5.11	2.0	19.11	−1.7
1986	9.9	4.8	8.60	2.6	25.90	2.5
1987	8.6	2.9	6.69	4.3	22.49	−3.1
1988	7.6	4.8	6.63	5.5	24.53	4.3
1989	5.5	8.8	7.69	5.9	27.89	−8.9
1990	4.4	9.2	7.74	6.2	27.54	−13.1

Notes: [a] Rates are proportions of subsidy values to exports.
   [b] Direct payments include tax rebates and cash premium payments. Duty allowances include subsidies from duty-free importation and foreign exchange allocations. Tax allowance includes subsidy from corporate tax allowance.
Source: Uygur (1993).

222

Table 9.3 Turkey: exports by sectors and destination and volume of manufacturing exports

Years	Exports by sectors							Volume index, manufac. exports 1980 = 100
	$ million				% distribution			
	AGRX^a	MINX^b	MANX^c	Total	AGRX^a	MINX^b	MANX^c	
1977–9	1309	127	664	2100	62.1	6.2	31.8	78.9
1980	1672	191	1047	2910	57.5	6.6	35.9	100.0
1981	2219	193	2290	4703	47.2	4.1	48.7	234.6
1982	2141	175	3429	5746	37.3	3.1	59.7	377.3
1983	1881	189	3658	5728	32.8	3.3	63.9	425.3
1984	1749	240	5145	7134	24.5	3.4	72.1	642.7
1985	1719	244	5995	7958	21.6	3.1	75.3	762.6
1986	1886	247	5324	7457	25.3	3.3	71.4	743.1
1987	1853	272	8065	10190	18.2	2.7	79.2	982.8
1988	2341	377	8944	11662	20.1	3.2	76.7	1043.7
1989	2126	413	9086	11625	18.3	3.5	78.2	1014.8
1990	2388	332	10240	12960	18.4	2.6	79.0	1036.1

Exports by destination, % distribution

	OECD countries		Middle East		East Eur. and USSR	Others
	EC	Other	Gulf	Other		
1979	50.0	13.9	9.3	8.8	14.7	3.3
1980	44.7	13.1	11.8	10.7	17.7	2.0
1981	32.0	16.2	22.6	19.2	7.8	2.2

Year						
1982	30.5	14.0	32.6	15.3	6.1	1.5
1983	35.1	13.1	33.0	12.9	4.6	1.3
1984	38.3	14.1	30.9	11.1	4.5	1.1
1985	40.3	11.3	34.1	8.7	4.6	1.0
1986	43.8	13.8	22.1	12.9	5.8	1.6
1987	47.8	15.4	20.5	9.8	4.3	2.2
1988	43.7	13.8	18.5	11.7	7.1	5.2
1989	46.5	15.2	14.0	10.7	9.5	4.1
1990	52.8	15.2	9.5	9.7	8.1	4.7

Notes: [a] AGRX = agricultural exports.
[b] MINX = mining exports.
[c] MANX = manufacturing exports.

Sources: State Institute of Statistics, *Summary of Monthly Foreign Trade*, several issues, and Uygur (1993).

On the other hand, the performance of exports in the 1988–90 period can be described as one of stagnation or, at best, marginal growth. Export performance until 1987 was strong, especially if it is considered that it was achieved in an international environment that was affected adversely by the second oil shock and the recession of the early 1980s. Turkish exporters were able to take advantage of this environment by making use of the geographical proximity to the oil-exporting countries of the Middle East. The war between Iraq and Iran also increased the demand for Turkish exports. Export volumes almost multiplied by 10 during the period 1980–7.

The existence of excess production capacity in manufacturing, created in the 1970s and not fully utilized as a result of reduced domestic demand, was another significant factor that contributed to the supply response of exporters to foreign demand. Consequently, there has been a considerable rise in the exports of relatively new products such as basic metals. iron and steel, and chemicals. Yet, in spite of incentives for diversification, textiles and food, beverages and tobacco, which are among the most labour-intensive industries, have kept their large share of about 60 per cent in total exports, as can be observed in Table 9.4. This presumably is a reflection of the comparative advantage of Turkey in labour-intensive industries, but it also reflects the fact that diversification has not been achieved to the extent desired.

Table 9.4 Turkey: percentage shares of industries in manufacturing exports

Years	Sectors (ISIC CODES)					
	31	32	35	36	37	38
1977–9	50.0	39.8	2.4	3.9	2.4	2.5
1980–2	36.8	34.7	9.8	6.3	4.1	7.0
1983–5	22.8	37.9	12.5	3.7	11.1	9.4
1986–8	19.9	37.3	14.1	2.6	12.9	11.1
1989–90	17.7	40.9	14.1	3.2	15.0	8.0

Notes: (1) Sums of rows do not add up to 100 due to the exclusion of industries 33, 34 and 39.
(2) 31: food, beverages and tobacco; 32: textiles and clothing; 35: chemicals and petroleum refining; 36: cement and other soil products; 37: basic metals; 38: machinery and transport equipment.

Sources: Uygur (1991) and (1993).

Export Growth and Productivity Growth

Export growth depends, *ceteris paribus*, on output growth and the latter can result firstly from increased use of the factors of production, secondly from the reallocation of factors across sectors, and thirdly from increased productivity in the use of resources. Since it provides a direct competitive edge, productivity growth is the most important factor, not only for export growth but also for its sustainability.

In the case of Turkish growth, especially during the 1960s and the 1970s, it is often contended that growth was largely based on increased factor use and that the strategies followed had not encouraged the achievement of higher growth by way of higher productivity. The argument goes on to say that the outcome has been a relatively inefficient manufacturing industry, where productivity growth lags behind the fast-growing developed and developing countries (see, for example, Krueger and Tuncer, 1980 and 1982; and Nishimizu and Robinson, 1984). Nishimizu and Robinson compare growth rates of total factor productivity in manufacturing for the period 1963–76 in Japan, Korea, Turkey and Yugoslavia and find that they are lower in Turkey than in Korea and Japan but higher than in Yugoslavia.

The growth rates of labour, capital and multifactor productivity in Turkish manufacturing industries for 1965–76 (which can be typified as one of 'import substitution'), 1976–81 (the 'crisis' period), and 1981–8 (the 'export-orientation' period) show that there is little difference between the productivity performance of the earlier 'import-substitution' and the later 'outward-oriented' periods (see Table 9.5).[5] Thus, the import-substituting development strategy worked well up to a point and productivity growth was relatively high. This phase could indeed be considered necessary for the building of an industrial base for future exports. The strategy reached its limits, however, and export orientation became the only feasible policy.

In spite of the improvement relative to the 1976–81 period, the growth of multifactor productivity in the 1980s can be considered low. Two explanations can be given. First, education and the general well-being of the labour force were relatively neglected. Secondly, manufacturing investment stagnated and the increase in output was achieved largely through higher utilization of a capital stock that had been created earlier. This had two results: production technology remained relatively old; and economies of scale, which could have resulted from larger plants, could not be exploited.

Table 9.5   Turkey: labour, capital and multifactor productivity growth in manufacturing industries[a]

	1965–76	1976–81	1981–8	1965–88
Labour productivity: Public + Private				
3 Total manufac.	6.4	−1.6	4.9	4.2
Capital productivity: Public + Private				
3 Total manufac.	3.5	−4.4	4.1	2.0
Multifactor productivity: Public				
3 Total manufac.	1.2	0.9	1.0	1.1
Multifactor productivity: Private				
3 Total manufac.	1.6	−2.8	2.0	0.7
Multifactor productivity: Public + Private				
31 Food, bev. and tobac.	0.5	−0.4	2.0	0.7
32 Textiles and clothes	1.8	−2.9	0.2	0.2
33 Forest prod.	1.2	−3.4	2.1	0.5
34 Paper print	1.7	−1.7	2.6	1.1
35 Chemical and petr. refin.	2.1	0.3	1.1	1.5
36 Soil prod.	1.5	1.5	1.0	1.3
37 Basic metals	1.6	−3.4	3.6	1.2
38 Machin. and transp. equip.	3.0	−3.8	2.3	1.2
3 Total manufac.	1.5	−1.4	1.5	0.8

Note: [a] Total manufacturing includes Industry 39 (other manufacturing).
Source: Uygur (1991).

This second source of productivity growth is particularly relevant, since it is shown by Kwon (1986) and Dollar and Sokoloff (1990) for Korea and by Chen and Tang (1990) for Taiwan that economies of scale were the main determinants of the growth of total factor productivity in those countries. In particular, Dollar and Sokoloff (1990) show that the most significant variable explaining multifactor productivity growth in Korean manufacturing is establishment size. It is interesting to note that there has not been a significant change in establishment size in the Turkish manufacturing sector over the last two decades.

There is a high correlation between labour productivity (LPi) and exports (Xi) in manufacturing industries in the 1975–88 period. When one looks at correlations between total factor productivity (TFPi) and exports (Xi) for the same period, significant positive relationships are observed for four (e.g. basic metals and machinery and transport equipment) out of eight industries. Two correlations are positive but insignificant. Another two correlations, those relating to textiles and clothing and forest products, are found negative, though both insignificant at the 5 per cent level of significance (Uygur, 1991). This result can be explained by the relatively high rate of growth of the capital stock in these industries in the final years of the sample period and which is not yet reflected in the rate of growth of output.

With the stagnation in manufacturing investment in general and the accompanying low productivity growth rates, the sustainability of export growth and of the export-oriented growth strategy becomes doubtful. The uncertainty created by macroeconomic polices, particularly exchange rate and export promotion policies, is one of the key factors explaining poor investment performance.

Comparative Evaluation of Export Policies

Export promotion schemes carry direct and indirect costs. The direct cost of a scheme would be equivalent to its subsidy value, which in turn is an income transfer from public funds to exporters. Indirect costs are more difficult to assess. An important one is the increase in public-sector spending which may make the public deficit more difficult to control, with attendant inflationary effects. In order to be able to make inferences concerning the effects of export promotion schemes, quarterly manufacturing export equations were estimated. In these equations, the values of incentives schemes appear either within the relative export price variable or as separate explanatory variables. The estimation results are provided in the Appendix at the end of the chapter.

The estimated equations, which relate to three different periods, indicate that, at the beginning of the 1980s, exports were quite responsive to relative price changes, through both exchange rates and subsidies. The results are, therefore, supportive of the view that, at the beginning of an export drive, the compensation, through export incentives, of the overhead costs of entry to world markets is important. In addition, estimations show that the presence of excess supply also played a significant role in the export drive. Thus, the data support the contention that it was the decline in domestic demand, as well as the change in relative export prices, that produced the fast growth in exports.

After exporters are established in world markets, however, relative export prices (determined primarily by exchange rates) and perceived demand become the most significant factors in the growth of exports. More explicitly, the results imply that exchange rate policy is more effective than specific export incentives in determining export growth in the longer run. This finding is in agreement with that of Arslan and van Wijnbergen (1990), who conclude that the real depreciation of the exchange rate contributed by far the most to the explanation of Turkish export growth.

The greater long-run effectiveness of an appropriate exchange rate than export incentives can also be understood intuitively. Export promotion schemes, which are usually numerous and have intricate details, create bureaucracy and require time and energy for correct interpretation and understanding. Equally importantly, they contribute to the ineffectiveness of the tax system and add to budget deficits, which are of vital importance in inflationary economies like Turkey. Incentive schemes do play a crucial role at the beginning of an export promotion programme, but they should not considered as a substitute for an appropriate exchange rate.

IV IMPORT AND CAPITAL ACCOUNT LIBERALIZATION AND ECONOMIC PERFORMANCE

Liberalization of Imports and the Capital Account

The 1970s were characterized by various import restrictions, including bans, quotas, tariffs and other charges such as stamp duties, surcharges and advance-guarantee deposits. Imports were regulated through annual (or sometimes six-monthly) import programmes. The latter generally included a 'free import list', a 'restricted list', and a 'quota list'. These were 'positive lists', in that only those commodities that appeared on the lists could be imported. All imports carried tariffs, other charges and advance deposits.

For balance-of-payments reasons, the adjustment programme approached import liberalization in a gradual and cautious manner. At the start of the programme in January 1980, the stamp duty was lowered and in 1981 the quota list was partly eliminated. But the major change came at the end of 1983 with the replacement of the 'positive list' by a 'negative list' approach. In May 1985, the number of items in the latter was reduced from about 500 to 3. There was also a 'permission list', for imports requiring official permission. From about 1,000 in 1984, the number of goods in this list fell to 33 at the beginning of 1988.

Alongside, with the removal of quantitative restrictions (QRs) on a large proportion of imports, tariffs were lowered in December 1983 and again in January 1984. Tariff reductions concentrated especially on raw materials, intermediate goods and certain capital goods. Under the new system, about 60 per cent of the value of total imports was liberalized in the sense that QRs were removed, even though tariffs on most imports of consumer goods were raised (see Table 9.6).

In 1984, a tariff surcharge was introduced on a limited number of goods. In 1986 and 1987 the coverage and the rates of this surcharge were raised considerably in response to the worsening trade balance. Again in 1986 and 1987, two additional surcharges were imposed on most imports. These raised protection rates in certain sectors to some extent. Nominal and effective protection rates (NPRs and EPRs) computed in different studies agree that they have declined since 1984, but the magnitudes are quite different for different sectors; in the case of EPRs, this is largely a result of the differences in access that exporters had to duty-free imports.

The overall tariff plus surcharge rates were lowered in 1989 and 1990 as part of an anti-inflationary policy which aimed to divert demand increases towards imports. The outcome of these recent tariff reductions was a jump in imports, mainly of consumer goods, and a phenomenal trade deficit of over $10 billion in 1990, to which the Iraqi crisis also contributed. At present, given these large deficits, further import liberalization is unlikely. Although quantitative infor-

Table 9.6   Turkey: elimination of QRs and tariff rates (percentages)

	QRs	Average tariff rates	
	Elimination in 1984	*Before Dec. 1983*	*After Jan. 1984*
Consumer goods	93.6	18.0	26.2
Intermediate goods	69.2	40.8	18.6
Capital goods	23.5	44.0	25.3
Total	60.1	38.8	25.3

Sources: Baysan and Blitzer (1988) and (1991).

mation is not available, the process of import liberalization appears to have reduced the anti-export bias only slightly, since the various schemes discussed above already gave exporters access to duty-free imports.

Together with the liberalization of the current account, changes were made in the direction of capital account liberalization in 1984, when some restrictions on foreign exchange transactions were eased. Major policy changes in this area have been in effect since August 1989. Turkish nationals are now permitted to purchase foreign securities abroad and foreigners can buy Turkish securities; Turkish banks are entitled to extend foreign currency credits with a maturity of over three years to foreign trade companies; Turkish nationals are no longer required to obtain government permission to borrow abroad; and foreigners can now open lira accounts convertible into foreign exchange. These changes have made it easier for Turkish corporations to borrow abroad, and this has been reflected in an increasing foreign debt. The changes have made it possible for foreign capital to exploit arbitrage opportunities arising from interest rate differentials. Partly as a consequence of speculative inflows, the Turkish lira appreciated in real terms in both 1989 and 1990.

Macroeconomic Performance in 1980–90

The fight against inflation was given top priority in the adjustment programme. Partly owing to increases in government-controlled price hikes, inflation reached nearly 110 per cent in the first year of the programme. With the help of restrictive monetary and fiscal policies, inflation fell in the following years, but these policies were relaxed after 1983 and especially in 1987, owing to electoral considerations. Consequently, inflation accelerated and hovered around 65 to 70 per cent in 1988 and 1989, declining marginally to 55 per cent in 1990. Thus, inflation was lowered after 1980, but success in this area was rather short-lived, and the variability of inflation remained high. The view that the basic cause of this outcome is the growing deficits of the public sector is generally accepted. Policy-makers in Turkey have not solved the domestic transfer problem over the last decade through an efficient fiscal system.

The growth record of the 1980s is relatively better than the inflation record, but there are reservations concerning its stability and sustainability. Table 9.7 indicates that, in the period 1980–90, the Turkish economy experienced an average GDP growth rate of 4.6 per cent, but

Table 9.7 Growth, employment, investment, savings and sectoral indicators in Turkey[a]

	1977–9	1980	1981	1982	1983	1984	1985	1986	1987	1988	1989	1990
GDP Growth	2.0	−0.7	4.4	5.0	3.7	5.7	5.1	8.3	7.4	3.9	1.1	9.2
Manufacturing	1.1	−3.9	9.4	6.4	7.5	9.3	5.7	10.5	10.1	1.8	3.1	9.9
Agriculture	1.5	1.7	0.1	6.2	−0.1	3.5	2.7	7.6	2.1	7.9	−10.5	11.4
Empl Growth	1.9	1.2	0.8	−0.5	0.9	1.4	1.6	1.7	2.1	2.4	2.1	1.7
Fixed INV/GNP	23.2	19.7	18.9	18.8	18.8	17.9	20.0	23.1	24.0	24.0	22.5	21.3
Private	12.0	9.3	7.9	7.3	8.3	8.2	8.4	9.8	11.2	12.6	12.3	11.6
Public	11.3	10.4	11.0	11.5	10.5	9.7	11.6	13.3	12.8	11.4	10.2	9.7
Savings/GNP	17.3	16.0	18.6	15.9	16.2	16.5	18.9	21.9	24.1	26.3	23.6	21.1
Private	10.8	10.6	9.5	9.2	8.4	9.2	9.1	11.3	15.6	17.5	17.2	17.0
Public	6.5	5.4	9.1	6.7	7.8	7.3	9.8	10.6	8.5	8.8	6.4	4.1
Exports/GNP	5.2	6.4	10.2	14.6	15.7	19.5	20.7	17.9	20.7	24.6	23.5	20.3
Imports/GNP	10.1	13.9	15.2	17.6	19.6	23.1	23.5	20.6	22.3	22.1	24.0	26.8

Note: [a] The figures for employment and expenditure components of the GNP are provisional. All the ratios are calculated in terms of current prices.

Sources: State Institute of Statistics, *Statistical Yearbook of Turkey* (several issues); OECD (1991b); SPO (1985 and 1990b); Uygur (1987) and (1991b).

its variability increased after 1986 when economic policies themselves became more variable and uncertain. Moreover, the growth rate for the 1980s is lower than the average 5.6 per cent achieved from 1961 to 1980. On the other hand, the post-1980 growth performance of Turkey is decisively better than that of most other semi-industrialized developing countries or that of the Southern European countries (Greece, Italy, Portugal and Spain).

Industrial growth in 1980–90 was definitely not investment-led. Manufacturing investment, private and public alike, stagnated in this period. The adjustment programme relied on the assumption that financial liberalization would stimulate private savings and that greater funds would be available for fixed productive investments. These did not materialize. The decline in private manufacturing investment needs to be taken seriously, since the sustainability of outward orientation and liberalization processes critically depends on investment growth. There are several reasons for the stagnation of private manufacturing investment, and policy uncertainty is clearly one of the most important factors.

Foreign borrowing and foreign debt increased considerably in the second half of the 1980s; however, foreign exchange reserves reached an all-time high at the end of the 1980s. Employment growth was sluggish, particularly in the first half of the decade. Employment growth picked up after 1986 but high real-wage increases in 1989 and 1990 have already put a damper on further increases in employment. The functional and the size distribution of income worsened considerably between 1980 and 1988 (Celasun, 1989). It was only in 1989 and 1990 that there was a significant improvement in income distribution, when real agricultural prices and real manufacturing wages rose significantly.

V CONCLUDING REMARKS

By the late 1970s, the import-substitution model previously followed by Turkish policy-makers was in crisis. The year 1980 marks the beginning of an outward-oriented growth strategy which worked well until 1986. In 1980–6, there were improvements in most macroeconomic variables, especially foreign trade, against a background of real depreciation of the Turkish lira. However, real wages and agricultural incomes declined during this period. The years since 1986 have been marked by uncertainty in macroeconomic policies. During the last years of this period, real wages increased, the lira appreciated in real terms, exports stagnated and erratic changes in domestic absorption resulted in larger variability of growth rates.

Turkey's export performance has been impressive, especially in the first half of the 1980s. A combination of the following factors can explain this performance: (a) a substantial real depreciation of the lira, especially in the first year of the adjustment programme; (b) the introduction of new export promotion schemes and the improvement of existing ones; and (c) a considerable reduction in domestic demand and the shift of production from domestic to foreign markets. Capital inflows from the multilateral organizations and individual OECD countries at the start of the adjustment programme helped finance the required transfer of resources to the export sector.

The outward orientation programme was implemented with relative ease and without much conflict. One reason was the climate created by the emigration of workers to Western Europe since the 1960s. Policy-makers were successful in conveying to the private sector the message that, if the economy was to overcome the crisis, there was no alternative to the programme, and that the programme would shape the future course of the economy. From the mid-1980s onwards, however, policies became more erratic. Ironically but understandably, uncertainty and the loss of credibility intensified with the advent of elections and with democratization.

Policy uncertainty hit the most vulnerable variable, namely private productive investment, particularly in manufacturing. The result was that manufacturing productivity growth was not as high as expected. The relatively low growth of multifactor productivity in manufacturing casts doubt on the sustainability of the growth of Turkish exports. Given also the negative effect of the real appreciation of the Turkish lira since the end of 1988, it was no surprise that exports stagnated from 1988–9 onwards. In order to encourage exports, policy-makers turned to export promotion measures such as subsidized export credits. This may not be sufficient, however, especially in the medium and long run. Export promotion schemes played a significant role in the initial growth of exports but, as argued in this chapter, they are not as effective in determining sustainable long-term export growth.

The liberalization of imports and the capital account was approached gradually and at later stages of the adjustment programme. It is, therefore, too early to make a full assessment of these changes. One result of import liberalization is that it led to an increase in the imports of consumer goods. Capital account liberalization, on the other hand, contributed to the real appreciation of the lira. In 1990, further import liberalization measures were introduced at a time of real exchange appreciation, with the result that there was a sizeable trade and current account deficit. It is clear that the Turkish economy cannot afford this 'simultaneity problem' much longer.

APPENDIX: ESTIMATION OF EXPORT SUPPLY EQUATIONS

The basis for the estimated equations was an export supply function, where in the short run exports are determined by relative export price, export potential and perceived world demand. Estimations were done by ordinary least squares using quarterly data, first for the period from 1978I to 1983IV, then for 1984I to 1990IV and finally for the whole sample period of 1978I to 1990IV. The first estimation period was chosen on the grounds that at the beginning of 1984 there was a regime change in export promotion. Estimation results for the 1978I–1983IV period are given in Table A9.1.

In the first estimated equation of the table, LRELEXP is a relative export price variable that incorporates the effect of direct subsidy payments (tax rebates and cash premiums) only. In the second equation, the relative export price variable LRELMXP incorporates the effects of all the incentive schemes except that of the export credit scheme. The latter, when included in the relative price variable, did not add to the explanatory power of the equation. This result is understandable since export growth continued unabated in the first half of the 1980s in spite of the decline in subsidies from export credits. In the third equation, the relative export price LRELMAP does not incorporate the effects of export promotion schemes at all, and subsidy variables are included separately. Here, it was not possible to estimate correctly the effects of different export promotion schemes and exchange rate policy, basically because of multicollinearity.

Estimation results of the export equation for the period from 1984I to 1990IV are given in Table A9.2. In these estimations, the excess demand variable LEXDEMA became insignificant and, thus, it does not appear in the estimated equations. During this period, there appears to have been a considerable increase in the relative price elasticity. However, export promotion schemes, whether included within the relative export price variable or separately, did not significantly contribute to the explanation of manufacturing exports.

Table A9.1 Estimation of manufacturing export equation, dependent variable: LRMANX, period: 1978I–1983IV

Variable	Coeffic.	T-statistic					
Constant	4.924	6.429	n	24	SEE		.177
LROECDM	1.733	2.557	R**2	.951	Adjusted R^2		.943
LRELEXP (−1)	.745	2.277	D−W	1.731			
LEXDEMA (−2)	−1.673	−17.362					
Constant	4.917	6.543	n	24	SEE		.176
LROECDM	1.667	2.558	R**2	.951	Adjusted R^2		.935
LRELMXP (−1)	.787	2.362	D−W	1.726			
LEXDEMA (−2)	−1.664	−17.241					
Constant	5.072	6.294	n	24	SEE		.190
LROECDM	1.555	2.068	R**2	.943	Adjusted R^2		.935
LRELMAP (−1)	.600	1.267	D−W	1.420			
LEXDEMA (−2)	−1.709	−13.242					
RXREBAT (−1)	.851	1.595					
DUTALLO (−1)	1.020	.484					

DUTALLO: Manufacturing subsidies from corporate tax allowances, foreign exchange allocations and duty-free importations as a proportion of manufacturing exports.

LEXDEMA: Logarithm of Excess Demand Index. Excess Demand Index = (Capacity Utilization Rate)/(% of firms which report insufficient demand as the reason for underutilization of capacity). Capacity utilization itself may not be an accurate indicator of excess demand if there are supply constraints, as there were in Turkey in the late 1970s.

LRELEXP: Logarithm of relative manufacturing export price RELEXP which contains the effect of direct subsidy payments only, RELEXP-RELMAP * (1 + RXREBAT).

LRELMAP: Logarithm of relative manufacturing export price index RELMAP, where RELMAP = MXP * ER/MWPI, MXP: Manufacturing export US$ price index, ER: Nominal official US$ exchange rate, MWPI: Manufacturing domestic wholesale price index.

LRELMXP: Logarithm of relative manufacturing export price RELMXP which includes the effects of direct subsidy payments and duty allowances, RELMXP = RELMAP * (1 + RXREBAT + DUTALLO).

LRMANX: Logarithm of real manufacturing exports.

LROECDM: Logarithm of real non-petroleum imports of OECD.

RXREBAT: Rate of direct subsidy payments to manufacturing exports including tax rebates and cash premiums from extra-budgetary funds, as a proportion of manufacturing exports.

Table A9.2   Estimation of manufacturing export equation, dependent
variable: LRMANX, period: 1984I–1990IV

Variable	Coeffic.	T-statistic				
Constant	4.915	10.600	n	28	SEE	.105
LROECDM	1.416	6.673	R**2	.779	Adjusted R^2	.761
LRELEXP (−1)	1.075	2.801	D−W	1.379		
Constant	5.085	11.406	n	28	SEE	.107
LROECDM	1.236	7.378	R**2	.768	Adjusted R^2	.750
LRELMXP (−1)	1.048	2.529	D−W	1.301		
Constant	5.188	13.134	n	28	SEE	.088
LROECDM	1.111	4.496	R**2	.856	Adjusted R^2	.831
LRELMAP (−1)	1.918	4.510	D−W	1.670		
RXREBAT (−1)	−.831	−1.471				
DUTALLO (−1)	.492	.456				

Table A9.3   Estimation of manufacturing export equation, dependent
variable: LRMANX, period: 1978I–1990IV

Variable	Coeffic.	T-statistic				
Constant	4.170	14.297	n	41	SEE	.187
LROECDM	1.988	14.622	R**2	.964	Adjusted R^2	.961
LRELEXP (−1)	1.806	6.826	D−W	1.669		
LEXDEMA (−3)	−1.479	−14.455				
Constant	4.200	13.738	n	51	SEE	.194
LROECDM	1.808	14.058	R**2	.961	Adjusted R^2	.958
LRELMXP (−1)	1.891	6.350	D−W	1.516		
LEXDEMA (−3)	−1.473	−13.686				
Constant	4.267	14.567	n	51	SEE	.189
LROECDM	2.040	10.337	R**2	.965	Adjusted R^2	.961
LRELMAP (−1)	1.875	5.108	D−W	1.729		
LEXDEMA (−3)	−1.472	−13.427				
RXREBAT (−1)	.970	1.852				
DUTALLO (−1)	1.102	−.764				

Estimation results obtained by making use of the whole sample period from 1978I to 1990IV are presented in Table A9.3. Here again, the excess demand variable is negative and significant, but the variables that represent export incentives contribute only marginally to the explanatory power of the equation. In the case of this latter finding, though, part of the blame should go to multicollinearity.

Notes

1. I am grateful to Yilmaz Akyüz and Manuel Agosin, who made helpful comments and suggested improvements on this chapter. Any omissions and errors are obviously mine.
2. See, for example, Krueger (1984) and Edwards (1989).
3. The exchange rate is expressed as the Turkish lira equivalent of one unit of foreign currency.
4. An exhaustive list of export promotion measures in the 1980s is provided in SPO (1990b).
5. The total factor productivity growth rate of 1.5 per cent computed for 1965–76 falls between the 1.33 per cent rate obtained by Nishimizu and Robinson (1984) and the 1.96 per cent rate obtained by Krueger and Tuncer (1980) for 1963–76.

References

Arslan, I., and S. van Wijnbergen (1990), 'Turkey: Export Miracle or Accounting Trick?', World Bank Discussion Paper WPS 370, Washington, DC.

Balassa, B. (1984), 'Adjustment Policies in Developing Countries: A Reassessment', *World Development*, Vol. 12, No. 9, pp. 955–72.

Baysan, T., and C. Blitzer (1988), 'The Timing and Sequencing of a Trade Liberalization Policy: The Case of Turkey', Country Manuscript (Washington, DC: World Bank).

Baysan, T., and C. Blitzer (1991), 'Turkey', in D. Papageorgiou, M. Michaely and A. M. Choksi, *Liberalizing Foreign Trade*, Vol. 6 (London: Basil Blackwell, for the World Bank).

Celasun, M. (1989), 'Income Distribution and Employment Aspects of Turkey's Post-1980 Adjustment', *METU Studies in Development*, Vol. 16, Nos. 3–4, pp. 1–32.

Celasun, M., and D. Rodrik (1989), 'Debt, Adjustment and Growth: Turkey', in J. D. Sachs and S. M. Collins, eds, *Developing Country Debt and Economic Performance, Country Studies*, Vol. 3 (Chicago: NBER and the University of Chicago Press).

Celebi, I. (1991) 'Turkiyede 1980 Sonras; Ihracata Yonelik Sanayilesme Modelinde Ihracata Ozgu Tesviklerin Sanayilesme Acisindan Degerlendirilmesi', unpublished Ph.D. dissertation, Dokuz Eylul Universitesi, Izmir.

Chen, T.-J., and D.P. Tang (1990), 'Export Performance and Productivity Growth: The Case of Taiwan', *Economic Development and Cultural Change*, Vol. 38, No. 2, pp. 577–85.

Dervis, K., and P.A. Petri 91987), 'The Macroeconomics of Successful Development: What Are the Lessons', *NBER Macroeconomics Annual 1987*, pp. 211–54.

Dollar, D., and K. Sokoloff (1990), 'Patterns of Productivity Growth in South Korean Manufacturing Industries, 1963–1979', *Journal of Development Economics*, Vol. 22, No. 2, pp. 303–27.

Edwards, S. (1989), 'On the Sequencing of Structural Reforms', unpublished paper prepared for the OECD.

Krueger, A.O. (1974), *Foreign Trade Regimes and Economic Development: Turkey* (New York: NBER).

Krueger, A.O. (1984), 'Problems of Liberalization', in A. Harberger, ed., *World Economic Growth* (San Francisco: ICS Press).

Krueger, A.O., and B. Tuncer (1980), 'Estimating Total Factor Productivity Growth in a Developing Country', *World Bank Staff Working Paper No. 422*, Washington DC.

Krueger, A.O., and B. Tuncer (1982), 'Growth of Factor Productivity in Turkish Manufacturing Industries', *Journal of Development Economics*, Vol. 11, No. 4, pp. 307–25.

Kwon, J. (1986), 'Capital Utilization, Economies of Scale and Technical Change in the Growth of Total Factor Productivity', *Journal of Development Economics*, Vol. 24, No. 1, pp. 75–89.

Milanovic, B. (1986), 'Export Incentives and Turkish Manufactured Imports', World Bank Staff Working Papers No. 768, Washington DC.

Nishimizu, M., and S. Robinson (1984), 'Trade Policies and Productivity Change in Semi-Industrialized Countries', *Journal of Development Economics*, Vol. 16, No. 2, pp. 177–206.

OECD (1991a), *OECD Economic Surveys, Turkey*, 1990/91, Paris.

OECD (1991b), *National Accounts: Main Aggregates*, Vol. 1, 1960–1989, Paris.

Onis, Z. (1986), 'Stabilization and Growth in a Semi-industrial Economy: An Evaluation of the Recent Turkish Experiment, 1977–1984', *METU Studies in Development*, Vol. 13, Nos 1–2, pp. 7–28.

Senses, F. (1989), *1980 Sonrasi Ekonomi Politikalari Isiginda Turkiye'de Sanayilesme* (Ankara: Verso Yayincilik).

SPO State Planning Organization (1985), *V. Bes Yillik Kalkinma Plani Oncesinde Gelismeler 1972–1983*, Ankara.

SPO State Planning Organization (1990a), *VI. Bes Yillik Kalkinma Plani Oncesinde Gelismeler 1984–1988*, Ankara.

SPO State Planning Organization (1990b), *Doviz Kazandirici Faaliyetlerin Tesviki Politikalari*, Ankara.

Uygur, E. (1987), *SESRTCIC Econometric Model of Turkey*, Turkey.

Uygur, E. (1991), *Policy, Productivity, Growth and Employment in Turkey, 1960–1989 and Prospects for the 1990s* (Geneva: ILO, Special Topic Study, MIES 90/4).

Uygur, E. (1993), *Policy, Trade and Growth in Turkey: 1970–1990*, UNCTAD Trade Policy Series No. 4 (Geneva, forthcoming).

10 Structural Adjustment in Mexico: Two Different Stories

Adriaan Ten Kate[1]

In this chapter the structural adjustment of the Mexican economy carried out during the 1980s is analysed from two different vantage points. The first of these analyses focuses on the radical changes that had to be made in macroeconomic policy in order to put the economy back on its feet after the series of crises it suffered in 1982, 1985 and 1987. The second addresses the thorough-going changes in trade policy that have transformed Mexico from a tightly closed economy at the start of the decade to one of the most open in the world. In the final section of the chapter an attempt is made to merge the two stories into one.

I THE FIRST STORY

The 1982 Crisis

The debt crisis, which broke out in full force in 1982, prompted Mexico to suspend its debt payments, thereby precipitating a crisis in the international financial system. When international reserves ran out in February, it became necessary to devalue the Mexican peso, and the exchange rate was raised from 26 to over 40 pesos to the dollar. Even this proved insufficient, however, and in September exchange controls were introduced, following a long history of full convertibility. At the same time, prior licensing requirements were instituted for all imports.

These measures proved insufficient, and in December the system of exchange controls was modified and a dual exchange rate was established: a controlled rate for trade and for the servicing of pre-existing debt, and a free-market rate for all other external transactions. The controlled exchange rate was set at 90 pesos to the dollar and a

239

crawling peg was introduced whereby the rate was allowed to slide by 13 centavos per day. The free rate started out at 150 pesos to the dollar and remained at that level until late 1983, by which time the controlled rate was nearing the same level.

All these events took the wind out of the economy's sails. Whereas GDP had grown by 8.8 per cent in real terms in 1981, in 1982 it shrank by 0.6 per cent and in 1983 it fell by 4.2 per cent. Fixed capital investment dropped from 26.4 per cent of GDP in 1981 to 22.9 per cent in 1982 and to 17.5 per cent in 1983 (see Table 10.1). In 1982, inflation reached an annual rate of 100 per cent, as compared to rates of around 25 per cent in earlier years. None the less, owing to the above-mentioned devaluations, the real exchange rate depreciated significantly (see Table 10.2).

The 1983–5 Stabilization Programme

As a consequence of the steps taken in 1982, imports fell sharply. During the first quarter of 1983, the level of imports was just one-fourth of what it had been in the final quarter of 1981. The upturn in non-oil exports was less dramatic but none the less significant: in the first quarter of 1984 they were double what they had been in the darkest

Table 10.1   Rate of growth of GDP and ratios of investment and imports to GDP: Mexico, 1980–90 (percentages)

Year	Growth of GDP	Investment[a]	Imports
1980	9.2	24.7	13.0
1981	8.8	26.4	12.9
1982	−0.6	22.9	10.3
1983	−4.2	17.5	9.4
1984	3.6	17.9	9.6
1985	2.6	19.1	10.5
1986	−3.7	19.4	12.6
1987	1.8	18.4	12.6
1988	1.4	19.1	14.4
1989	3.2	18.1	15.0
1990	3.9	20.3	16.4

Note: [a]Gross fixed capital formation.
Source: National accounts.

Table 10.2   Mexico: inflation and the real exchange rate

Quarter	Annual inflation[a] (percentage)	Nominal[b] Controlled	Free	Real (base:1978)[c] Controlled	Free
1980–1	22.6	–	22.8	140.8	88.4
2	25.1	–	22.8	–	85.9
3	28.4	–	23.8	–	83.7
4	28.9	–	23.1	–	82.4
1981–1	27.9	–	23.5	–	79.5
2	28.4	–	24.1	–	78.7
3	26.8	–	24.8	–	76.4
4	28.5	–	25.7	–	76.4
1982–1	32.8	–	34.4	–	92.4
2	44.3	–	46.8	–	109.4
3	65.6	59.8	67.4	117.0	132.0
4	87.6	55.9	80.1	91.8	131.6
1983–1	112.9	102.4	148.7	132.2	192.0
2	114.7	114.2	148.6	126.9	165.2
3	100.8	126.1	148.4	124.7	146.7
4	87.4	138.0	155.4	122.0	137.3
1984–1	73.0	149.9	167.3	114.5	127.8
2	67.8	161.7	179.2	109.7	121.5
3	63.3	173.7	191.1	107.2	117.9
4	60.4	185.7	203.2	104.0	113.8
1985–1	59.4	200.4	217.9	96.7	105.1
2	55.0	218.6	236.0	96.6	104.3
3	55.8	275.3	336.2	109.7	134.0
4	60.6	333.5	451.1	118.0	159.6
1986–1	66.7	422.9	463.7	122.3	134.1
2	77.0	522.1	554.3	128.0	135.9
3	91.5	664.2	686.8	135.8	140.4
4	103.1	836.2	846.7	142.9	144.7
1987–1	109.4	1015.9	1019.2	140.5	140.9
2	124.3	1229.1	1232.3	137.7	138.1
3	134.2	1450.6	1454.3	130.9	131.2
4	148.4	1775.9	1917.3	125.5	135.5
1988–1	177.4	2240.4	2265.8	113.9	115.2
2	147.8	2257.0	2297.5	104.2	106.0
3	107.3	2257.0	2297.5	100.7	102.5
4	66.8	2257.0	2297.5	98.6	100.4
1989–1	26.9	2308.6	2343.1	97.2	98.6
2	18.4	2407.7	2434.0	99.3	100.4
3	17.0	2502.4	2525.5	99.8	100.7
4	18.7	2593.9	2630.9	100.1	101.5
1990–1	23.5	2681.6	2762.9	96.1	99.1
2	25.2	2789.3	2818.7	95.0	96.0
3	28.0	2851.3	2881.0	93.3	94.3
4	29.6	2918.7	2923.4	92.5	92.7

Notes overleaf

Table 10.2 *cont.*
Notes: [a] Percentage increase in consumer prices.
     [b] Pesos per U.S. Dollar.
     [c] The real exchange rate was calculated using a consumer price index
       for Mexico and a wholesale price index for the United States. Since
       70 per cent of Mexico's trade is with the United States, only the
       exchange rate against the dollar was computed.
Source: Banco de México.

hours of 1982 (see Table 10.3). With these measures and the restructuring of external financial obligations, the authorities regained control over the balance of payments, and in 1983 the servicing of the external debt, which had been suspended since 1982, was resumed.

One economic variable that did not respond so satisfactorily to these advances, however, was inflation, which declined more slowly than expected or desired. In fact, the annual rate of inflation, which had been almost 100 per cent at the end of 1982, dropped to 80 per cent in December 1983 and to about 60 per cent in late 1984. Consequently, it remained far above the inflation tax implicit in the fiscal deficit, probably as a result of the huge price differentials between Mexico and the international market that were created by the devaluations of 1982.

Improved fiscal discipline was reflected in the reduction of the financial deficit from 17.3 per cent of GDP in 1982 to 9.5 per cent in 1985 (see Table 10.4). This reduction was achieved largely at the expense of public investment, but sizeable adjustments were also made in the prices of goods and services supplied by the public sector. The dismantling of state companies was also begun during this period. Although this process initially consisted primarily of the closure of companies that could not be sold, its impact was none the less felt more generally via the reduction of the subsidies needed to keep such firms in operation (Córdoba, 1990).

Throughout this period the rate of devaluation remained substantially below the rate of inflation, and the real exchange rate therefore steadily appreciated. The result, in 1984, was that imports were on their way back up, while export growth was losing momentum. Consequently, early in 1985 difficulties began to arise once again in connection with the external balance. A slight increase in the pace of the crawling peg proved ineffective in counteracting the above trends, and by mid-1985 it became necessary to act. A lesson from the 1982 crisis was that it was better to act in time, rather than waiting until international reserves evaporated.

Table 10.3   The trade balance: Mexico 1980–90[a] (in millions of dollars)

| Quarter | Exports | | Imports | | Balance | |
	Petroleum products	Total	Private sector	Public sector		Total
1980–1	2.022	3.421	2.365	1.269	−213	3.634
2	2.574	3.789	2.791	1.691	−693	4.482
3	2.882	4.042	3.132	2.017	−1.107	5.149
4	2.940	4.259	3.509	2.121	−1.371	5.630
1981–1	3.924	5.489	3.724	2.131	−366	5.855
2	4.004	5.370	3.944	2.262	−836	6.206
3	2.981	4.206	3.478	2.321	−1.593	5.799
4	3.664	5.035	3.900	2.190	−1.055	6.090
1982–1	3.165	4.427	3.373	1.690	−636	5.063
2	5.008	5.105	2.649	1.495	961	4.144
3	4.627	5.650	1.885	1.257	2.508	3.142
4	4.677	6.049	1.129	958	3.962	2.087
1983–1	3.780	5.183	730	908	3.545	1.638
2	4.054	5.557	1.007	1.303	3.247	2.310
3	4.044	5.539	1.255	1.112	2.367	3.172
4	4.140	6.023	1.252	982	3.789	2.234
1984–1	4.283	6.436	1.267	1.092	4.077	2.359
2	4.121	6.051	1.458	1.125	3.468	2.583
3	4.129	5.867	1.782	1.310	2.775	3.092
4	4.068	5.846	1.957	1.264	2.625	3.221
1985–1	3.916	5.699	1.960	1.271	2.468	3.231
2	3.291	4.915	2.244	1.135	1.536	3.379
3	3.827	5.342	2.272	962	2.108	3.234
4	3.734	5.708	2.351	1.024	2.333	3.375
1986–1	1.677	4.009	2.067	902	1.040	2.969
2	1.407	3.769	2.246	817	706	3.063
3	1.446	3.667	1.962	731	974	2.693
4	1.777	4.587	1.814	596	2.177	2.410
1987–1	2.030	4.828	1.910	603	2.315	2.513
2	2.228	5.360	2.238	679	2.443	2.917
3	2.342	5.211	2.545	762	1.904	3.307
4	2.030	5.260	2.750	736	1.774	3.486
1988–1	1.801	5.274	3.007	720	1.547	3.727
2	1.814	5.439	3.793	792	854	4.585
3	1.620	4.981	4.064	1.100	−183	5.164
4	1.572	4.963	4.479	940	−456	5.419
1989–1	1.853	5.404	4.299	868	237	5.167
2	2.033	6.046	4.987	998	61	5.985
3	1.913	5.536	4.895	934	−293	5.829
4	2.076	5.779	5.458	972	−651	6.430
1990–1	1.983	6.157	5.009	633	215	5.942
2	1.484	5.369	5.703	954	−1.288	6.657
3	2.934	7.085	7.026	1.080	−1.021	8.106
4	3.703	8.162	7.814	1.280	−932	9.094

Note: [a] Does not include the inbond assembly (maquila) industry.
Source: Banco de México.

Table 10.4 Fiscal balance: Mexico, 1982–90 (as a percentage of GDP)

Year	Financial balance	Primary balance[a]	Operating balance[b]
1982	17.3	−7.2	−5.1
1985	−9.5	3.4	−3.8
1986	−16.1	1.6	−2.4
1987	−16.0	4.7	1.8
1988	−12.3	8.0	−3.5
1989	−5.6	8.4	−1.7
1990	−3.5	8.2	1.1

Notes: [a] Excludes interest payments.
        [b] Excludes the inflationary component of the interest paid on Mexican peso-denominated debt.
Source: Grupo de Economistas y Asociados (GEA).

A Change of Course in July 1985

The orientation of macroeconomic policy changed dramatically in July 1985 when the government launched a programme of outward-oriented trade reforms which will be described in greater detail in the course of the second 'story'. From that point on, the exchange rate ceased to serve as a means of curbing inflation and became instead the chief tool for seeking balance of payments equilibrium. Policy-makers were confident that competition would moderate inflation.

Towards the end of July 1985, the nominal exchange rate was devalued by 22 per cent and from that point until December 1986, the rate of change in the crawling peg was consistently higher than inflation, which meant that the real exchange rate began to depreciate once again (see Table 10.2).

Exports responded very well to the devaluations. In fact, non-oil exports doubled in just three years from US$ 7 billion in 1985 to US$ 14 billion in 1988. Despite the outward-oriented trade reforms, imports fell – no doubt as a result of the steep depreciation of the real exchange rate. This trend was reversed in early 1987 when exchange rate policy was altered.

As a matter of fact, little attention had been paid to inflation in 1985, which rose even higher than it had in 1982. This was primarily the result of two factors: first, the expansion of the fiscal deficit caused by the drop in oil prices;[2] and secondly, the severe undervaluation of the

Mexican peso. After all its devaluations, Mexico had become very inexpensive compared with other countries, and external prices pulled domestic prices up after them. Paradoxically, during this period the reforms spurred inflation rather than reducing it, as local producers made contact for the first time with the outside world – where prices (expressed in national currency) were far higher than in the domestic economy.

With external accounts on a solid footing but with prices rising sharply, inflation again became a first priority. This gave rise to a change in exchange rate policy early in 1987 and, from then on, the rate of change in the crawling peg was kept below the inflation rate, with the result that the real exchange rate started to appreciate once again (see Table 10.2). This did not stop inflation from worsening, however, and by the end of 1987 – following the stock market crash on Wall Street and another steep devaluation of the Mexican peso – the situation had deteriorated to such an extent that it again became necessary for the government to step in.

The Economic Solidarity Pact

In order to redress this situation, the Economic Solidarity Pact (ESP) was launched in December 1987. This heterodox stabilization programme consisted of an agreement between the government, trade unions and industry that set forth five courses of action:

(i) A sharp adjustment in the prices of goods and services supplied by the public sector and greater restraint in respect of government spending with a view to lowering the fiscal deficit;

(ii) An adjustment of the controlled exchange rate in order to close the gap with the free-market rate that had been opened up by the depreciation of the latter in November 1987, and a freeze on the controlled rate until June 1988, after which the exchange rate was to serve as an 'anchor' for inflation;

(iii) A one-time wage increase at the start of the Pact and a commitment to index wages to inflation from March 1988 onwards;

(iv) A commitment on the part of industry not to raise prices and a commitment on the part of the trade unions not to demand wage increases above and beyond those agreed to; and

(v) The acceleration of the trade reform programme (described in the following section) with a view to curbing inflation.

The ESP was originally signed for a period of six months, but it was later extended on various occasions.

In other developing countries similar programmes had not had the desired effects. Save for a few exceptions (Bolivia and Israel), the outcome of such programmes had been an enormous amount of friction. Sooner or later, these programmes had been cut short by an inflationary surge that obviously hurt the credibility of the next stabilization attempt.

In Mexico, however, the programme worked. In 1988 the monthly rate of inflation slowed from 15 per cent in January to about 1 per cent in September. One of the reasons for this was that the fiscal balance improved considerably. The government's operating deficit (i.e. excluding the inflationary component of interest on the peso-denominated debt) shrank from 5.4 per cent of GDP in 1987 to just 0.7 per cent in 1988 (see Table 10.4). All this was achieved against the backdrop of a moderately recessionary situation coupled with exchange rate stability. After a year of self-discipline in respect of prices and wages, shortages of goods were not a major problem and the economy continued to function on the basis of what were essentially free-market principles.

There is no consensus of opinion as to why the Mexican pact worked so well. Certainly, part of its success was a result of the flexibility with which it was implemented. For example, when frictions became too great, incidental price and wage increases were granted, but care was always taken to ensure that such increases would not spread to the rest of the economy. The Pact's success can also be attributed to the heavy concentration of political and economic power, which played a significant part in bringing the main parties concerned together at the bargaining table. Another factor is the high level of international reserves, which shielded the programme from speculative attacks on the exchange rate. Last but not least, part of the reason may be luck, pure and simple – luck in the sense that the levels of relative prices, wages and the exchange rate at the start were not too far off from levels that proved to be sustainable over the medium term.

The Resumption of Growth

During 1989 the Mexican economy continued to stabilize. Inflation remained below 20 per cent and the growth rate was positive, although still modest (3.1 per cent). The fiscal balance showed an operating surplus and the exchange rate was relatively stable. These trends strengthened in 1990. Perhaps the most outstanding event of the year was the renegotiation of the public sector's external debt with commercial banks under the terms of the Brady Plan (in fact, Mexico was the first to benefit from this plan). The renegotiations exorcised the spectre of the external debt from the scene and laid a foundation for future growth. One of the chief consequences was a spectacular drop in domestic interest rates, which gave the government much more breathing space than it had enjoyed since 1982. Indeed, in order to counterbalance widespread uncertainty and check capital flight, it had been necessary to keep domestic interest rates at very high levels throughout the entire post crisis period.[3] This situation changed in 1990 when, finally, even the most wary economic agents realized that the adjustment programme was a success. Other factors contributing to the change were: (a) the statement of intent to reach a free-trade agreement with the United States and Canada; (b) the announcement that the banking system would be returned to private ownership; and (c) the temporary rise in oil prices sparked by the conflict in the Persian Gulf. These events heralded the beginning of a new era marked by the return of capital to the country and the consolidation of economic growth, which amounted to 3.9 per cent in 1990.

The slight upturn in inflation seen in 1990 – the annual rate rose to 30 per cent – seems to have been brought under control in 1991. Moreover, economic growth is accelerating and the government is tackling the enormous task of rebuilding the country's infrastructure, which deteriorated noticeably during nearly a decade of austerity measures in the area of public investment. Private investment levels are apparently recovering as well, although reliable statistics are not yet available to confirm this. The greatest cause of concern at present is the trade deficit, which is mounting rapidly. However, this deficit is more than offset by inflows in the form of returning capital and foreign direct investment. With international reserves of over US$ 15 billion, no major difficulties are expected in the short run.

In sum, macroeconomic stabilization has been successful. Fiscal accounts are balanced. Interest rates are now at levels that do not impede growth. Inflation is moving downward once again, and the external accounts are under control. Everything seems to indicate that Mexico is heading for a period of strong, sustained growth.

II   THE SECOND STORY

The Trade Policy Reforms

The 1980s were a time of major change in terms of the conventional
wisdom as to what trade policies developing countries should follow in
order to further their economic development (see Chapter 1 in this
volume). In the three decades following the Second World War, these
policies had been based, in large part, on an abiding mistrust in the
merits of leaving international trade to the free play of market forces. A
number of developing countries (including Mexico) had considerable
success with such policies over protracted periods of time. Yet by the
1970s it was becoming increasingly clear that few protected industries
could keep pace with the ever swifter flow of international technological progress.[4] In most cases, rather than falling into step with their
counterparts in the international market after having gone through the
necessary learning process, these firms fell further and further behind
and became increasingly dependent on the protection that had been
given to them to help them set themselves up in business.

When by early 1985 the stabilization measures described in the
preceding section proved unsatisfactory, the lack of growth was
attributed to an inefficient, obsolete production structure, and the
blame was laid at the door of protectionist policies, the excessive
involvement of the public sector in production and the regulations
concerning foreign direct investment. This entailed the need for trade
liberalization, the privatization of state companies and a more flexible
attitude towards foreign direct investment, rather than mere austerity
measures in respect of public expenditure.

Before trade liberalization, Mexico's import regime consisted
primarily of a system of *ad valorem* tariffs which were supplemented
by official prices to counter under-invoicing and a system of
quantitative controls, whether in the form of quotas or simply import
licences. Although for some products the *ad valorem* tariffs were as
high as 100 per cent, it is generally agreed that the system of
quantitative controls was the most restrictive aspect of the import
regime (see Balassa, 1983).

The trade liberalization programme began in July 1985 with the
elimination of quantitative controls on a large number of tariff items.
The corresponding decree also did away with prior licensing requirements for almost all intermediate goods and for many capital goods as

well. Only 908 tariff items (out of a total of 8,000) remained subject to controls, and most of these were final consumer goods.

The second step was the announcement of a tariff reduction timetable in March 1986 which provided for stage-by-stage reductions in all tariffs. According to this timetable, the tariff ceiling – which, following the elimination of the 100 per cent rate early in the year, had fallen to 50 per cent – would be lowered in four equal stages to 30 per cent by October 1988.

The third major step was taken in the summer of 1986 when Mexico acceded to the General Agreement on Tariffs and Trade (GATT). Although, generally speaking, the commitments made upon joining GATT did not go beyond what had already been done under the reforms of July 1985 and what was already set forth in the tariff reduction timetable, accession to GATT was a sign of the Mexican authorities' determination to see the outward-oriented reform programme all the way through, or, in other words, it was a signal that there was no turning back. This sign was considered to be important in order to increase the credibility of the programme which until then had not been strong enough.

One of the 'admission fees' to GATT was the commitment to eliminate the system of official prices by the end of 1987. This system, whose coverage had been broadened following the suppression of the import licensing system, had already begun to be pared down as early as January 1986 and was in fact phased out of existence in the course of 1986 and 1987.

The last major step was taken in December 1987 with the launching of the ESP described in section I of this chapter. One of its provisions called for larger tariff reductions than those stipulated in the abovementioned timetable. Indeed, as a result of the pact, tariff rates were lowered quite evenly to approximately half their former level. The result was an *ad valorem* tariff structure containing five rates ranging from 0 to 20 per cent.

This last measure brought the programme of import reforms to a close. Since that time, some quantitative controls have been eliminated and some adjustments have been made in the tariff structure, but the bulk of the reforms were completed in the period between July 1985 and December 1987. This can be seen in Tables 10.5, 10.6 and 10.7, which show the trends in import licensing coverage (Table 10.5), official prices (Table 10.7) and average tariff levels (Table 10.6) during the second half of the 1980s.

Table 10.5 Mexico: domestic production protected by import licensing (percentages)

Sectors	1980 Apr.	1985 June	1985 Dec.	1986 June	1986 Dec.	1987 June	1987 Dec.	1988 June	1988 Dec.	1989 June	1989 Dec.	1990 June	1990 Dec.
1. Agriculture	95.1	95.8	62.4	57.6	57.6	42.2	44.3	42.2	42.2	42.2	38.4	38.4	33.5
2. Petroleum and natural gas	100.0	100.0	100.0	100.0	100.0	100.0	100.0	100.0	100.0	100.0	100.0	100.0	100.0
3. Other mining	27.4	51.8	4.3	4.3	4.3	4.3	0.0	0.0	0.0	0.0	0.0	0.0	0.0
4. Food	68.5	98.1	56.0	55.8	38.2	31.7	25.9	25.9	23.0	25.3	20.5	20.2	16.6
5. Beverages and tobacco	18.3	99.5	99.4	99.4	62.6	20.6	20.6	19.8	19.8	19.8	19.8	19.8	19.8
6. Textiles	80.4	90.7	9.6	9.6	9.6	9.6	7.0	2.4	3.1	3.1	1.0	1.1	0.1
7. Wearing apparel and footwear	92.6	99.1	81.4	81.4	81.4	78.1	52.9	0.0	0.0	0.0	0.0	0.0	0.0
8. Wood products	76.7	99.1	81.4	81.4	78.1	52.9	0.0	0.0	0.0	0.0	0.0	0.0	0.0
9. Paper and printing	30.7	74.5	6.7	6.7	6.7	6.7	6.3	0.3	0.3	0.3	0.3	0.3	0.0
10. Petroleum products	90.4	94.3	87.4	87.4	87.2	87.2	87.2	87.2	87.2	87.2	86.4	86.4	86.4
11. Chemicals	41.3	86.8	24.8	24.8	21.9	18.0	2.5	2.5	2.4	2.4	2.1	1.6	0.5
12. Non-metallic mineral product	31.2	95.6	15.3	15.3	10.3	3.6	2.1	2.1	2.4	2.4	0.0	0.0	0.0
13. Basic metals industry	49.6	86.8	0.4	0.4	0.0	0.0	0.0	0.0	0.0	0.0	0.0	0.0	0.0
14. Metal products	21.8	74.0	8.3	8.6	2.6	1.6	1.0	1.0	1.1	1.1	1.1	1.1	1.1
15. Machinery and equipment	54.8	85.6	19.2	15.6	6.7	6.1	3.0	2.4	4.8	4.8	2.8	2.1	2.1
16. Electrical equipment	51.3	97.2	40.8	36.9	31.6	24.0	0.0	0.0	0.0	0.0	0.0	0.0	0.0
17. Transport	77.3	99.0	77.0	76.8	64.2	64.0	58.0	57.4	41.4	41.4	41.0	39.4	39.4
18. Other manufactures	51.8	91.8	22.9	22.8	18.3	17.0	0.0	0.0	0.0	0.0	0.0	0.0	0.0
Total production of goods	64.0	92.2	47.1	46.9	39.8	35.8	25.4	23.2	21.3	21.8	19.8	19.6	17.9

Source: Secretaría de Comercio y Fomento Industrial.

Table 10.6 Mexico: average tariffs weighted by output[a] (percentage *ad valorem*)

Sectors	1980 Apr.	1985 June	1985 Dec.	1986 June	1986 Dec.	1987 June	1987 Dec.	1988 June	1988 Dec.	1989 June	1989 Dec.	1990 June	1990 Dec.
1. Agriculture	8.8	8.6	12.9	12.1	13.2	12.9	7.4	6.4	6.5	9.3	9.2	9.2	8.3
2. Petroleum and natural gas	0.0	0.0	0.0	0.0	0.0	0.0	0.0	0.0	0.0	10.0	8.6	8.6	8.6
3. Other mining	12.4	19.1	18.5	17.7	17.8	16.4	8.0	8.0	7.9	11.0	11.0	10.9	10.9
4. Food	24.0	22.6	31.5	29.2	28.8	26.4	13.6	11.6	8.7	11.6	11.9	11.9	12.5
5. Beverages and tobacco	72.9	77.0	77.0	41.4	40.1	37.4	19.7	19.7	19.7	19.7	19.7	19.7	19.7
6. Textiles	21.7	32.5	44.5	37.2	37.2	33.3	14.7	14.7	14.2	14.8	14.8	14.8	14.8
7. Wearing apparel and footwear	32.0	46.8	48.2	41.4	41.4	37.1	18.7	18.7	18.1	18.5	18.5	18.5	18.8
8. Wood products	29.2	37.0	41.2	37.0	37.0	33.5	17.7	16.8	16.7	16.9	16.9	16.9	16.9
9. Paper and printing	21.7	19.6	22.1	19.3	18.7	18.3	9.6	4.6	4.8	6.8	6.7	6.8	6.8
10. Petroleum products	2.2	2.2	3.0	2.3	2.1	2.0	1.0	1.1	1.1	10.2	4.4	4.4	4.4
11. Chemicals	30.8	28.7	30.8	26.5	27.7	26.0	13.1	12.9	11.7	13.5	13.4	13.4	13.5
12. Non-metallic mineral product	32.6	31.7	39.4	33.1	33.2	29.8	15.0	14.2	14.6	14.9	14.9	14.9	14.9
13. Basic metals industry	12.4	15.1	22.2	19.7	19.8	18.9	8.0	8.0	8.5	10.6	10.6	10.6	10.6
14. Metal products	37.3	35.7	38.8	30.1	30.1	27.7	15.1	15.0	13.8	14.6	14.6	14.6	14.6
15. Machinery and equipment	23.8	21.5	32.6	29.0	30.9	28.2	15.4	15.6	14.4	15.7	15.7	15.7	15.7
16. Electrical equipment	30.6	35.5	46.2	38.4	38.5	34.9	17.4	17.4	17.2	17.4	17.4	17.4	17.4
17. Transport	41.6	39.2	41.6	29.0	31.9	28.6	14.4	14.8	14.4	16.0	16.0	16.0	16.0
18. Other manufactures	44.4	50.8	53.1	37.9	37.8	33.8	17.7	17.6	17.2	18.0	18.0	18.0	18.0
Total production of goods	22.8	23.5	28.5	24.0	24.5	22.7	11.8	11.0	10.2	12.6	12.5	12.5	12.4

Note: [a] These averages do not include the uniform 5 per cent surcharge, which was eliminated in December 1987.
Source: Secretaría de Comercio y Fomento Industrial.

Table 10.7 Mexico: domestic production protected by official import prices (percentages)

Sectors	1980 Apr.	1985 June	1985 Dec.	1986 June	1986 Dec.	1987 June	1987 Dec.	1988 June	1988 Dec.	1989 June	1989 Dec.	1990 June	1990 Dec.
1. Agriculture	0.2	0.7	2.6	0.1	0.2	0.2	0.2	0.0	0.0	0.0	0.0	0.0	0.0
2. Petroleum and natural gas	0.0	0.0	0.0	0.0	0.0	0.0	0.0	0.0	0.0	0.0	0.0	0.0	0.0
3. Other mining	0.2	7.5	13.7	8.2	8.2	7.8	0.0	0.0	0.0	0.0	0.0	0.0	0.0
4. Food	2.0	7.2	8.7	3.5	3.5	2.5	1.2	0.0	0.0	0.0	0.0	0.0	0.0
5. Beverages and tobacco	42.2	57.7	57.5	30.4	15.5	0.0	0.0	0.0	0.0	0.0	0.0	0.0	0.0
6. Textiles	0.3	37.9	67.1	67.1	67.1	58.2	0.0	0.0	0.0	0.0	0.0	0.0	0.0
7. Wearing apparel and footwear	0.3	29.6	40.2	15.4	15.4	14.4	0.0	0.0	0.0	0.0	0.0	0.0	0.0
8. Wood products	2.6	8.0	31.4	30.3	30.3	10.7	6.5	0.0	0.0	0.0	0.0	0.0	0.0
9. Paper and printing	11.2	26.9	43.4	34.3	32.9	27.7	0.0	0.0	0.0	0.0	0.0	0.0	0.0
10. Petroleum products	0.7	0.3	1.7	1.7	1.7	1.7	0.0	0.0	0.0	0.0	0.0	0.0	0.0
11. Chemicals	22.4	21.3	31.0	29.6	27.0	15.5	0.0	0.0	0.0	0.0	0.0	0.0	0.0
12. Non-metallic mineral product	29.5	30.4	31.5	31.7	31.0	26.6	0.0	0.0	0.0	0.0	0.0	0.0	0.0
13. Basic metals industry	20.0	19.1	49.0	39.5	40.2	31.9	1.9	0.0	0.0	0.0	0.0	0.0	0.0
14. Metal products	36.2	40.6	47.5	40.4	40.4	26.6	3.3	0.0	0.0	0.0	0.0	0.0	0.0
15. Machinery and equipment	28.2	27.1	33.3	26.7	29.1	23.5	0.1	0.0	0.0	0.0	0.0	0.0	0.0
16. Electrical equipment	30.5	37.3	42.0	21.3	25.0	16.8	0.0	0.0	0.0	0.0	0.0	0.0	0.0
17. Transport	56.7	55.5	55.8	54.1	54.3	44.0	0.0	0.0	0.0	0.0	0.0	0.0	0.0
18. Other manufactures	17.6	19.6	20.2	16.6	16.6	8.5	0.0	0.0	0.0	0.0	0.0	0.0	0.0
Total production of goods	13.4	18.7	25.4	19.6	18.7	13.4	0.6	0.0	0.0	0.0	0.0	0.0	0.0

Source: Secretaría de Comercio y Fomento Industrial.

After the completion of the reform programme, a series of complementary measures were adopted which were extremely important to the continuation of the structural adjustment process. These measures included: (a) reforms in the customs system; (b) some liberalization measures in the financial market; (c) the modification of the regulations applying to foreign investment in order to make them more flexible; (d) the deregulation of some services, including cargo services; and (e) the re-privatization of state-run companies and, particularly, the de-nationalization of the banking system.

Some Early Results

As was to be expected, the results of these reforms were not immediately apparent. The mechanism by which outward-oriented reforms are supposed to give rise to a more efficient and more competitive production apparatus is not very direct. During an initial stage, trade liberalization is supposed to result in an increase in imports – but this increase does not always materialize. For example, when the liberalization of imports is coupled with an excessive depreciation of the real exchange rate, as occurred in Mexico in 1986, imports may fall rather than increase, and the effects of liberalization then remain in abeyance. In fact, in Mexico the liberalization programme did not lead to a rise in imports until 1988, when the appreciation of the real exchange rate finally made this possible.

During a second stage the increased competition generated by the expansion of imports is supposed to prompt changes in relative prices that will eliminate the distortions created by past protectionist policies. But these changes do not come about immediately either. The lack of adequate distribution channels and the restrictive practices of the private sector preclude a smoothly operating form of arbitrage and impede the transmission of price signals from external markets to the domestic market. A number of studies have been conducted in Mexico which indicate that, years after the import liberalization process was completed, price differentials persisted that can in no way be accounted for by the remnants of the former trade regime (Ten Kate and de Mateo Venturini, 1989a and 1989b).

In a third stage, domestic industry is supposed to undergo a structural adjustment process in which increased competition will act as a spur for greater efficiency while a new system of relative prices leads the way. Such a process entails a reallocation of resources both within and between industries. Investments have to be made in fixed capital, which in turn involves the design of new projects, their economic and financial evaluation, and their execution. All this takes time, especially when doubts persist as to the definitiveness and irreversibility of the reforms. Therefore, the benefits of trade reforms cannot be expected to become evident immediately. Mexico's experience indicates that one must allow for a lag of between five and ten years.[5]

During the first years of the reform process, major disequilibria remained. In 1987 – i.e. two years after the start of the trade reform programme – inflation was still at 150 per cent and the peso was devalued by 120 per cent against the dollar, which did not exactly create an attractive setting for the investments needed for industrial adjustment. Meanwhile, economic growth remained flat. It was not until 1989 that, for the first time since the 1982 crisis, a significant rate of economic growth rate was recorded (see Table 10.1).

A preliminary assessment of Mexico's trade reform effort leads to the conclusion that it has been a success. First of all, everything seems to indicate that the outward-oriented reforms were indeed carried out. Credibility problems seem to have been overcome.[6] Secondly, the reforms are being reflected in a significant increase in foreign trade relative to GDP. Thirdly, industrial adjustment is in full swing. Investment levels are rising and the orientation of manufacturing is clearly shifting towards export markets. Although the increase in imports is outstripping the expansion of exports by an ample margin, the latter continues to be satisfactory. Last but not least, after six years of near zero growth, the economy has begun to grow again. Although the rates may not yet have reached their targeted levels, the rate of growth appears to have picked up.

III SYNTHESIS

The Pivotal Question

The pivotal question to be posed in this section is: 'What has enabled Mexico to resume its economic growth?' Is it the macroeconomic stabilization programme, as suggested in the first story? Or is it the trade liberalization programme, as suggested in the second?

The two factors are not entirely separable. On the one hand, it is hard to imagine the trade reform programme being a success if it had not been linked to macroeconomic policy, and particularly exchange rate policy. On the other hand, trade reform probably contributed to the success of the macroeconomic stabilization programme by, among other things, enhancing the credibility of the entire policy package. Indeed, there are those who say that liberalization and stabilization measures are so closely related that any attempt to separate their effects is doomed to failure.

In the following discussion, a slightly different interpretation will be proposed. The argument that will be made here is that exchange rate policy has, in fact, been of crucial importance in terms of the continuity of the trade reform programme. Yet the contribution made by trade reforms to the macroeconomic stabilization effort has been limited.

This is by no means intended to detract from the importance of the trade reform process. On the contrary, it is clear that the reforms and the accompanying deregulation measures have transformed the Mexican economy from a heavily regulated economy into a less bureaucratic and more competitive one. However, only recently have the first benefits of this change become evident. Their full effect will not be felt until the end of the 1990s.

Exchange Policy and Outward-Oriented Reforms

Restrictive policies on imports and currency devaluations are largely substitutes for each other. The imposition of a 20 per cent import tax has the same effect on the prices of importables as a 20 per cent devaluation. Thus, the effect of eliminating import barriers can be offset by devaluing the local currency.

This is exactly what was done during the early years (1985–7) of Mexico's trade reform programme. The impact of the elimination of import barriers was softened with the help of such a thick exchange rate "cushion" that the impact of the trade reforms on Mexican industry was almost entirely cancelled out. Consequently, imports shrank rather than expanded in response to the reforms; it took until the last quarter of 1987 for imports to recover from the exchange-rate blow they had been dealt and to regain their pre-reform levels (see Table 10.5). Throughout this period, the protection that had been provided by the trade regime was replaced by exchange-rate protection.

The exchange rate cushion had some extremely important implications for the reform process. Perhaps the most significant of all was that it blunted political opposition to the reforms. The opponents of the reform programme had argued that the liberalization would lay the economy bare to a wave of imports that would swamp the domestic market and ruin Mexican industry. As time passed these arguments appeared groundless and the government then had a free rein in continuing its implementation of the reforms. By 1988 when the wave of imports actually did arrive, the reforms were already an accomplished fact and were irreversible.

Another consequence of the extreme undervaluation of the Mexican peso[7] during the period 1985–7 was that the industrial adjustment that was to be brought about by the liberalization of trade was postponed indefinitely. Since imports did not increase, Mexican industry was not exposed to the invigorating effect of external competition.

The reverse was true for exports. With the depreciation of the real exchange rate, the previous anti-export bias was transformed into a pro-export bias. The shift towards export activities, which had already begun after the 1982 devaluations, gathered steam in the early years of the reform process. However, even though exports responded dramatically, there is no question that, in the beginning, price signals went beyond what would be sustainable in the medium and long terms. In fact, the export boom of the early days of the programme was in large part attributable to transnational corporations with well-established international distribution networks which temporarily transferred certain production processes to Mexico in order to save on costs. When the real exchange rate appreciated again in 1988 and 1989 to more realistic levels, many of these exports evaporated; after the smoke had cleared, however, the permanent effects of adjustment remained.

A final consequence of the marked undervaluation of the Mexican peso in 1985–7 that should be mentioned is the absence of an anchor for inflation. In fact, since international prices were far higher than domestic prices, the former pulled the latter upward, thereby considerably exacerbating the difficulties faced in late 1987.

It now appears to be generally agreed that the depreciation of the real exchange rate in 1985 and 1986 was excessive. It is likely that with a less steep depreciation it would have been possible to reduce the costs of the transition, to further the process of industrial adjustment, and to avoid much of the increase in the rate of inflation observed in 1986 and 1987.

Outward-Oriented Trade Reforms and Inflation

At the start of the reform process, the liberalization of imports was presented as a powerful tool for holding down inflation. If Mexican producers and traders were exposed to external competition, they would supposedly be unable to raise their prices above a level equal to the corresponding international price plus the tariff. This argument was strengthened in 1987 when selective reforms were being applied to products whose domestic prices had been rising at a faster than average pace. The accelerated tariff reductions of December 1987 were also part of the ESP package, whose chief aim was to lower inflation.

There are two conditions, however, that must be fulfilled in order for these types of anti-inflationary measures to work. First, there must be a free flow of arbitrage so that price signals can be transmitted effectively from external to domestic markets. Secondly, the barriers to imports must be of an active nature. When, for example, domestic prices are already below external price levels, the elimination of import restrictions will probably not cause domestic prices to drop even lower. On the contrary, in such a case the reforms might well lead to an increase in domestic prices as a consequence of greater inter-market communication.

It would seem that neither of these two conditions were present during the early years of Mexico's outward-oriented trade reforms. On the one hand, because of the lack of distribution channels, restrictive practices in the private sector, and the widely held view that the price ratios of the moment were transitory, arbitrage between external and domestic markets was very patchy. On the other hand, as a result of the devaluations and a policy designed to curtail aggregate demand, domestic prices had lagged behind external prices, and the effect of lifting import barriers was therefore hardly noticeable. Consequently, it comes as no surprise that in its early years the reform process did not dampen inflation, or did so in the case of only a few products.

The situation changed in 1988 when the appreciation of the real exchange rate brought it back to its pre-reform levels, which caused many of the negative price differentials that had existed until that time to disappear. Since that time, it is likely that the reforms, in conjunction with the level of the real exchange rate, have had a moderating effect on inflation.

Outward-Oriented Reforms and Credibility

Even though the reform process may not have contributed a great deal to bringing inflation under control, it did engender a new economic policy stance which helped to boost the credibility of the adjustment programme. If, in 1985, exclusively macroeconomic measures had been adopted and there had been no trade reforms, a feeling of 'déjà vu' would probably have prevailed. A completely new trade policy added the welcome element of 'pas encore vu'. After the traumatic experiences of the 1982 crisis and the relative failure of the 1983–4 stabilization programme, the country had reached a point where familiarity bred contempt.

This is not to say that the adjustment programme enjoyed a high degree of credibility from the very outset. On the contrary, during the first years the outward-oriented trade reforms were heavily criticized. The programme's credibility has been built up very slowly by giving signal after signal pointing in the same direction. These signals included the March 1986 tariff reduction timetable, accession to GATT, the ongoing elimination of prior licensing requirements, the accelerated tariff reductions of December 1987, the deregulation of the transport sector, the dismantling of state enterprises, the liberalization of interest rates in the financial market, the privatization of the banks, and, last but not least, the decision to enter into negotiations with the United States and Canada concerning the establishment of a North American Free Trade Agreement.

The hardest tests that the reforms have had to face came in late 1987 when the free-market exchange rate plummeted and, in December of that year, when inflation skyrocketed, but thanks to the favourable response to the ESP, this crisis was brought under control and the credibility problem seems to have been laid to rest.

IV CONCLUSIONS

We now return to the question of the relative importance of outward-oriented trade reforms and the macroeconomic stabilization programme. It is the macroeconomic programme that has actually led the Mexican economy to the threshold of what will probably become a new era of growth. The influence of the trade reforms has been indirect and has had more to do with the growing credibility of the adjustment programme than with its contribution to the moderation of inflation.

This is not intended to detract from the merits of the trade reform process. Trade reforms lead to a reallocation of resources both within and between industries and therefore raise the productivity of various industries and of the economy as a whole. This being so, liberalization may also give rise to greater economic growth. However, its benefits only become apparent in the long term, which is why such reforms should not be expected to contribute to the stabilization of an economy undergoing a short-term crisis. This is just as true for Mexico as it is for any other country.

Therefore, if the Mexican economy turns out to be the *wirtschafts-wunder* of the 1990s, with growth rates approaching 10 per cent – and the initial conditions needed for such a feat are, it would seem, taking shape – then the credit should go primarily to its outward-oriented trade reforms, rather than to macroeconomic policy measures.

Notes

1. I am grateful to Fernando de Mateo Venturini for his comments on a preliminary version of this study.
2. For Mexico, the drop in international oil prices prompted a loss of foreign exchange and of public-sector revenues equivalent to 5 per cent of GDP. This accounts for the growth of the fiscal deficit in 1986 (see Table 10.4 on p. 244).
3. The reader is reminded that, since the government lacked access to external credit, it had to cover fiscal deficits either by using domestic savings or by adding to the money supply.
4. The import substitution model can only function satisfactorily if the internal learning process is proceeding at a faster pace than international technological advances. One of the reasons for the failure of this model in the 1980s was precisely the international technological revolution of recent decades.
5. Papageorgiou *et al.* (1990) are more optimistic as regards an economy's response time to the changes brought about by trade reforms. However, they do not distinguish between the effects of trade reforms and the effects of macroeconomic adjustment programmes.
6. The importance of credibility for an adjustment programme's success can scarcely be overestimated. See Rodrik (1989).
7. The undervaluation of the peso is defined as the extent to which domestic prices of tradeables are lower than external prices. For an estimate of the extent of the peso's undervaluation, see Ten Kate and de Mateo Venturini (1989a).

References

Balassa, B. (1983), 'Trade policy in Mexico', *World Development*, Vol. II, No. 9, pp. 795–811.
Córdoba, J. (1990), 'Diez lecciones de la reforma económica en México', *Nexos*, No. 158.

Papageorgiou, D., A. M. Choksi and M. Michaely (1990), *Liberalizing Foreign Trade in Developing Countries: The Lessons of Experience* (Washington, DC: World Bank).

Rodrik, D. (1989), 'Credibility in Trade Reform: A Policymaker's Guide', *The World Economy*, Vol. 12, No. 1.

Ten Kate, A., and F. de Mateo Venturini (1989a), 'Apertura Comercial y Estructura de la Protección en México: Estimaciones Cuantitativas de los Ochenta', *Comercio Exterior*, Vol. 39, No. 4, Mexico City, pp. 312–29.

Ten Kate, A., and F. de Mateo Venturini (1989b), 'Apertura Comercial y Estructura de la Protección en México: Un Análisis de la Relación Entre Ambas', *Comercio Exterior*, Vol. 39, No. 6, Mexico City, pp. 497–511.

11 Trade Liberalization in a High-Inflation Economy: Argentina, 1989–91[1]

E31

F13

O19

Mario Damill and Saúl Keifman

The intensive trade reform effort made by Argentina over the last few years has taken place within a context of severe macroeconomic instability, and the present analysis of its trade liberalization programme therefore focuses mainly on the relationship between stabilization policies and trade policy. In so doing, it examines the difficulties involved in implementing outward-oriented trade reforms in an economy where agents are fully adapted to high inflation. Under such circumstances, an initiative of this type should be accompanied by a consistent set of income policies designed to put a halt to the economy's inflationary inertia. The lack of just such a policy package throughout 1990 sparked an extremely sharp rise in the value of the local currency, thereby raising doubts as to whether the present combination of trade and short-run policies can be maintained without major changes.

I INTRODUCTION

At the start of the 1990s, Carlos Menem's administration launched a series of measures designed to liberalize Argentina's trade with the rest of the world. The average tariff was lowered substantially, specific duties were eliminated, and almost all quantitative restrictions were discontinued. Taxes on agricultural exports were sharply reduced as well.

Although the trade reform process was initiated quite some time ago, under the administration of Raúl Alfonsín, the changes made in 1990–1 were so sweeping that it is more accurate to talk about a change in course, rather than the continuation of an existing programme. In addition to the differences to be observed between this new initiative and the programme that went before it in terms of the intensity and pace of the reforms, which were stepped up considerably, the ways in which trade policies are linked with short-term macroeconomic policies are also strikingly different.

This latter aspect is of particular importance because these trade reforms have been pursued during a period in which the instability of the Argentine economy has been particularly severe. Fluctuations in relative prices have been so great in recent years that the discussion of the allocative effects of changes in trade regulations is in danger, at least for the moment, of appearing somewhat irrelevant. In the presence of such severe disequilibria, the interaction between trade liberalization and stabilization policies is of particular interest and will be one of the chief subjects dealt with in this analysis of recent changes in Argentina's trade regulations.[2]

This approach to the problem is amply justified considering the fact, for example, that the costly failure of liberalization initiatives launched in the Southern Cone of South America in the late 1970s can be attributed to just such a series of problems in relation to the short-run growth of the economy. Thus, although there has been relatively little disagreement as to the wisdom of moving towards a more open economy,[3] a number of very important questions as to *how* to go about accomplishing this in each individual country have yet to be resolved. In this regard, various aspects of Argentina's recent experiences make it appear unlikely that the particular combination of trade reforms and short-term macroeconomic policies implemented at the start of the 1990s can continue to be pursued without major changes.

In the following section the macroeconomic environment in which Argentina's trade reforms have been implemented is outlined and the outlook with regard to the short-term policies being applied by the government as of mid-1991 is analysed. Then, in the second section, the specific features of the reforms being introduced in order to open up the economy are described, starting with their background. This discussion of the events that led up to this movement towards an outward-oriented economic stance begins with the external adjustment that followed upon the debt crisis of the early 1980s. The study ends with a series of concluding remarks in which the main aspects of Argentina's trade reforms and their interaction with short-term policies are evaluated.

II MACROECONOMIC INSTABILITY AND TRADE LIBERALIZATION

A High Degree of Instability

Since the start of the 1990s Argentina has been going through a period of great macroeconomic instability. Two outbreaks of hyper-inflation within the space of a year and a deep, protracted recession have been the most conspicuous outward signs of a crisis unlike any ever before experienced by the country. During this crisis, a series of attempts to use shock treatments as a means of stabilizing the economy have achieved no more than fleeting success. Meanwhile, the room for manoeuvre available to economic policy-makers has steadily dwindled.

The intractability of these problems is a result of the exacerbation, since the early 1980s, of two basic disequilibria that were already ingrained characteristics of Argentina's post-war economic development: its external and fiscal deficits (see Table 11.1). The marked increase in these deficits was chiefly a consequence of the external debt crisis and the specific form taken by the subsequent adjustment to the country's altered payments position. The balance-of-payments current

Table 11.1 Argentina: main macroeconomic indicators, 1980–90 (rates in percentage annual change; values in billion US$)

	Growth of GDP	Rate of inflation[a]	Balance of payments		External debt		Fiscal deficit as % of GDP
			Trade balance	Current account	Value	% of GDP	
1980	1.1	87.6	−2.5	−4.8	27.2	30.9	7.5
1981	−6.7	131.2	−0.3	−4.7	35.7	40.1	13.3
1982	−4.6	209.7	2.3	−2.4	43.6	53.7	15.1
1983	2.8	433.6	3.3	−2.5	45.1	53.6	15.2
1984	2.6	686.8	3.5	−2.4	46.2	52.2	11.9
1985	−4.5	385.4	4.5	−1.0	49.3	59.2	6.0
1986	5.3	81.9	2.1	−2.8	51.4	59.7	4.7
1987	1.6	131.3	0.5	−4.2	58.3	64.5	6.7
1988	−2.8	342.9	3.8	−1.6	58.3	63.8	8.6
1989	−4.6	4,924.0	5.4	−1.3	63.3	70.0	7.2
1990	−0.8	1,343.9	8.3	1.8	61.3	...	4.9

Note: [a] As measured by the consumer price index.
Sources: CEPAL, Banco Central de la República Argentina, and Secretaría de Hacienda.

account began to exhibit a structural deficit owing to the level of the interest payments on the country's external debt, and this was further compounded by capital flight.

The external sector's recessionary (and incomplete) adjustment in 1981-2 led to higher inflation and lower tax revenues, and this, in conjunction with the high level of interest payments on the public debt, generated a marked financial imbalance in fiscal accounts. Traditional policy tools proved to be inadequate or ineffective under these new circumstances, and the public sector of the economy deteriorated visibly, as did the government's ability to manage the situation. Furthermore, the country's already fragile web of domestic financial relations began to come apart. The economy became both demonetized and dollarized.

The country's deepening external and fiscal deficits destabilized its financial and exchange markets and were a major source of inflationary pressures, and these pressures were, in their turn, magnified by the existence of a high-inflation regime. This regime is a structural trait of Argentina's economy which needs to be borne very much in mind by macroeconomic policy-makers, since it can strongly influence the outcome of such policies. It is also particularly important to an understanding of the links between outward-oriented trade policy reforms and short-term macroeconomic policies, and it is therefore worth pausing here to outline it.[4]

The most salient feature of high-inflation economies is the presence of a system of both explicit and implicit contracts and of a way of forming expectations that are extremely well adapted to high inflation. Unindexed contracts expressed in nominal terms have virtually gone out of existence or cover a period of no more than a few days. Indexation becomes very widespread in labour markets and in other services. Contract adjustment intervals have been shortened as much as the supply of price information permits, and the formation of expectations is linked with the establishment of contracts. In the absence of shocks or any other major event, expectations regarding future inflation will be based on the latest available information (in Argentina, the last monthly rate).

Short-term macroeconomic dynamics under these conditions differ from those of an economy that is less well adapted to high inflation. Indexed contracts 'transfer' past inflation to the present, thereby giving it an inertial aspect. In addition to gathering momentum, inflation also gains in volatility. The effects of shocks (e.g. a nominal devaluation) are swiftly transmitted to the rest of the pricing system through indexation mechanisms. Hence, the overall result of the procedures and practices generated by an array of microeconomic defence mechanisms is greater economic instability.

In Argentina, the tendency for high inflation to slip over the edge into hyper-inflation, the persistent fiscal deficit, the financial fragility of the economy and the country's difficulties in negotiating with its external creditors have all added to economic agents' already high degree of uncertainty and have been clearly reflected in its performance indicators.

Thus, for example, GDP fell in 1990 to a level similar to that of 1982, which was the lowest to be recorded in the 1980s. Gross domestic investment slipped to between seven and eight points of GDP, which, in addition to being an all-time low, indicates that net investment was, in fact, negative. Urban open unemployment rates reached an unprecedented high in the first half of 1990 of nearly 9 per cent of the economically active population. The available statistics indicate that there had never before been so low a rate of capital formation nor so high a rate of labour underutilization in the country's history.

The levels of monetization and domestic financial intermediation were also at a low ebb, particularly during the country's bouts of hyper-inflation. Although they did recover somewhat after those episodes, they failed to regain their previous levels.

Fluctuations in relative prices have also been unusually sharp in recent years. The real exchange rate, for example, climbed to record highs in 1989, but during 1990 the rapid appreciation of the local currency pushed the exchange rate to its lowest level in the last decade[5] (see Table 11.2). In 1990 real wages in the manufacturing sector were only 7 per cent higher than their 1982 average (the lowest of the 1980s) and were 20 per cent below the peak levels attained in 1984 during the early days of the Alfonsín administration.

The gloomy picture painted by these performance indicators stands out in sharp contrast, however, to the country's achievement of a record trade surplus in 1990 of over US$ 8 billion, which gave Argentina a surplus on the balance-of-payments current account for the first time since 1978. This was partly attributable to the deep recession being experienced by the country (which, along with the high average real exchange rate in 1989, led to a drop in imports of intermediate goods), but it was also partly a result of higher exports; in fact, the dollar value of Argentina's merchandise exports climbed at an average annual rate of nearly 25 per cent between 1987 and 1990.[6]

Table 11.2 Argentina: real exchange rates, 1980–91 (1990, second quarter = 100)

		Real exchange rate for imports[a]	Free market real exchange rate
1980		50.4	50.4
1981		60.6	77.2
1982		100.2	141.9
1983		117.3	160.3
1984		106.7	167.4
1985		120.1	141.8
1986		107.4	119.8
1987		109.0	139.5
1988		110.8	127.7
1989		140.2	192.8
1990		93.7	93.9
1990	Q1	100.2	131.3
	Q2	100.0	100.0
	Q3	90.7	82.4
	Q4	74.5	61.7
1991	Q1	69.8	69.7
	Q2	68.9	68.8

Note: [a] Nominal exchange rate for the US dollar (units of national currency per dollar), multiplied by US wholesale prices and deflated by an average of domestic consumer and wholesale prices (excluding foodstuffs).

Source: Based on data of CEPAL and INDEC.

Despite this trade surplus, since the primary fiscal balance was not large enough to permit the government to 'buy' this surplus by means other than money creation, the surplus contributed to the steep appreciation of the austral observed from March 1990 onwards. Although a small part of this rise was 'corrected' by a run on the currency early in 1991, the low real parity as of mid-1991 constituted a major problem in terms of the stabilization effort and, of course, the process of opening up the economy by means of outward-oriented trade reforms.

These sharp fluctuations have been associated with a rapid succession of events and policy changes during the past three years. A brief description of these events may be useful in order to illustrate the nature of the macroeconomic framework for the trade liberalization process.

The Period 1989–91

This section will provide an overview of the major events affecting the Argentine economy in 1989–91.[7]

The first hyper-inflationary episode

In February 1989 an acute shortage of foreign exchange put an end to the Alfonsín administration's last stabilization attempt, which was known as the 'Spring Plan'. With its foreign exchange reserves almost exhausted, the Central Bank ceased dealing in the open exchange market, where it had been regulating the exchange rate by selling off dollars that it bought on the 'official' market. Following its withdrawal from the open market, the dollar set out on an upward spiral that eventually triggered the first hyper-inflationary episode of this period.

It should be noted that, in addition to certain inconsistencies in the stabilization programme and the political frailty of Raúl Alfonsín's administration at the time, another of the underlying causes of the foreign exchange shortage was the political and economic uncertainty caused by the approach of general elections, which were scheduled for May. Everything seemed to indicate that the elections would be won by the Peronist candidate, who, at the time, was following a populist line that did not rule out the possibility of repudiating the public sector's domestic debts, nationalizing the banking system and declaring a moratorium on external payments. Under these circumstances, there was little that economic policy-makers could do to ward off the general public's flight from austral-denominated assets. The probability of a stampede was great, and traders found themselves trying to gauge when it would happen so that they could 'get out of australs' just before it did.

The hyper-inflationary surge that followed on the heels of the foreign exchange crisis was to last until the end of the second quarter of the year. The economy was plunged into a period marked by a loss of control and frequent policy shifts. A series of different exchange schemes, in particular, followed one another in quick succession in the period from February to June.

The new administration's first stabilization plan

In June 1989, in view of his inability to bring the economic situation under control, President Alfonsín announced his decision to resign and to hand over the reins of government ahead of time to the incoming administration, which was scheduled to take office in December. President Menem was inaugurated in early July, whereupon he immediately launched a new stabilization plan (the 'BB' plan) based on an agreement between the government and a prominent group of entrepreneurs from among whom the key members of the new administration's economic team were then drawn. When the new plan was unveiled, a great deal of emphasis was placed on the 'structural reforms' that were to be undertaken in the near future. Particular importance was attributed to the privatization of public companies, which would be accompanied by steps to decentralize and deregulate economic activity. The policy package marked for immediate implementation, however, was quite similar to the contents of earlier stabilization attempts which had relied heavily on economic shock treatments. The BB plan combined an incomes policy scheme designed to quell the inertial component of inflation with measures to provide the government with a greater measure of fiscal and monetary control. The authorities retained the exchange-rate scheme that had been established in June by the preceding administration, which provided for a single exchange rate fixed by the Central Bank (which was devalued by about 170 per cent in relation to the average rate for the month before).

At first the BB plan was successful in bringing down inflation, but residual inflation and an ineffective monetary policy led to the reappearance of a significant gap between exchange rates. Accordingly, in early December the country's economic leadership opted for a large devaluation, which aligned the exchange rate set by the Central Bank with the going rate on the parallel market. The shock of this December devaluation was coupled with a major adjustment of rates and charges and with the rescheduling of a portion of the public debt. The announcement of this rescheduling sharply reduced confidence in the securities issued by the Treasury, and this explosive combination of measures sparked a sharp acceleration in the rate of price increases which, in its turn, ushered in a second round of hyper-inflation that lasted until March 1990.

It having proved impossible to maintain a fixed exchange rate, the authorities made the announcement that the currency would be allowed to float and that all private-sector price controls would be lifted. With inflation surging upward, the pressure on the foreign exchange market did not abate, and in order to forestall a full-blown run on the banks in the midst of swiftly circulating rumours that the austral was about to be made fully convertible,[8] the government decided on a 'drastic' solution, which became known as the 'BONEX Plan'. On 1 January 1990 the public's fixed-term time deposits in the financial system were converted into external debt notes, as was the public sector's domestic debt, much of which was made up of interest-bearing bank reserves deposited with the Central Bank. Since this conversion was based on the face value of the external debt paper, the capital losses sustained by those holding the converted assets were enormous. Following a brief 'lull' in the exchange market in the wake of the brutal liquidity squeeze caused by the BONEX Plan, the run on the dollar and the acceleration of inflation gathered speed once again.

The appreciation of the exchange rate

In February and March 1990, a succession of drastic monetary and fiscal measures (the latter being focused on curbing expenditure, especially wages) burst the exchange bubble. The relative stability of the nominal exchange rate that ensued put an end to the second hyper-inflationary episode. In fact, in March 1990 the rate of inflation began to fall steeply, although it then tended to level off at around 10–15 per cent per month. This was partly a result of the existence of a significant inertial component, which was attributable to the re-establishment of the mechanisms associated with a regime of high inflation. Against this backdrop, the demand for money rebounded from the extremely depressed levels to which it had fallen in the first quarter of the year. The increase in the demand for money enabled the Central Bank to buy foreign exchange without exerting upward pressure on the exchange rate. On the contrary, although disposable liquid reserves increased appreciably, the real exchange rate was falling sharply. Between March and December the government's efforts to fight inflation were based almost entirely on fiscal and monetary tools, and price and incomes policies were not used for this purpose. Faced with a floating exchange rate and an exchange market that had an excess supply of foreign exchange ever since the close of the second round of hyper-inflation, at some points the Central Bank chose to step into the market now and then in order to slow the drop in the exchange rate. When it later decided to withdraw from the market in order to gain greater control over the money supply, the exchange rate began to fall even more steeply. The persistent appreciation of the austral combined with the steady deterioration of the fiscal accounts (for which the outlook was very dim towards the end of the year) to create a new exchange bubble in early 1991.

This new crisis, following as it did upon the heels of a series of failed stabilization attempts, prompted the Menem administration to change its line of attack. The decision was finally taken to abandon the floating exchange rate, which was a particularly unsuitable system for an economy with such a tendency towards instability.[9] Policy-makers did not return to a fixed exchange rate set by the Central Bank, however. The pivotal element of the new stabilization plan was to make the austral fully convertible at an exchange rate set by law.

The convertibility plan

The new stabilization plan that went into effect on 1 April 1991 includes the following basic components:

(i) A set of measures to improve the *fiscal accounts*, which had deteriorated markedly since mid-1990. These include a variety of tax provisions passed by Congress in February as well as new rate adjustments. The government also announced that it would undertake a major enforcement effort in order to lower the country's high levels of tax evasion and would pursue a very strict policy to curb public expenditure. Tax reductions were made, however, as part of the negotiation of price agreements with business sectors. Taxes on foreign trade were also lowered.

(ii) The establishment of the *convertibility* of the austral, by act of Congress. This requires the Central Bank to maintain reserves of gold, foreign exchange or securities denominated in foreign currency equivalents (at the legally established exchange rate) to at least 100 per cent of the monetary base.

(iii) The opening of the economy through *tariff reform* (which will be discussed later on) and the elimination of specific import duties; and

(iv) A ban against the inclusion of *indexation* clauses in any sort of contract after 1 April. This prohibition was coupled with the establishment of guidelines concerning price adjustments, particularly for certain types of services (schools, pre-paid medical plans, real-estate rents) which tended to *roll back* prices or at least to prevent April prices (i.e. at the start of the plan) from reflecting the high rates of inflation registered ever since the start of 1991.

By setting the exchange rate to be used for the austral under this convertibility scheme, freezing public-sector rates and charges and de-indexing contracts, the plan sought to achieve a steep reduction in inflation.[10] It was also hoped that the increased purchasing power of wages, the reappearance of commercial credit and the drop in interest rates as a result of this policy package would lead to a strong upswing in economic activity. This, in turn, would boost tax receipts, thanks to the large proportion of taxes that are highly income elastic, and this increase in tax revenues would help the authorities to improve the fiscal accounts substantially. Such an improvement was absolutely essential, since under these new circumstances the public sector would not be able to rely on the Central Bank to help it finance its deficits through money creation.

Generally speaking, the effects of the plan were as expected, with one important exception: apart from in a few isolated cases, nominal prices did not fall. Inflation eased considerably, nominal and real interest rates fell substantially, the purchasing power of wages rose, and commercial credit reappeared on the scene. Thanks to the upturn in aggregate demand and economic activity, tax receipts also climbed appreciably. This made it possible to raise public spending somewhat (which had been excessively 'repressed' as part of the above-mentioned plan) while at the same time marking up an operating surplus on the public sector's consolidated balance sheet. The plan failed, however, to achieve the *deflation* that was needed in order to correct a serious congenital defect of the convertibility scheme: the extremely low starting point for the real exchange rate.

III TRADE POLICY: 1989–91

Background: 1983–8

A brief review of the major events of the past decade will be helpful in order to arrive at a better understanding of the trade policy pursued in 1989–91. The years following the debt crisis can be divided into two very different phases: 1982–4 and 1985–8.

In 1982–4 trade policy was dominated by the exigencies of the adjustment to the presence of an external debt overhang. The need to generate rapidly large trade and fiscal surpluses in order to service the debt gave rise to an adjustment process (initiated, actually, in 1981) of a type that heightened the country's macroeconomic instability.[11] Its corollary in the realm of trade policy was a series of measures that reduced the microeconomic efficiency of the system of incentives. Meanwhile, the authorities resorted to the widespread use of quantitative import restrictions in order to save foreign exchange while, in order to bring in more resources for the Treasury, also raising import duties and taxes on traditional exports. Tax rebates on non-traditional exports were reduced as well.

Later, in 1985–8, within an economic environment marked by a degree of macroeconomic instability that, although considerable, was less marked than during the preceding phase, and under pressure from multilateral lending agencies within the framework of the Baker Plan, the democratic government embarked upon a programme of gradual outward-oriented trade reforms. The nature of this process, at its height, found expression in the terms and conditions of the two loans granted by the World Bank in 1987–8 to help the country implement trade reforms (Tussie and Botzman, 1989). The trade policies pursued during this phase were aimed at the sequential achievement of two objectives: first, a reduction of the incentive system's anti-export bias (which had become notably stronger during the 1982–4 period); and, secondly, the rationalization of the protection provided for domestic production activities.

In order to reduce the trading system's anti-export bias, the following measures were adopted: (a) the elimination of the taxes on agricultural exports, which had been levied not only on agricultural commodities but also on many agriculturally based manufactures;[12] (b) the establishment of a stable system of tax rebates on exports of manufactures which included three different rates for exports of industrially based manufactures (10, 12.5 and 15 per cent) and a 5 per cent rebate for a variety of agriculturally based manufactures; and (c) the reinstatement of an automatic system for temporarily clearing inputs through customs for use in the production of 7,370 manufactures intended for export (this system had been discontinued in 1983).

The two main steps that were taken in order to rationalize the protective structure were: (a) reduction of the number of import items subject to quantitative restrictions (bans or licensing requirements), and (b) reduction of the level and range of protective tariffs. Thanks to these measures, the proportion of manufactures, in terms of value, subject to quantitative restrictions dropped from 62.3 per cent of total manufacturing output at the start of 1987 to just 18 per cent during the second half of 1988.

In the case of some widely used inputs (petrochemicals and iron and steel), the elimination of quantitative import restrictions was coupled with a reduction of tariffs. In other cases (such as textiles), additional specific duties were introduced.

The tariff reforms reduced the level of legal protection from a range of 15–53 per cent to 5–40 per cent. Thus, the average tariff decreased from 43 per cent to 30 per cent. Special regulations concerning motor vehicles and computers were retained, however, and these product groups remained subject to tariffs of over 40 per cent.

Another important factor in the effort to open up the economy during the period 1985–8 was exchange rate policy. Economic policy-makers were quite successful in maintaining the real exchange rate at relatively high, stable levels (considering the very high levels and volatility of inflation) during this period. Even the cumulative appreciation of the local currency during what became known as the 'Spring Plan' (August 1988–January 1989 – spring in the southern hemisphere) seems moderate in comparison to the fluctuations later seen in the real exchange rate (see Table 11.2).

The Trade Liberalization of 1989–91

The effort that was made during the period 1989–91 to open up the economy to trade took place within a very different macroeconomic setting than had existed during the preceding phase, and this circumstance strongly influenced the types of policies that were adopted. These years have been marked, as was noted in the first section of this chapter, by a notable increase in the instability of the economy. The need to halt the economy's slide towards hyper-inflation has forced the authorities to pursue a much more restrictive fiscal policy; meanwhile, it is becoming even more difficult to balance the budget because flagging economic activity and increased tax evasion are eroding tax receipts. Furthermore, the new authorities' *Weltanschauung* includes a firm belief in the universal efficiency of market mechanisms. The dual pressures on trade policy arising out of fiscal needs and ideological imperatives help to account for the changes in this policy.

The way in which exports have been treated provides a clear example of how this pressure has influenced policy. The relatively high taxes on exports between mid-1989 and late 1990 attest to the pre-eminence of budgetary exigencies during that period. However, although there were some reversals, export taxes were gradually brought down to a very low level[13] (a 3 per cent 'statistical surcharge') by April 1991. On the other hand, exporters of manufactures have still not managed actually to obtain payment of the tax rebates on such exports, which were suspended in mid-1989. Although the government has acknowledged that it owes exporters the rebates corresponding to the entire period (except March–June 1990), it has not actually paid them (by issuing the relevant vouchers). What is more, in March 1991 the government announced its decision to reduce these tax rebates on exports of manufactures by 33 per cent, thereby lowering them from 15, 12.5 and 10 per cent to 10, 8.3 and 6.7 per cent, respectively, and from 5 to 3.3 per cent. Meanwhile, the government's promise to pay these lower tax rebates in cash, which it made at the same time that it announced their reduction, has not yet been honoured because the government has expressly stated that it is contingent upon an improvement in the fiscal accounts. Finally, the system for automatically clearing inputs through customs on a temporary basis was also suspended and was replaced by a drawback system (reimbursement, after the fact, of the taxes incorporated in inputs). It should be noted that a drawback system had been established earlier, but was not used by exporters because of its greater financial cost.

The import policies implemented during this most recent phase have undergone much more dramatic changes, particularly in respect of tariffs. The process of reducing the number of quantitative restrictions, which had been begun by the preceding administration, was completed by President Menem's government. The two major milestones in this process, in October 1989 and February–March 1990, can be seen in Table 10.3. Virtually all such restrictions had been eliminated by the end of 1990 (restrictions remained in place for only 25 tariff items – corresponding to motor vehicles and spare parts – out of a total of 10,000). Tariffs, for their part, were reduced on a step-by-step basis until the current structure was arrived at in April 1991. This includes three rates: zero for raw materials and food products, 11 per cent for inputs, and 22 per cent for final goods. Special rates were maintained, however, for motor vehicles and electronics, which are subject to 35 per cent tariffs. At the same time, the specific duties that protected certain goods (such as textiles) were eliminated, and these products became subject to the highest of the new tariff rates. The magnitude of the change brought about by the tariff reforms can be gauged by noting that the average tariff, weighted by industrial output, dropped from 30 per cent in October 1988 to just 9 per cent in April 1991. This is one of the lowest rates in the developing world. Thus, the recent trade policy reforms have been strikingly different in both pace and scope from the 1985–8 liberalization programme.

The 1989–91 reform programme has also coincided with a sharp rise in the value of the local currency. This represents yet another major difference between it and the 1985–8 plan.

Table 11.3 Argentina: evolution of trade policy indicators, 1988–91

		Tariffs		Percentage of tariff lines with:		Number of tariff lines subject to:		
	Average[a]	Maximum	Minimum	Maximum tariff	Minimum tariff	Specific duties	Import licensing	Tariff surcharges
Oct. 88	28.9	40	5	22.7	8.2	119	1,056	845
Oct. 89	26.5	40	0	22.3	7.5	129	122	807
Dec. 89	20.7	24	0	22.5	7.6	327	118	801
Jan. 90	16.4	24	0	30.6	7.6	327	118	802
Mar. 90	15.5	24	0	29.5	13.8	325	27	800
Apr. 90	16.2	24	0	30.4	7.6	325	27	800
May 90	18.3	24	5	30.3	7.8	329	27	759
Jul. 90	18.5	24	5	30.4	7.8	328	27	788
Aug. 90	18.0	24	5	30.3	7.8	326	27	788
Oct. 90	17.3	24	5	34.3	8.3	324	25	0
Jan. 91	18.2	22	0	82.5	17.5	279	0	0
Apr. 91	9.7	22	0	32.4	44.0	0	0	0

Note: [a] Weighted by import values.
Source: Secretaría de Industria y Comercio Exterior.

IV A PRELIMINARY EVALUATION

An analysis of the sequencing and speed with which these liberalization measures have been implemented and their impact in terms of short-term economic growth points up a number of noteworthy aspects of Argentina's recent experiences. Three of these aspects are as follows: first, the contrast between the rapidity, scope and nature of the most recent changes made in trade policy and the gradual approach used in 1985–8; secondly, the fact that they coincided with a steep increase in the value of Argentina's currency; and thirdly, their adverse impact on the fiscal accounts.

Other more specifically trade-related and sectoral aspects of the reform include: (a) the anti-export bias which is reflected in the *de facto* elimination of tax rebates on exports of manufactures; and (b) the absence of selective sectoral policies in the current tariff structure, which attests to the lack of an industrial policy strategy. The graduated tariff structure favours all final goods producers, especially those who use unprocessed raw materials. The different regulations applying to motor vehicles and electronics fall far short of constituting anything that might be likened to a coordinated strategy. It is true, however, that the preceding administration did not have such a strategy either.

The first issue that should be raised with regard to the 1989–91 trade reforms relates to the levels of protection provided. One classification that is commonly used in this connection distinguishes between 'outward orientation', on the one hand, and 'liberalization', on the other (see Sachs, 1987; and Bhagwati, 1987). From this standpoint, the intensity and nature of the trade reforms recently introduced in Argentina are more properly of the latter type. In 'outward-oriented' strategies, the average effective exchange rate for exports is similar to the rate for imports, and the incentives for sales on the external and domestic markets are therefore similar, on average. This type of strategy is perfectly compatible with the existence of significant sectoral deviations from that average (usually as a result of high but uneven levels of protection), however, and it therefore does not necessarily imply that relative prices on the domestic market are equivalent to those prevailing on the international market. 'Liberalization', or laissez-faire strategies, on the other hand, seek to arrive at a relative-price vector on the domestic market close to that found on the international market, which necessarily involves setting very low levels of protection for the domestic market and keeping them within a fairly narrow range.

The Argentine government's choice of a strategy that approximates this concept of 'liberalization' is clearly in line with its overall economic policy orientation. It has also been in keeping with the tenets of the Washington Consensus. Nevertheless, the theoretical and empirical basis for choosing a liberalization strategy are questionable. From a theoretical standpoint, there are no models that support the superiority, measured in terms of growth rates, of an extreme liberalization strategy. As for the empirical evidence, it is to be noted that the so-often cited success stories of East Asia (the Republic of Korea, Japan and Taiwan) clearly fit into the 'outward-oriented reform' category rather than the 'liberalization' group. On the other hand, it is difficult to find such success stories among the countries that have chosen laissez-faire strategies (see Chapter 4 in this volume).

A second issue raised by the Argentine government's trade strategy concerns the pace of reform. The question as to the optimum speed of reform can be approached from three different angles: its fiscal effects, its effects in terms of employment and growth, or its impacts on the trade balance. From a fiscal perspective, gradual reforms are clearly preferable, especially once quantitative restrictions on imports have been eliminated. This is a result only of the obvious fact that lowering tariffs and export taxes will tend to reduce tax receipts, but also of the fact that the public sector will have to spend a great deal on infrastructure investments (ports, communications and transport) in order to prepare for the increase in export activity which is expected to occur. In this connection, it should be noted that customs duties represented about 20 per cent of government revenues at the outset of the trade reforms of early 1991.

The trade-off between opening up an economy and having a balanced fiscal position takes on particular importance in the case of economies suffering from serious macroeconomic disequilibria and high inflation, such as Argentina. From this vantage point, the wisdom of undertaking drastic reforms before the government shows signs of having consolidated its fiscal position and before some degree of macroeconomic stability has been achieved is questionable at best. In view of the financial straits in which the Argentine government finds itself, the recent reforms' initial adverse impact on public-sector revenues is especially damaging.

When it comes to minimizing the costs in terms of employment and growth that are usually associated with outward-oriented trade reforms, it is generally agreed that gradual reforms are preferable (see, for example, Edwards, 1989). Along these lines, it has been argued that a strategy calling for more gradual reforms in respect of imports and an initially more aggressive stance on exports might enjoy greater credibility and, hence, greater chances of success (Berlinsky, 1986). This argument is based on the idea that the expansion of exports would help to cushion the economy from the recessionary effects of the reforms and would thus bolster the strategy's viability. This certainly appears to be what happened in the case of a number of 'Asian dragons'. In the Argentina of today, the problem posed by the speed of the tariff reforms is exacerbated by the fact that its export policy is not in keeping with the reduction of import barriers. As a matter of fact, until tax rebates on exports of manufactures are once again being paid on a regular basis, or the drawback system comes into widespread use,[14] Argentina's export policy in 1989–91 cannot be placed in the same category as its import policy. Strictly speaking, it is actually more in line with an import-substitution strategy.

Finally, it is clear that the faster a trade reform process is, the more it will (in the short run) hurt a country's trade performance. In economies such as Argentina's, which are faced with an external debt overhang that obliges them to maintain a large trade surplus, this is no minor consideration. Consequently, it is highly likely that rapidly implemented trade reforms – unless they are coupled with other policies that will help to raise the trade surplus – will soon fail. This presents policy-makers with a dilemma, however, since an effort to make outward-oriented trade reforms more viable on the external front will either heighten inflationary pressures (via major devaluations) or deepen the recession (via policies designed to curb aggregate demand). Be that as it may, in the case of Argentina, policies that would offset the trade effects of a swift reform process have been conspicuously absent.

The combination of these three types of adverse impacts, which is typical of a rapid trade reform process, poses serious problems of credibility with regard to its continuity, and these problems are greatly exacerbated when such reforms are undertaken in the presence of high inflation. Indeed, there is a great deal in the literature concerning the problems that arise when an attempt is made to 'open up' a high-inflation economy. The failure of the stabilization-plus-liberalization initiatives launched in the Southern Cone in the second half of the 1970s has become something of a classic example in this regard (see, for example, Bruno, 1988; Edwards, 1989; Frenkel, 1983; and Ramos, 1986). These problems become particularly acute when the economy in question suffers from macroeconomic imbalances that are magnified by an external debt overhang. Furthermore, the advisability of opening up an economy only after it has been stabilized is supported by a certain amount of empirical evidence (see Chapter 4 in this volume).

This does not complete the list of the Argentine trade liberalization programme's difficulties, however. The rapid implementation of outward-oriented reforms in a context of high inflation coupled with orthodox stabilization policies opens up a whole new range of possible conflicts. Actually, the speed of the liberalization process seems to be closely linked to the illusion that it will contribute to the stabilization effort. As was also the case in 1979–80, the acceleration of the reform process appears to have been motivated largely by a desire to lower inflation (the reasoning in this regard being that the competition of foreign products would help curb the increase in nominal prices in the domestic market). Moreover, in the case of the convertibility plan, tariff reductions were aimed at the even more ambitious goal of helping to bring about the deflation of industrial prices. As mentioned earlier, however, the government's hopes in this regard were dashed and the ultimate outcome was a substantial reduction of protection together with a sharp appreciation of the local currency. In fact, the combined impact of the decrease in the average level of tariff protection and the drop in the real exchange rate amounted to 46 per cent between the fourth quarter of 1988 and the second quarter of 1991.[15]

In these respects Argentina's experiences with trade reforms in 1979–80 and in 1989–91 have some visible similarities. It is true that an appreciation of the local currency has been an initial result of most recent stabilization programmes, in Argentina as well as in other countries, regardless of whether they have ended in success or failure. The most striking aspect of this phenomenon in such cases, however, is how steeply the real exchange rate has fallen. The combination of a rapid trade liberalization process and an overvalued local currency can lead to a serious downturn in expectations and can prove to be an explosive mixture in terms of both the stabilization effort and the trade reform process itself.

In order to understand the reasons for this sharp appreciation of the local currency, one has to consider the long process by which economic agents in Argentina have adapted to high inflation, thereby leading to the formation of the high-inflation regime described in the first section of this chapter.

In a high-inflation economy, the stabilization of the nominal exchange rate does not provide a sufficiently strong 'anchor' for nominal prices, wages and inflationary expectations in the short run – not even when a trade liberalization programme is making rapid progress (which should, theoretically, bring domestic inflation into line with the international rate of inflation). If there is a substantial lag in the materialization of the effects of outward-oriented reforms, then the persistence of indexation mechanisms in a significant portion of the non-tradeables sector will, if the exchange rate is fixed, tend to produce a sharp decline in the real exchange rate. The key point here is the absence of a consistent package of incomes policies which would help stabilize the nominal exchange rate while, at the same time, making it possible to do away with such indexation mechanisms in order to forestall a rapid change in relative prices in favour of non-tradeables. The lack of such an incomes-policy package is a feature that the trade-reform programmes of the late 1970s and early 1990s share.[16] What is more, in both cases trade reforms were coupled with the deregulation of private-sector wages and prices, in keeping – in this regard, too – with the Washington Consensus. The rise in the value of the local currency prompted by these policies reveals an ambiguity in the Consensus, however, since, in the discussion concerning the types of policy reforms that should be used by developing countries (particularly those that applied the import-substitution-based model of capital formation) in order to resume their economic growth, the Washington Consensus states in no uncertain terms that a 'high and stable' exchange rate is a prerequisite for a successful trade liberalization programme.

Notes

1. Translation by Diane Frishman is gratefully acknowledged.
2. The relationship between the trade reforms and other sets of policies, such as sectoral policies, also merits attention. These policies, which have fallen far short of constituting a consistent package of measures, have been weakened so much that they have virtually disappeared from the scene in recent years.
3. As is proposed in the agenda of reforms of what is known as the 'Washington Consensus'. See Williamson (1990). For a critical discussion of the Consensus, see Fanelli *et al.* (1990).
4. The concept of a high-inflation regime is set forth and discussed in Frenkel (1990).
5. The real exchange rate is here defined as the domestic currency price of the dollar, adjusted by the US wholesale price index and deflated by a combined index of consumer and wholesale prices (excluding food).
6. At 1970 prices, exports rose from slightly more than 15 per cent to nearly 25 per cent of GDP within a span of two years. Despite its improved trade performance, Argentina maintained a *de facto* moratorium on the

servicing of its external financial debt with commercial banks between
April 1988 and mid-1990, during which time it accumulated considerable
arrears.

7. A detailed description of the events and policies discussed in this section
   may be found in CLADEI-FEDESARROLLO (1990 and 1991) and in
   Situación Latinoamericana (1991). See also Damill and Frenkel (1991).

8. This would have resulted in a steep devaluation, given the relative levels of
   the monetary base and the Central Bank's foreign exchange reserves at
   the time.

9. Ever since December 1989, the government had characterized the float as
   just another of the series of free market policies which headed up its
   agenda. From the government's vantage point, the uncertainty associated
   with this type of scheme – which clearly magnifies price uncertainty in
   highly volatile economies – was a virtue, however. One manifestation of
   that virtue was the fact that the Central Bank did not have to bear the
   supposed costs of fixing the exchange rate.

10. The government actually expected to see a fairly considerable deflation of
    prices. The new authorities supposed that this would be the result of a
    reduction of exchange uncertainty, and that it would pave the way for an
    improvement in the currency's real parity. Economic policy-makers did,
    in fact, acknowledge the exchange rate lag, however, when they used the
    prices prevailing during the second quarter of 1990 as their point of
    reference for price negotiations with business sectors and for the
    formulation of price-adjustment guidelines for some services. The idea
    was for the 'negotiated' prices to return, in March 1991, to the levels (in
    dollars) observed during that period.

11. This stage of the adjustment has been described as 'chaotic' because of its
    strongly destabilizing effects on short-run economic growth and the
    inconsistencies apparent in the economic policies implemented during
    that period. See Fanelli *et al.* (1990).

12. The only exceptions were some raw materials, which continued to be
    taxed in order to encourage producers to process them locally before
    shipping them abroad (e.g. soybeans, cuts of beef, hides). Agricultural
    exports also pay a 1.5 per cent specific tax to support the National
    Institute of Agricultural Technology. Actually, although the reduction of
    export taxes was a long-term goal, in the short term it tended to have an
    adverse effect on the fiscal accounts, and the authorities consequently
    went back and forth on this issue from 1985 onwards. First the drop in the
    prices of exportable goods (which prompted the government to take
    compensatory measures) and, later, the pressure brought to bear by the
    agricultural sector (especially towards the end of the Radical Party's time
    in office, when its position in dealing with various power groups was
    particularly weak) also gave momentum to the move to lighten the tax
    load on exports.

13. The exceptions listed in note 12 continue to apply.

14. If the government's failure to pay tax rebates and its elimination of the
    system of temporary import clearance have been due to its straitened
    fiscal situation, then there is no reason to expect it to behave differently in
    regard to the system of export drawbacks.

15. Moreover, the level of the real exchange rate during the fourth quarter of 1988 fell far short of the peak levels of the past decade.
16. The situation in this regard changed early in 1991 when a new stabilization plan based on the full convertibility of the austral was launched. At that time, the Menem administration decided to move forward on the suppression of indexing practices, as noted in the section where the plan's contents are summarized. Price agreements were also negotiated and guidelines for price adjustments in various service activities were formulated. The incomes policies implemented in 1991 slowed the appreciation of the local currency, but did not manage even to reverse partially the steep cumulative decrease in the real exchange rate that had occurred between March and December 1990.

References

Berlinsky, J. (1986), 'La Elección de una Estrategia de Crecimiento: Los Regímenes de Comercio Exterior y la Promoción de Exportaciones en América Latina', *Documento de Trabajo*, No. 122, Instituto Torcuato Di Tella, Buenos Aires.

Bhagwati, J. (1987), 'Outward Orientation: Trade Issues', in V. Corbo, *et al.*, eds, *Growth-oriented Adjustment Programs* (Washington, DC: International Monetary Fund and World Bank).

Bruno, M. (1988), 'Opening-Up', in R. Dornbusch and L. Helmers, *The Open Economy* (Washington, DC: World Bank).

Cladei-Fedesarrollo (1990 and 1991), *Coyuntura Económica Latinoamericana*, Nos. 1 and 2, Bogotá.

Damill, M., and R. Frenkel (1991), 'Hiperinflación en Argentina: 1989–1990', *Documento CEDES*, No. 62, Buenos Aires.

Edwards, S. (1989), 'Structural Adjustment Policies in Highly Indebted Countries', in J. Sachs, *Developing Country Debt and Economic Performance* (London: National Bureau of Economic Research, University of Chicago Press).

Fanelli, J. M., R. Frenkel and G. Rozenwurcel (1990), 'Growth and Structural Reform in Latin America. Where We Stand', *Documento CEDES*, No. 57, Buenos Aires.

Fanelli, J. M. and R. Frenkel (1990), *Políticas de Estabilización e Hiperinflación en la Argentina*, Editorial Tesis, Buenos Aires.

Frenkel, R. (1983), 'Mercado Financiero, Expectativas Cambiarias y Movimientos de Capital', *El Trimestre Económico*, Vol. L, No. 200.

Frenkel, R. (1990), 'El Régimen de Alta Inflación y el Nivel de Actividad', in J. P. Arellano (comp.), *Inflación Rebelde en América Latina*, CIEPLAN-Hachette, Santiago, Chile, 1990.

Ramos, J. (1986), *Neoconservative Economics in the Southern Cone of Latin America, 1973–1983* (Baltimore: Johns Hopkins University Press).

Sachs, J. (1987), 'Trade and Exchange Rate Policies in Growth-oriented Adjustment Programs', in Corbo *et al.* (see Bhagwati, 1987).

Situación Latinoamericana (1991), Nos. 1 and 2, Madrid.

Tussie, D. and M. Botzman (1989), 'Las Negociaciones de la Argentina con el Banco Mundial: La Condicionalidad en los Préstamos de Política Comercial', Documentos de Trabajo e Informes de Investigación, No. 85, FLACSO, Buenos Aires.

Willliamson, J. (1990), *The Progress of Policy Reform in Latin America*, (Washington: Institute for International Economics).

Index